College-Prep Homeschooling

Your Complete Guide to Homeschooling through High School

David P. Byers, Ph.D.,
and Chandra Byers

Mapletree Publishing Company
Denver, Colorado

Printed in the United States of America
13 12 11 10 09 08   1 2 3 4 5 6 7

Cover design by Tamara Dever   www.tlcgraphics.com

Library of Congress Cataloging-in-Publication Data
Byers, David P., 1963-
  College-prep homeschooling : your complete guide to homeschooling through high school / by David P. Byers & Chandra Byers.
     p. cm.
  Includes bibliographical references and index.
  ISBN-13: 978-1-60065-100-7 (alk. paper) 1. Home school-ing—United States. I. Byers, Chandra, 1964- II. Title.
  LC40.B94 2008
  371.04'2—dc22

                          2007015271

Legal Disclaimer: Author and Publisher offer the infor-mation contained in this book without guarantee of any kind. The information provided in this book, while use-ful, is not guaranteed to produce any particular results, and the advice given may not be suitable for every individual. Author and Mapletree Publishing Company disclaim all liability in connection with the use of this book.

Printed on acid-free paper

Mapletree Publishing Company
Denver, Colorado 80130
800-537-0414
www.mapletreepublishing.com
The Mapletree logo is a trademark of Mapletree Publishing Company

We dedicate this book to our children,
who love without limits.

Table of Contents

ACKNOWLEDGMENTS

FIRST AND FOREMOST, NONE OF WHAT we have or have been able to do in life would have been possible without God's love and guidance.

We wish to acknowledge our children, to whom we've dedicated this book. Without their willingness to trust us and to learn at home, none of this would have been possible. We especially wish to acknowledge our oldest two children, Holly and Cameron, who were our guinea pigs, so to speak. They paved the way for their siblings, who will be in high school sooner than we would care to imagine.

A special thanks goes out to David Hall and the folks at Mapletree Publishing for giving us this chance to share our experiences with other homeschoolers. We also wish to thank our editors, who patiently walked us through the process of making our work ready for publishing.

INTRODUCTION

THIS BOOK IS THE RESULT OF YEARS of experience, study, and research. It began when my wife, Chandra, and I first started teaching our children at home in 1992 and continued through my dissertation about homeschooling. Since I devoted a great deal of my doctoral studies to the subject of homeschooling—particularly homeschooling and higher education—I decided that it was time to share what we've learned in a book.

Will this book provide all the answers you may be seeking? No. If we could write a book that would make everyone equally successful with homeschooling through high school, we'd end up creating "Stepford" homeschoolers, but where's the fun in that? The fun really is in the diversity of homeschooling families and how they customize their learning environments to meet their children's individual needs. After all, that is more than likely one of the reasons you decided to homeschool in the first place.

This book describes just one aspect of homeschooling: using the high school years effectively in order to prepare children for college. Many high school graduates will not go to college for one reason or another. Many will go back to college at some later point in their lives. However, the skills that students need for college are beneficial throughout life. We hope this book provides some insight and direction as you teach your children through high school, whether you are preparing them for college or for life choices.

Of course, no book can guarantee that you'll be successful in your program. Yet, we can assure you that the information presented in this book is educationally sound and based on thorough research and practical experience. Our hope is to give the best information we can about a variety of related subjects so you can make decisions about educating your child in a way that works best for your family.

Certain portions of the book include information from my doctoral research papers and dissertation. In these portions, I've included information in parentheses that indicates ideas written by educators and researchers who preceded us. The parenthetical information also corresponds to the list of references at the end of the book in case you want to locate and read any of the articles or books that we refer to.

In the list of references at the end of the book, I've also included the titles of materials that may not have been mentioned directly in any of the chapters, but which are nonetheless interesting to read and applicable to homeschooling. And yes, I've read all of the articles and books listed (and more) while working on my Ph.D. and so did Chandra, by default, as she read and edited all of my papers.

At the end of most chapters, we've included a short list of key points from the chapter. These lists highlight specific actions you can take to begin implementing the ideas we present. We hope these lists help you in developing your own program and preparing your child for college.

We recommend that you read the entire book. However, because we realize that you may have particular interests or needs, we've tried to make it easy for you to find the information you need right away. The book is organized topically into sections, each with several chapters. The information below provides an overview of each section for quick reference. Please refer to the table of contents for more specific chapter information.

Section I: Making the Choice To Homeschool Through High School

Here we review some arguments for and against homeschooling through high school, and we include several pros and cons you might experience.

This section also includes information to help you evaluate your qualifications for teaching high school at home, which is often a concern. We help you answer the questions "How do I know what to teach?" and "How can I be sure that I'm teaching the right stuff?"

Since high school isn't just about academics, this section addresses other activities you should include in your program. We look beyond the twelfth grade by considering your role in preparing your child for the life choices—attending college or entering the workforce—that every high school student has to make after graduation. And finally, we offer a short chapter about "intelligence" as it relates to success in higher education.

Section II: Academic Discipline— Building Skills for Success in Higher Education (And in Life)

After high school many young people are unprepared for college and for life. Drawing upon my experiences as a college professor, the third section describes how to use the high school years to help prepare your child for the independence and academic rigors of higher education. We identify several important skills students need to succeed in college. These academic skills can also be useful life skills.

So even if college isn't right for your child, the information may be helpful anyway. You may find it worthwhile to have your high school student read this section too.

Section III: Homeschool Teaching Approaches—What Works and What Doesn't to Prepare Your Child for Higher Education

There are many teaching and learning approaches, especially with homeschooling. However, from the perspective of preparing your child to succeed in higher education, some approaches may work better than others. This section reviews educational approaches used in homeschooling as compared to those used in higher education so that your homeschool program can more effectively prepare your child for college.

Section IV: Creating Your High School Program

This section evaluates some of the pros and cons of buying curricula versus building or customizing your own. We describe various types of prepared curricula and offer suggestions on how to decide which components will best suit your needs. This section also reviews how to adapt purchased curricula to your child's needs and ideas for those who prefer to create their own from scratch. Since we generally prefer to create or customize the curricula for our children, we've devoted considerable effort to sharing our knowledge and experiences with you.

This section also provides a look at your educational goals. We offer practical suggestions on determining what you want your child to learn by creating educational objectives. We have provided sample objectives for possible high school courses.

Additionally, we provide information about implementing your program that is applicable whether you prefer to buy or to create your own curriculum. Topics include selecting courses for your program, figuring credits, and setting up basic schedules. We offer in-depth information about daily, weekly, and yearly schedules. We then provide several examples of how to create assignments, establish due dates for homework, and develop a syllabus. We also offer strategies for evaluating and grading your child's work.

Section V: Preparing for the End

If your child plans to go to college, detailed record keeping is a must. Many parents forget this important step until their child starts to submit college applications—and then the scrambling begins. We describe the types of records colleges want and provide some tips on developing and maintaining these records throughout your program rather than waiting until the end.

SECTION I

MAKING THE CHOICE TO HOMESCHOOL THROUGH HIGH SCHOOL

CHAPTER 1

Homeschooling in the United States Today

THE PRESENT-DAY VERSION OF HOMESCHOOLING, a choice by parents to educate their children at home rather than sending them to public or private schools, began as a grassroots social movement in the 1960s. The movement increased in popularity and acceptance in the United States during the latter half of the twentieth century—particularly during the last two decades.

In 1985 Patricia Lines, then a researcher with the US Department of Education, estimated that 50,000 children in the United States were being taught at home. In 1990 Lines revised her estimate of the number of homeschoolers to be between 250,000 and 355,000. In a later report, she indicated that the number of homeschoolers increased to about 700,000 in the five-year period between 1990 and 1995 (Lines, 2000). While the specific figures remain speculative, current estimates place the number of children being taught at home in the United States at over one million (Rauchut and Patton, 2002).

Although children being taught at home are still in the minority compared to their public or private school counterparts, their numbers continue to grow each year. In 2000 Lines estimated the number of homeschoolers to be between 3–4% of school-age children nationwide.

The exact number of homeschoolers is difficult to pinpoint because each state has different homeschool registration requirements. Additionally, many homeschoolers continue to teach their children covertly and do not voluntarily register with their state officials.

For example, according to the Indiana Department of Education, the number of children reported as being homeschooled tripled between 1998 and 2002 because parents were becoming more aware that they were required to register with the state. Similarly, the actual number of students being homeschooled may be inflated if parents registered to homeschool, but then later sent their children back to public school and didn't inform the state (Zehr, 2003).

The popularity of homeschooling continues to grow not only in sheer numbers, but in diversity as well. Although the majority of homeschoolers are white, two-parent, single-income families with three or more children (Omaha World Herald, 2003), the cultural **The popularity of homeschooling continues to grow.** make-up of homeschoolers is changing. African-American families are five times more likely to be homeschooled than just five years ago (FOX News, 2003). The US Department of Education indicates that minority children who are homeschooled are scoring better in reading and math than minority children in public schools (Masland and Ross, 2003).

Our Homeschooling Story

Like many parents who teach their children at home, we knew little of the history behind homeschooling in the United States when we first started. In 1992 I read an article about homeschooling in a small publication that was distributed to local childcare centers. That was the first time I had ever heard about homeschooling, but I immediately became fascinated with the idea of teaching children at home. Chandra read the article too, but her reaction was considerably less enthusiastic than mine.

At that time we had only two children. Our oldest daughter was just months away from entering kindergarten. She was hearing impaired, so we were both worried about sending her off to school. Although she was an intelligent girl and had adapted well to using hearing aids, we knew she often missed information in a crowded and active environment, such as could be found in many elementary schools.

We were also concerned about sending our children to public school for reasons such as safety and academics. However, we knew we couldn't afford a private or parochial school, and public schooling seemed like our only option—until we read the homeschooling article.

As we continued to discuss the possibility of homeschooling, Chandra was unconvinced that we should go that route. After all, she would be the one to teach the children the majority of the time since she would be home with them, and she had never planned or prepared for being a teacher. On the other hand, I had been a teacher and administrator for several years and the thought of putting together a curriculum and carrying it out was second nature. I thought it was an equitable arrangement: I'd tell Chandra what to do and how to do it and she would merely have to follow my instructions. Chandra, however, had a somewhat contrary view.

In the end I convinced Chandra to try homeschooling for a few months at the beginning of our daughter's kindergarten year. Since kindergarten was not required by the state of Colorado (so my reasoning went), we knew the year wouldn't be a total waste if it didn't work out. We could always decide later to put our daughter in a regular kindergarten or first grade in the fall. Perhaps Chandra believed (or hoped) that's what would happen. Of course, I had other plans. Yet she was willing to go along as we began our homeschooling journey.

When we first started out, I created all of our curriculum from scratch. We didn't even know about A Beka or Bob Jones or any of the other homeschooling publishers. It was a great deal of work not only developing the lesson plans, but also writing out detailed instructions so Chandra could feel comfortable carrying them out. And she did carry them out, to the letter. If I had been able to teach the children myself, I would have preferred to "shoot from the hip" a little more and adapt the daily lessons as the children's interests dictated, but then again, I wasn't teaching.

I thought the first year was a tremendous success. Chandra was more reserved in her enthusiasm, but we both agreed that the children were happy and had undoubtedly learned a great deal, so we kept going. Now, even after all these years and the addition of four more children, we both are glad that we did.

In 1996 we moved from Denver to Omaha to work as Family-Teachers at Boys Town (it was still just *Boys* Town then and we still had just two children at the time). It seemed like God directed us to come to Omaha despite finding out a month into our training at Boys Town that their policies had changed and we would no longer be allowed to homeschool our children while we worked there as we had initially believed we would.

Despite a very generous offer from Boys Town to move us anywhere we would like to go, we decided to stay there since we had sold our Colorado home, moved out of state, and lacked the resources to do anything else at that point. As a result, we reluctantly enrolled our children in a local public school. The children were excited to try *regular* school.

Having our children attend public school was an enlightening experience for all of us. The children had wonderful teachers, the school had excellent administrators, and we all made some good friends. However, we were thankful the experience lasted just a few months because in the end, it just wasn't what we wanted to do.

When our third child was born, we left Boys Town. I found a new job, and we worked back into the routine of homeschooling. Despite being cooped up in a third-floor, two-bedroom apartment for a while, we all were happier as a result of being able to homeschool again.

We now have six children and continue to homeschool. As we write this book our oldest child is attending the University of Nebraska at Omaha (UNO) on an academic scholarship. The next oldest, our son, is a senior in high school and will soon attend UNO on an academic scholarship as well. The middle two are in grade school, and the youngest two are constantly learning despite being too young for formal schooling. Since it is our goal to teach all of our children at home through high school, we wrote this book to offer our combined experiences and education with other parents who might be considering doing the same.

Like most homeschooling parents, we have read many papers and books about homeschooling—some with political agendas and some with religious agendas. While we do not discount the validity of political or religious agendas, especially when it comes to homeschooling, neither was beneficial to the educationally objective research papers I wrote during my doctoral studies. Likewise, it is not our intention in this book to profess a religious or political agenda or to persuade anyone to join a cause. We want to present information about homeschooling as objectively as possible.

However, if you really try to read between the lines of this book, you might sense that we had our own agendas. As homeschooling parents, we have a certain amount of bias with regard to teaching children at home. We won't deny it. We are also advocates of higher education and have a certain amount of bias about the skills high school students should acquire in preparation for college.

Our true agenda is to report the facts of the matter—at least the facts according to a variety of experts—in an objective manner in order to let you come to your own conclusions. Throughout this book, we hope you will also get a sense that our purpose is to encourage you to teach your child at home through high school if you decide that it is in your best interest.

Although we strongly believe in the value of homeschooling from an educational perspective, as well as from a family perspective, we know that it's not for everyone. We also know that there are many valuable educational experiences for children that occur in private, parochial, and public schools. We have a great respect and admiration for the many teachers, administrators, and parents who daily strive to provide their students and their families with the best educational and support services possible in spite of numerous challenges and obstacles.

For those families who decide homeschooling is right for them, the good news is that homeschooling is now legal in all 50 states. Even better news is that colleges and universities are not just tolerating homeschoolers in their admission process, but many colleges are actively recruiting homeschooled children due to their advanced academic abilities. In addition, many formal studies are being conducted by qualified professionals who want to study the homeschooling phenomenon.

In order to fully understand the continued growth and popularity of homeschooling, it is important to know its history. It is equally important to understand some of the primary arguments of both homeschooling advocates and their opponents. A detailed history of homeschooling in the United States, as well as a review of the current homeschool debate, can be found in Appendix A.

Many colleges are actively recruiting homeschooled children.

CHAPTER 2

Should I Homeschool through High School?

MANY PARENTS CHOOSE TO RETAIN CONTROL of their children's education during the elementary school years because they are concerned about safety, moral development, and socialization, as well as education. However, parents are sometimes content to return educational control to the public schools during the high school years. This is often for a variety of reasons, but usually it comes down to a lack of confidence in their abilities to teach their children through the twelfth grade.

For some families, homeschooling through high school may be the best choice. For some, even those who have successfully homeschooled during the elementary years, the decision to send their children "away" for high school may be a good one. In order to decide if homeschooling through high school is right for you and your family, there are many questions you should ask yourself. In this section we will review what we feel are the most important ones.

There are certainly other questions that you can ask yourself before you decide to homeschool through high school. We hope the rest of the book will help you find some of the answers. No matter what questions you have, it is important to at least consider them, but don't be overly concerned if you don't have *all* the answers before you get started with your high school program—sometimes things have a way of working out.

Making the Decision

Parents who haven't taught their children at home prior to high school are probably less likely to consider homeschooling in high school than those who already have some homeschooling experience under the belt. For some parents who have educated their children at home through grade school, continuing through high school seems like the appropriate and normal thing to do.

For non-homeschoolers, the decision to consider homeschool at any grade level is often influenced by a dissatisfaction with the traditional school setting, such as problems with one or more teachers, worries about the child's safety, or concerns with the curriculum. For some families, homeschooling may seem to be a quick and easy solution to whatever problems they are having. However, many families end up sending their children back to traditional schools when they find that homeschooling is more difficult and time consuming than they had believed.

The decision to consider homeschool is often influenced by a dissatisfaction with the traditional school setting.

Even for experienced homeschoolers, there may actually be any number of reasons why parents decide to stop homeschooling when their children are ready to enter high school. Competitive sports, the lure of social activities, scholarship opportunities, and preparation for college are just some of the reasons.

Another valid reason may be that some parents and children are burned out on homeschooling, especially if they have homeschooled for any length of time. Many parents are concerned about what their children may miss by not attending a traditional school, particularly when it relates to socializing and opportunities to prepare for college and life.

Yet perhaps the primary reason even some experienced homeschooling parents choose not to homeschool through high school is fear. Teaching high school can be intimidating and overwhelming, especially if you don't consider yourself qualified to teach certain subjects. However, just because you may not be an expert in every high school subject doesn't mean you aren't qualified to teach your child at home. In fact, there may be no one better qualified than you to teach your child through the twelfth grade.

However, before you jump into it, you may want to carefully think about what homeschooling in high school really means. Here are fifteen questions we recommend you ask yourself:

1. **Can I describe in one or two sentences why I want to teach my child at home through high school?**

   Think of this exercise as writing a thesis statement. If you can clearly and succinctly state your "thesis" for wanting to teach your child at home through high school, then you are more likely to be certain it is the right thing for you to do. It may also help you defend your choice to friends and family members.

2. **Does my child want to be taught at home through high school?**

   While this may seem silly to some, it is nevertheless a legitimate question. Your child may have a variety of concerns about homeschooling, such as being "different," being taught by (gulp) parents, or appearing incapable and making mistakes in front of you. In the end you are the parent and you must make the best decision you can for your child, but at least considering your child's feelings seems like the logical and ethical thing to do.

3. **Do I have the support of my spouse or other family members with this decision?**

There are some families in which one parent has chosen to homeschool the children but the other parent does not support the decision nor help with the effort. However, it is much easier for everyone if the parents are in agreement about homeschooling. In addition, having the understanding, if not support, of extended family members (grandparents, aunts, uncles, and so forth) can make everyone feel much more comfortable. If not, are you ready or willing to "go it alone"?

4. **Have I given this decision careful thought, or am I making a rash decision based on emotion rather than logic?**

Sometimes the decision to homeschool a child results from problems with one or more teachers, the curriculum, or the child's academic performance in a traditional school. For current homeschoolers, sometimes fear for the child's safety or concern that the child's needs will not be met in a traditional school are the motivators. While these are all legitimate concerns, there are strong emotions attached to each that may cause parents to react in a way they may later regret. We encourage you to make your decision carefully, based on logic rather than just emotion. The rest of the questions here may help you.

5. **Have I investigated and am I willing to comply with the laws in my state related to homeschooling through high school?**

The laws in each state vary and are subject to change, which is why we did not attempt to review them all in this book. Nevertheless, it is in your best interest to comply with homeschooling laws to avoid problems for both you and your child. In the mid-twentieth century, in the early days of homeschooling, many homeschooling families had to go "underground." That is no longer necessary. All fifty states allow homeschooling. Contact your state's department of education for more information.

6. **Am I willing to spend time with my child each day in the roles of parent, teacher, academic counselor, school administrator, and disciplinarian?**

A homeschooling parent wears many hats—all of them authoritarian to some extent. It is sometimes difficult to separate being a parent and being everything else you need to be in the educational setting. It can be done, but it is best that you recognize this aspect of homeschooling up front.

7. **Am I willing to devote my time and energy to plan an effective education for my child, including actively learning about teaching and learning styles?**

Homeschooling in high school doesn't mean simply buying a few books and having your child work through them at the kitchen table. A solid educational program requires a great deal of planning and effort on your part—perhaps even more than from your child. If you choose to homeschool, you should be willing to learn about teaching and learning. Your child deserves the best educational program possible.

8. **Am I willing to devote time, money, and energy to developing, or locating and buying, high school-level materials for my child for one to four years?**

There are a variety of options for homeschooling materials, but finding one program that meets all of your child's needs isn't always possible. You may find that using a variety of materials or approaches is necessary, which means you need to be ready and willing to find them. You may also have to create your own courses and materials. We offer some suggestions about buying and creating materials in some of the later chapters.

9. **Am I willing to devote time and energy to teach my child, grade her work, and provide feedback and corrective instruction?**

You can assign the work. Your child can complete the work. But will it be completed correctly? If not, how will you help your child learn from her mistakes? Sometimes the most tedious part of teaching is grading, but it is one of the most essential parts—along with providing feedback and corrective instruction. Are you willing to do all of these things?

10. **Am I willing to devote time, money, and energy to locate sources for classes that I don't feel qualified to teach and then transport my child to and from these classes?**

If you don't have the knowledge or skills to teach certain subjects, will you do what is necessary to find someone who can? Even when you do, it won't do your child any good if you don't ensure that he gets to the classes and completes them.

11. Am I willing to devote time, money, and energy to take my child to and from extracurricular activities and social activities with other teenagers?

Most teenagers are social creatures, which is a great way for them to learn about themselves and others in order to prepare for life after homeschooling. It is often possible to find other parents who need to provide social experiences for their children, and you only have to put forth enough effort to get your child to the activities they plan. However, sometimes you may have to plan and implement activities yourself.

12. Am I willing to devote time, money, and energy into helping my child investigate colleges or career opportunities for when she completes high school?

What will your child do after high school? Perhaps she already has some clear ideas. Perhaps, like many students, she doesn't really know. Your job is to help your child identify and investigate options for life after high school, whether that is college or career. We provide some ideas in this book that may help you be your child's college and career counselor.

13. Am I willing to devote time and energy to keep the necessary records for helping my child apply for college?

Record keeping, like grading, can be tedious, but it is essential—especially if your child is going on to college. We devote quite a bit of space in this book to help you know how to keep effective records.

14. Am I willing to seek help with any of these items?

You don't have to do it alone. Throughout this book we offer step-by-step guidance for most of the practical concerns listed above. We also encourage you to seek out other expert advice—some of which can be found just by talking with other homeschoolers.

15. Am I willing to make sacrifices and enjoy the benefits of homeschooling through high school?

In the next few pages we'll review some of the sacrifices and benefits of homeschooling through high school. We're sure you can think of a few more. We encourage you to carefully consider all of them and to discuss them with your child and your family prior to making your final decision.

Of course, there are other questions you can ask yourself, but those listed above encompass most of the major issues related to homeschooling—especially through high school. It is easy to determine from this list of questions that time and energy are two primary requirements for an effective homeschooling program. If you aren't able or willing to devote the time and energy necessary to developing and implementing an educationally solid homeschool program, then other alternatives for educating your children may be more appropriate.

Costs

Although many of the questions mentioned the subject of *money*, cost does not have to be a major roadblock for teaching your children at home. Yearly costs for teaching your children depend greatly upon the resources or materials you choose.

Some research seems to indicate that the average cost of teaching a child at home is about $500 per year for books and materials. If there is more than one child in the home, the cost will obviously increase. If the child enrolls in extracurricular activities, classes offered outside the home, or college courses, the cost will probably be higher. Similarly, the use of tutors, consultants, distance educators, or correspondence schools will increase cost.

Parents who engage in cooperative schools or who create their own curriculum may spend less money than the average homeschooling family. Using the library, the Internet, and free community resources may also save money.

Sacrifices of Homeschooling in High School

Over the years many people have asked us if we plan to teach our children through high school. Our response has always been, "As long as we feel like we are doing well by our children, then by all means, yes!" As we write this book, our oldest child is in college and our second oldest will start college in a few months. We also have a third-grader, a second-grader, a pre-kindergartener, and a preschooler at home. We know we have many more years of teaching ahead of us if we are committed to teaching all of them at home through the twelfth grade. Although we can't say what the future will bring, we intend to teach all of our children at home through high school.

Teaching our children at home involves sacrifices beyond the time, money, and effort it takes to do the job well. They may not attend the local high school prom. They won't participate in a state-level football or volleyball game, be part of the school band, or join any of the clubs or groups available at traditional schools. They also won't have the benefit of an academic counselor to help them track down scholarships for college. However, there are many other activities available to them. So far, our high school children have enjoyed a combined co-ed formal dinner and activities night, homecoming dances and proms, teen game nights, competitive flag football, a bonfire outing, physical education classes, bowling, swimming, participating in mock presidential elections, and volunteering in various settings, just to name a few. Many dedicated homeschooling parents have helped make these and other activities possible, providing themselves and their children opportunities to socialize with other homeschooling children and families.

Our children have also been involved in a variety of individual activities throughout high school, including entering various writing and art contests, taking music and art lessons, and being an active part of our homeschooling program by working with their younger siblings.

There are numerous activities available to homeschooled youth today. Good friends of ours have their oldest boys take piano lessons, and we've been privileged to attend their recitals and listen to them play wonderful and extensive classical pieces from memory. Whatever options are available to you, it is important to have your child be involved with whatever interests him the most and what you can afford to do.

As for academics, we are confident all of our children will be as prepared for college and life as many of their traditionally schooled counterparts, if not more so. Our daughter's success in her

> **There are numerous activities available to homeschooled youth today.**

first semester of college (she took a full load of courses and earned a 4.0 GPA) is a testament to her being well prepared for higher education. In her second semester she is taking nineteen credit hours in subjects ranging from creative writing to astronomy, which tells us she is a confident learner and ready for any challenge.

If you are truly dedicated to your child's education, you must spend time reviewing and grading their work, which can be tedious at times, especially when you would rather be doing something else. Yet, to help your child become a better student and to prepare her for college and life, you must provide positive feedback about lessons or correction and follow-up instruction, as the case may be. This all takes time and energy, but it is a small sacrifice that reaps huge rewards.

Fortunately, Chandra and I have different strengths when it comes to math, science, and other subjects, so between the two of us, we have most of the bases covered. When it comes time for trigonometry or calculus, it may be a different story! There are many available resources to assist you in the areas you feel you are lacking skills or knowledge. Consultants, community college courses, and curriculum supplements can all be beneficial. Take the time to locate and learn about the options available to you, and academics will not have to be an area of sacrifice for you or your child.

There are, however, other sacrifices that you, your high school student, and your other family members may need to make while teaching your child at home through high school. You will have to juggle your time and attention between the needs of your older child and your younger children. There are times when you will need to focus on teaching one child while the other children go it alone until you can work with them. If you have very young children, you may be teaching while you fix lunch, change diapers, tend to a crying child, and other such activities. There are days when you may also have to teach longer into the evening.

When our oldest two children started high school, we had a two-year-old and a three-year-old in the house, and during the next two years we had two more children. Peace and quiet and uninterrupted teaching time just didn't exist very often. Despite having a very small house, we were able to do some creative rearranging of room assignments so that the oldest two got rooms of their own downstairs, which at least gave them somewhat of a quiet, private place to study. We also set up our daily schedule so the older children would alternate baby-sitting the youngest ones. While Chandra worked with one on his math or sciences lessons, the other kept the little ones entertained.

Younger siblings may feel a little like luggage after a while as you tote them along while dropping your older child off at various activities. If you have elementary-age children, they sometimes have to interrupt their day or bring their studies along with them for such excursions. Of course, children are normally resilient and don't think too much about this sort of thing, but once in a while they get a little burned out. Chandra minimized our children's discomfort by packing snacks or fun lunches if they were going to be gone for a long period of time. She also planned extra fun activities for the young ones whenever possible, such as stopping at a playground while waiting for their older siblings.

We did our best to manage these interruptions by adhering to a regular schedule, which is something we will address further in a later chapter. Yet, even the best schedule falls by the wayside when the children are ill or something unexpected comes up. In these situations you cope the best you can and then use your schedule to get back on track as soon as possible.

Overall, the sacrifices we make in our homeschooling are not a big deal. After all, we are a family and sometimes that's what families need to do. From that viewpoint we consider it a privilege to make whatever sacrifices we need to in order to help prepare our children for college and life.

Giving up the Cons

What we hope to gain by homeschooling through high school definitely outweighs any sacrifices we might have to make. Although there is a tendency to look at all of the potentially negative or difficult aspects of homeschooling through high school, we encourage you to also consider all of the benefits before you decide. For example, we know that while we may be sacrificing some good things by not sending our children off to high school, we are also giving up some harmful things, including:

- Peer pressure
- Bullying
- Violence
- Unethical teachers and administrators
- Sexual predators (adults and peers)
- Drugs and alcohol
- Direct teaching or exposure to subject matter we would find highly questionable or in direct conflict with the moral, religious, and ethical principles of our family

By giving up all of the good *and* the bad of going to school elsewhere, our children have gained the safety and security of a loving home and the companionship and admiration of their siblings. Homeschooling helps our children to be better friends than if they were apart six to eight hours a day at a school outside the home. Our children also enjoy a variety of close and casual friendships in safe environments through homeschooling, church, and family activities.

Why We Homeschool

Homeschooling through high school can be fun for you *and* your children. When you teach your child at home—even in high school—you can set up the curriculum to help identify and explore topics your child will enjoy to a greater depth than he could in many other school settings. High school at home doesn't have to be drudgery for your child or a time of doubt for you. It is really a wonderful opportunity for you to take your homeschool program and your relationship with your child to new heights.

High school is also a great time to help children develop college-level skills such as critical thinking and self-directed learning. Not only are these skills essential for success in college, but they are also important life skills.

Although our society tends to rush teenagers into the role of adults, teenagers are still children. Yes, they are much more intelligent and capable than their elementary-age peers, but teenagers also are still in great need of guidance and nurturing—although they may adamantly deny it. We deliberately held off allowing our children to get part-time jobs until late in their high school years so they had more time to enjoy life. They will spend the rest of their lives working, so why make them start sooner than necessary?

The high school years provide great opportunities for you to help your child continue to explore and develop the values and morals that are important to your family. Teenagers can be taught how to use critical thinking and self-directed learning skills not only for academics, but also for dealing with peer pressure; coping with issues like drugs, alcohol, and sex; and developing their views of the world around them. You will have no better opportunity to influence the life choices of your children than in high school.

Although it might seem trite to say so, we realize that our children are growing up and will soon be on their own. While we hope to stay close as a family even after they leave home, we know that this time with them will never come again. For us homeschooling gives us that much more time to spend with them.

When we started homeschooling we had more than our share of serious doubts. Now we are confident that homeschooling is right for our family and we look forward to teaching our remaining children through the end of their high school years.

Key Points

- ☐ Review the fifteen homeschooling questions to help you make an informed decision on whether or not to homeschool through high school.
- ☐ Consider the sacrifices of homeschooling during the high school years: added expenses, no competitive sports, fewer social activities, no counselors for help with college preparation, and so on.
- ☐ Review the benefits of homeschooling through high school: activities with other homeschoolers, avoiding dangers and bad influences at traditional schools, closer family relationships.

Post-High School Life Choices of Homeschool Graduates

For my doctoral dissertation, I conducted a survey of homeschooled students in order to determine what life choices they made after completing high school. The study focused on the rationale behind the choices of graduates 18 years of age or older who completed high school in a homeschool program in Nebraska.

A majority of the respondents, 84%, indicated that they chose to continue their education after high school, while 16% indicated a different choice. Students who went on to college were enrolled in a variety of disciplines, including mechanics, computer science, paralegal-commercial and family law, liberal arts, computer systems management, communications/journalism, intercultural communications/ media studies, nutrition, elementary education, communications, equestrian science, horticultural landscape design, and biology. Some students indicated they were simultaneously pursuing courses related to either Bible studies or youth ministry.

The responses of the individuals who made choices other than attending a post-secondary school also indicated they had specific goals in mind when making their decisions. While these respondents chose to work after high school in lieu of college, some of their reasons included the following: to take a break from school, to experience a certain amount of independence, to pursue a business opportunity, to earn money, and to decide what to do. Two of the four respondents indicated a desire to return to school, and one respondent indicated she had already returned to school.

Overall, the homeschool graduates in the survey considered homeschooling to have been beneficial in relation to their life choices and goals. In some instances homeschooling helped students achieve their goals sooner because they were able to attend two-year schools during high school or were able to complete basic courses required to transfer to four-year schools. Other responses indicated that homeschooling had helped students be academically prepared to attend post-secondary school and also helped them be generally prepared for pursuing either work or further education.

CHAPTER 3

Am I Qualified to Teach High School?

SOME PARENTS MAY DECIDE NOT TO TEACH their children at home through high school because they don't believe they are qualified to do so. There may be legal requirements involved, and we can't address those because there are just too many variations from state to state to list here. We recommend you check with your state's education department for more information on qualifications for teaching high school. However, this chapter addresses two of the more common concerns parents have about being qualified to teach high school: 1) They don't know how to teach high school, only grade school, and 2) They aren't an expert in *every* high school subject.

How Do I Teach High School?

Let's face it, teaching grade school seems a lot less overwhelming than teaching high school. You may feel that you have a pretty good grasp of elementary-level subjects and skills or that you can quickly get up-to-speed in areas where your knowledge or skills may be rusty or deficient. You may also feel comfortable at the grade-school level because your children are less likely to question what they are being taught. They may consider you to be the subject-matter expert who *knows it all.*

Teenagers, on the other hand, are often more aware of the extent of your knowledge and skills (and your limitations), which may make you feel uncomfortable as a teacher. You may also figure that you can't *mess up* your children too much at the grade-school level, but there's a lot more at stake in high school, with college and life looming on the horizon.

You may also feel more comfortable teaching at a grade-school level because, after all, they are just children. But when those children become young adults, you may not be sure you know *how* to teach them anymore. And you are right that the teaching techniques will be different. The way to teach elementary-age children isn't necessarily the best way to teach high schoolers.

In the early twentieth century, as researchers— primarily psychologists—studied how children developed physically, mentally, and emotionally, educators began to apply this knowledge to better understand how children learned. Subsequently, various methods for teaching children were developed and later unofficially grouped under the term *pedagogy,* a word with Greek origins that loosely translates as "leading children" (Hiemstra and Sisco, 1990).

The pedagogical model is based on the teacher being a subject-matter expert who directs all the learning that occurs in the classroom. The teacher determines what will be learned, when it will be learned, and the best method for teaching and learning any given subject. From the pedagogical viewpoint, it is assumed that children know very little about anything, including how to learn, and that they require a teacher to lead them through their learning experiences. Since children have little or no experience from which to draw when learning about a new subject, they are sometimes described as blank slates to be written upon or empty vessels into which knowledge can be poured (Hiemstra and Sisco, 1990).

The pedagogical model is often appropriate when children are in grade school, since, due to their lack of knowledge and experience, they often need to be directly taught. For many parents this is an agreeable situation because they feel like they know enough about elementary mathematics, science, history, and English to teach their children.

The pedagogical model is often appropriate when children are in grade school.

However, when it comes time to teach algebra, geometry, advanced composition, chemistry, or a variety of other high-school level subjects, parents begin to doubt their teaching abilities. Later we will address teaching high-school subjects that aren't your strengths, but for now we will review a method of teaching that often works better for teaching older students than the method just described.

At the college level, many professors use a teaching approach called *andragogy*, which was popularized by Malcolm Knowles in 1970 (Hiemstra and Sisco, 1990). The andragogical model considers mature learners to be responsible for their own learning and for helping direct their own learning experiences. This model assumes mature learners have had real-life experiences and want to incorporate new knowledge for immediate application in their lives. We say "mature" learners and not simply "adult" learners because an andragogical approach may be appropriate for students when, at any age, they become actively involved in

The andragogical model considers mature learners to be responsible for their own learning.

their learning experiences, including deciding for themselves what will be learned, how, and why.

When a child reaches high school, the pedagogical model is appropriate for some subjects or certain aspects of some subjects, but not for others. Yet some homeschoolers continue to use the pedagogical approach almost exclusively throughout high school. Technically, there is nothing inherently wrong with this. However, as children progress through high school, the pedagogical approach can be somewhat limiting in helping them develop critical thinking and self-directed learning skills they need for higher education and life on their own.

What this means to you is that you don't have to teach high school like you taught grade school— as the subject-matter expert. Instead, your job is to help guide your high-school student to be more of an independent learner. By taking this approach, you can help your child develop self-directed learning skills.

In other words, you don't have to be an expert in every subject. What matters more is that you are able to help your child take an active part in deciding *what* to learn and how, rather than just being passively *taught*. In Section III we will discuss how to set up your program to achieve this goal.

You Don't Have to Be an Expert

What children should be taught in high school is regulated in part by the state in which they live, but is primarily driven by the knowledge and skills that colleges and universities want incoming students to have. This in turn is influenced by the needs of society and employers.

Many colleges want students to have a certain number of years (or credits) in social studies, English, science, a foreign language, and mathematics. While you may feel qualified to teach some of these subjects, you are probably less comfortable teaching others, and that's okay.

There are many options you can explore to supplement your weak areas. Community college courses often allow high school students to satisfy state requirements as well as college admission criteria. If you don't have access to a local college, there are also online college courses, computer programs, textbooks, video courses, consultants, co-op schools, and other resources. Even if you are not knowledgeable about or comfortable with teaching some subjects, this doesn't have to be an insurmountable roadblock to teaching your child at home through high school.

Chandra's Perspective

When we first started teaching our children at home, I felt so completely unqualified that it made me nervous. I really lacked the self-confidence I needed to enjoy what I was doing. Now, although I wouldn't go so far as to say that I feel like a "teacher" in the same way as someone who has earned a teaching degree, I do feel much better about teaching our children than I did when we first started.

For me, part of feeling comfortable is simply being an experienced homeschooler now. Another factor is reading the newspaper or watching the news reports of the bad things happening to children in traditional schools and knowing that our children are much safer at home.

However, I know that keeping children safe doesn't necessarily mean that they are well educated. So from a practical standpoint, we feel like we've been doing something right when we look at our children's standardized test scores over the years, which show them far above the national average in every subject for their grade levels. When our oldest daughter took the ACT test and scored 28 out of 36 possible points, and even did well in the mathematics portion (a subject I was directly responsible for teaching her), I was both proud of her and relieved that I hadn't messed things up along the way.

When we first started teaching our oldest two in high school we ran our program like we did during grade school, which worked only for a short while. We then looked at other options for high school instruction and settled on the approaches described throughout this book.

When we first started teaching our children at home, I felt so completely unqualified that it made me nervous. I really lacked the self-confidence I needed to enjoy what I was doing. Now, although I wouldn't go so far as to say that I feel like a "teacher" in the same way as someone who has earned a teaching degree, I do feel much better about teaching our children than I did when we first started.

For me, part of feeling comfortable is simply being an experienced homeschooler now. Another factor is reading the newspaper or watching the news reports of the bad things happening to children in traditional schools and knowing that our children are much safer at home.

However, I know that keeping children safe doesn't necessarily mean that they are well educated. So from a practical standpoint, we feel like we've been doing something right when we look at our children's standardized test scores over the years, which show them far above the national average in every subject for their grade levels. When our oldest daughter took the ACT test and scored 28 out of 36 possible points, and even did well in the mathematics portion (a subject I was directly responsible for teaching her), I was both proud of her and relieved that I hadn't messed things up along the way.

While we're not experts in every subject, David and I drew on our strengths and interests to cover most of the subjects. Where there were gaps in what we felt comfortable teaching well, we relied on classes taught at our community college. In subjects such as advanced mathematics, I felt like I did a good job of teaching the children, but to reinforce their skills for college they took some math classes (like algebra) a second time at the community college.

Now, more than ever, I am totally committed to homeschooling our children all the way through high school. Our children are safe, happy, and learning not only academics, but also the values that we want them to learn. These values cannot be taught anywhere else or by anyone else.

Homeschooling is the best opportunity you will have to demonstrate what it means to be an adult and to provide a real-life example of the values you've been teaching your children for years. In many ways the high school years represent the last chance you have to directly influence your child's development before she graduates and begins pursuing college or a career.

Key Points

☐ Reevaluate your teaching methods as your child transitions from grade school to high school. What worked for a younger student may not be best for an older student.

☐ High school can be more daunting to teach due to more complex subject matter. Let your older student become responsible for his own learning, so you don't have to have all the answers.

☐ Find supplemental resources for subjects when your child needs extra help. These include co-ops, local colleges, online courses, computer programs, books, and consultants.

CHAPTER 4

What Do I Teach in High School?

You MAY HAVE SOME SPECIFIC IDEAS about what you want to teach your child in high school. Perhaps you want to make high school fun—more so than the boring lectures you endured. Or maybe you want to help her avoid the embarrassments that can occur during high school, such as being uncoordinated in a physical eductation class, having to explain a special need to teachers or peers, or having to be overly concerned with their physical development around the opposite sex. Perhaps you have visions of providing your child with customized learning opportunities, such as conducting in-depth historical research, performing complex scientific experiments, creating beautiful art work, or engaging in real-life apprenticeships. Maybe you plan on teaching academically challenging curriculum that will have every ivy-league school clamoring for your child. Or perhaps you are scared to death and don't have a clue where to start.

To some extent it doesn't matter what you want your child to learn because your state's department of education, along with colleges and universities, determines what you *must* or *should* be teaching—

that is, if you want to continue homeschooling and if you want your child to be admitted to college. While this may sound harsh, the requirements set by individual states and institutes of higher education in turn reflect the demands of our society and, to some extent, of the companies that will eventually employ our children. The reason for this is two-fold. First, it is the goal of higher education to produce well-rounded individuals who will become productive members of society in order to keep it running smoothly. Second, in both the academic world and in the workforce, individuals without sound basic skills are a liability because remedial education and training are both time-consuming and costly.

It's still possible to customize your child's learning experiences and curriculum to be interesting, fun, and challenging rather than routine and mundane. However, before you set out to create a wonderfully rewarding high school program, you should know what exactly your child has to learn in high school.

High School Readiness

Prior to starting your high school program, you need to determine whether any gaps in your child's knowledge exist so you can plan to teach these missing skills along with the required subjects. If your child needs additional help at the start of high school, don't despair. This is a very common occurrence. Many high school and college students need to take refresher courses to build their basic skills in one or more subjects before moving on to advanced courses. Often the need for refresher training is a result of the differences in our various school systems—differences ranging from a lack of standardized curricula to the teaching approaches employed at each school.

For example, I went to a parochial grade school, one of several schools in the city, each of which had strengths and weaknesses when it came to teaching certain subjects. My elementary school produced, for the most part, students who were very good at reading and writing and performing basic arithmetic.

A neighboring parochial school produced students who had already been exposed to concepts of algebra and geometry by the time they completed eighth grade. While they weren't as effective overall with reading and writing, my peers and I didn't know anything about algebra and geometry. So when we all ended up at the same high school, everyone had some catching up to do.

Checking Your Child's Academic Readiness for High School

Prior to starting high school, there are certain learning skills and types of knowledge that teenagers should already have. These skills can be categorized into the three "R's"—reading, writing, and arithmetic. Literacy is essential for success in high school, college, and life. It is immensely beneficial for elementary-age children to acquire, practice, and develop reading, writing, and arithmetic skills.

The skills listed below may seem terribly basic, but so often students don't have these skills when they enter high school—some don't have them by the time they reach college or enter the workforce. This is not meant to be a complete list. Rather it is intended to give you an idea of some of the more common reading, writing, and arithmetic skills and concepts students should have prior to high school:

Reading and Writing

- Alphabetizing skills
- Correctly using spelling, grammatical, and word usage rules
- Correctly using suffixes, prefixes, contractions, and abbreviations
- Understanding when and how to capitalize letters of words

- Recognizing and being able to write in complete sentences
- Knowing how to correctly identify, structure, and punctuate different types of sentences
- Using resources such as a dictionary, thesaurus, and encyclopedia to gather or check information
- Using resources within a textbook, such as the table of contents, index, and glossaries
- How to effectively read and use a textbook
- Reading well aloud—both poetry and prose
- Memorization of poems or brief excerpts of prose
- Using and understanding common expressions
- Deducing meanings of unknown words based on clues within the word
- Writing a variety of documents in detail, such as thank you notes, various types of letters, book reports, and thesis papers
- How to write creatively
- How to write in an expository style in the third person
- How to cite sources when writing
- Penmanship skills—both printing (manuscript) and cursive writing
- Identifying key ideas in a story
- Interpreting meanings of words, phrases, and sentences from prose and poetry
- Reading, retention, and discussion skills based on reading assignments with various types of materials

Arithmetic

- Counting skills and recognizing numbers
- Reading and writing numbers to at least the millionth place
- Sequencing and organizing
- Addition, subtraction, division, and multiplication
- Solving story problems

- Understanding American and some metric measures
- Understanding place values
- Using fractions, decimals, and percentages
- Reading and interpreting numerical data from various sources, such as graphs, charts, dials, rulers, scales, and tools
- Recognizing and using Roman numerals
- Averaging, estimating, and rounding
- Counting change, computing money totals
- Telling time
- Understanding greater and less than
- Recognizing geometric shapes
- Finding the unknown number in an equation
- Deductive reasoning

Other Subjects

- Understanding basic concepts of various fields of science—physical science, astronomy, biology, geology, earth science, and others
- Understanding basic concepts of maintaining personal health
- Understanding basic geography terminology—continents, oceans, poles, equator, and so forth
- Identifying locations of major countries and locations using a globe
- Using maps effectively
- Understanding basic concepts about US government
- Remembering basic events and key persons from US and world history

Other Skills

- Employing common sense
- Taking responsibility for their actions, especially their academic work
- Learning to communicate effectively, verbally and in writing

- Knowing when to ask for help
- Following instructions, verbal and written
- Avoiding unnecessary errors
- Checking and self-correcting their work
- Planning how to complete assignments
- Managing time to complete assignments adhering to deadlines
- Accepting and utilizing feedback

What about Other Subjects?

If you want to specifically define *by subject* the depth and breadth of information your child should acquire during the elementary years, there are a variety of resources you can use. Most of the major publishers of homeschool curricula, such as Bob Jones University Press (BJU) or A Beka, provide a framework of what subjects they think should be taught each year and to what extent. Some publishers refer to this framework as a *scope and sequence* or some other similar term. Quite often this information is available in their marketing packets, on their Web sites, or by request. You can even find this information by simply looking at the table of contents of any of their elementary school texts.

By reviewing scope and sequence information, you can see what a publisher believes should be taught at each grade level for each subject. If you like to create your own curriculum but are afraid that your child might miss learning something important as a result, you can still use the scope and sequence information to help you decide what is important for your child to learn in each grade from elementary through high school.

For example, A Beka lays out a nice framework for each of the elementary years that includes reading, literature, poetry, penmanship, phonics, writing/composition, spelling, grammar, arithmetic, health, safety, manners, science, social studies (history and geography), Bible studies, and morality. BJU offers the same primary topics as A Beka. Your decisions about publishers and curriculum should be based on the quality and usefulness of the materials, as well as which ones are most aesthetically pleasing to you and your child.

You can also check your assumptions about what your child needs to know by the time she starts high school by looking at the situation in reverse—look first at the scope and sequence for the high school courses she will be taking. This will allow you to define the skills and concepts your child should have learned in elementary school. If you use this approach it is important to remember that in high school new information will be presented, such as math skills and foreign languages, so what is taught in elementary grades may not be directly related to what is taught in high school. The best way you can prepare your child for everything new that she will learn is by developing her reading, writing, and reasoning (mathematical) skills.

In Section IV we will address the issue of buying curricula versus creating your own. For now we will review one major advantage of using standardized curricula. If you purchase curricula, especially from the same publisher each year, theoretically your child will acquire all the information and skills during the elementary years that he will need to successfully complete that publisher's curriculum for grades nine through twelve. We say "theoretically" because even if you've *taught* your child using the best resources available, it doesn't guarantee that he *learned* everything. Whether you purchase a curriculum or customize it to your child's needs, it may be challenging to be sure that your child learned all the necessary information.

One way to check your child's progress is through standardized testing. Children at traditional schools take standardized tests periodically, allowing teachers to objectively identify what their students have learned. Many states are attempting to require homeschooled children to take standardized tests for the same reason—to be sure they know what they are supposed to know.

The Iowa Test of Basic Skills and other cumulative assessments can provide similar information to at least let you know where your child stands in relation to the baseline norm across the United States, especially regarding what knowledge and skills she should have by a specific grade level. Some parents are qualified to administer these tests on their own. BJU Press offers various tests for different ages of children. The requirements for test administrators vary by test, and often one or more options to meet the administrator criteria are available. For example, to administer the Iowa Achievement Test from BJU Press, the administrator must be a state-certified teacher, have a bachelor's degree, have been a full-time academic classroom teacher in a conventional K5–12 school, or be listed as a pre-approved Iowa tester.

The stipulations for administering achievement tests vary. Typically parents can administer the test to their own children, but not to other children even if they are related to them in some fashion. Your state may have its own requirements for which tests your child has to take, when, and by whom they can be administered. Your child may be able to take required tests at a local private, parochial, or even public school, which may be useful in achieving a certain level of objectivity in the results. Contact your local schools or your state Department of Education to determine what options are available to you.

You can double check what you should be teaching in both grade school and high school by finding out what your local public, private, or parochial schools are teaching their students in each grade. The information from the public schools should be available to you by law—often it takes only a simple request to your state Department of Education or a visit to its Web site to find this information. Whatever option you choose, the more information you have, the more confident you can feel about your own curriculum.

If you determine your child needs to learn or refine the skills he needs, remember that most high school courses start out with a review of the basics of each subject at the beginning of the academic year. If your child needs more than a quick refresher, you may want to consider other resources, such as community college courses, tutors, summer courses, and computer-based learning programs to help fill in the gaps.

Required High School Subjects

As we mentioned earlier, every state has its own criteria and regulations for homeschooling and the curriculum you need to include, so we encourage you to check with your state's Department of Education for details. However, as a general rule of thumb, most states require a progressively challenging program that includes at least the following:

- Three to four credits in high school mathematics with an emphasis on algebra
- Three to four credits of English with an emphasis on reading and writing
- Three to four credits of social studies with at least one credit devoted to American History or American Government
- Three to four credits of natural science with at least one course having a hands-on lab
- Two to three credits of one foreign language with "proof" of a lab for practicing speaking and listening to the language

NOTE: Sometimes completing a certain number of credits or years of study in a subject, such as four years of study in the same foreign language through high school, fulfills the required credits for that subject that would otherwise have to be completed during college.

You may find these requirements are either clearly defined by your state or they are written with a certain vagueness that leaves them wide open to interpretation. In either case, be sure you understand what it is you have to teach, how you have to measure your child's learning, and how you have to report both. If the state requires your child to be tested periodically, you may want to know what your child will be tested on so you can include that information in your courses.

Another way to determine what your child should be learning in high school is to look at the admission requirements for colleges or universities your child hopes to attend. Again, the admission requirements are usually similar—at least in regard to the minimum subjects your child should have completed in high school. These generally include the same subjects listed above.

Keep in mind that every college and university has its own definition of credits. Typically a high school credit is considered to be a full academic year (two semesters)—about 150 instructional hours. How you define a credit may be different if your child is able to complete a year's worth of study in one semester.

Also remember that admission requirements vary. Some schools may require more math credits and fewer social-science credits while others want everything listed above, as well as three to four elective credits. Check periodically with the schools your child hopes to attend because sometimes admission requirements change.

Double Checking Your High School Curriculum

We've identified the general knowledge and skills your child will need prior to high school, as well as the general course requirements for high school itself. Unfortunately, there isn't any specific test that can identify in advance with 100% certainty if your child is ready to go out into the world and succeed. Your child can take a test at the end of high school to see if he learned enough for a GED (General Education Diploma). The military administers a battery of tests to check general aptitude in one or more subjects. However, both of these options are delivered after the fact. Once your child has completed high school, it's too late to fix your program.

Once your child has completed high school, it's too late to fix your program.

You may now be wondering how you can make sure your child is learning the right "stuff" *during* high school. There are a few ways you can somewhat measure the value of the content in your curriculum.

If attending college is the goal, the ACT and SAT can help identify whether your child learned enough during high school to be successful in college. Unfortunately, these tests are not usually taken until near the end of high school, which limits your ability to correct any problems. In addition, some experts think (and we agree) that the results of these tests are not necessarily an accurate predictor of success in college. For example, I earned a 16 on the ACT but later graduated with a Ph.D., Summa Cum Laude with a 4.0 grade point average.

While the actual questions that appear on the ACT and SAT are supposed to be carefully guarded secrets, you can use any number of resources to at least get a good idea of what is on them before your child takes the tests. Using computer-training programs, such as those by Kaplan, or any number of teacher-led programs to help your child prepare for these tests is a good way to double check your curriculum along the way and to identify what gaps may need to be filled in prior to college. Most of the ACT or SAT tutoring resources provide sample tests and scores to help your child estimate his potential score on the actual test. A simple search of the Internet, Amazon.com, your local library, or the computer section of your local bookstore or office supply store will give you a variety of choices in resources.

Some colleges and universities have their own admission and placement tests, and some schools may require homeschooled students to have a General Education Diploma (GED), which is simply a test given by your state Department of Education or other regulating body that evaluates one's knowledge about the required subjects for graduating high school students. Unfortunately, individuals who earn a GED are sometimes unfairly labeled as being inferior in some way to those who have a traditional high school diploma.

These perceptions come from the notion that an individual who dropped out of or for some other reason left high school couldn't complete the traditional curriculum and thus had to settle for the GED and is not as smart as her peers. Yet there is any number of reasons why someone might obtain a GED versus a traditional high school diploma; therefore, it is unfair to judge these individuals in any way.

Many colleges and universities no longer require the GED in lieu of a high school diploma.

Many colleges and universities are now fully versed on the values of homeschooling and no longer require the GED in lieu of a high school diploma. Many schools are now much more interested in the official record of the student's high school curriculum (transcript) and his score on the ACT, SAT, or other such test of knowledge and skill. If you have to have a diploma or if you are simply interested in the GED, we recommend you start with your state Department of Education to find more information.

It is important not only to know the required tests and minimum scores for your schools of choice, but to know what specific knowledge and skills will be evaluated on these tests so you can help your child prepare accordingly.

ACT: The ACT is a national college admission and placement examination that was first used in 1959 and now is used in all fifty states. ACT originally stood for American College Testing but now is simply known as ACT, which is the name of the organization that administers and scores the tests. Some schools require that incoming students take just the ACT, and some require the ACT and the SAT tests or additional tests of their own design.

The ACT test evaluates a student's knowledge in English, math, reading, science, and writing (the writing option was recently added and is not required by all schools, but it may either soon be required or highly encouraged by colleges and universities). Students typically take the test at least once during their junior or senior year, although many students will take it more than once. There is a fee for each time the student takes the test.

Test results are sent directly to the student and to the colleges/universities the student has identified she wants to receive the scores. The scores on the ACT can impact whether or not the student is accepted into a college, the types of courses the student may be eligible to take in college (such as honors courses), as well as her eligibility for scholarships. For more information about the ACT please refer to **http://www.act.org/aap/**.

SAT: SAT stands for Scholastic Assessment Test. The primary test, formerly called SAT I, measures language skills and mathematical reasoning abilities. A writing assessment has also recently been added. Like the ACT, the test is given on specified dates throughout the year at test centers in the United States and other countries and is required by many colleges. Test results are sent to the student and the schools of his choosing to determine admission, placement, and financial aid.

There is a second SAT formerly known as SAT II, but now called Subject Tests. These tests are designed to measure knowledge and skills in particular subject areas, as well as the student's ability to apply that knowledge. Students typically take the Subject Tests to demonstrate their mastery of specific subjects such as English, history, mathematics, science, and language. Some colleges require both the SAT I and II, and some require one or the other. There is a fee for both tests.

For more information on the SAT, there are two links that are most useful:
http://www.collegeboard.com/splash/

http://www.princetonreview.com/college/testprep/ testprep.asp?TPRPAGE=59&TYPE=NEW-SAT-ABOUT

GED: GED stands for General Education Diploma, which is an alternative for demonstrating knowledge equivalent to that required to earn a traditional high school diploma. GED tests are administered by some vendors and by the state where a student resides. We encourage extreme caution when signing up to take the GED through a vendor in order to ensure that you are taking the correct test and that it will be valid for your state and the colleges or employers to which you would like to apply. Your best bet is to contact your state's Department of Education for specific information or requirements about the test. There is a fee for the test, which may vary depending on location. A good resource we found that listed each state and its contact information is as follows: **http://www.passged. com/test_state.php?PHPSESSID=7c3f6d709b79a9e398 f4614c92b710c5#1**

ITBS: ITBS stands for Iowa Test of Basic Skills. It is a test typically administered in the school systems every other year or so to evaluate the school's curriculum based on the students' performance against the cumulative performance ratings of students throughout the country.

The test is typically grade specific, and the specific test administered to students corresponds to their grade or level at the time they took the test; for example, the start of third grade or halfway through the third grade.

The test is administered according to the schedule determined by your local school system. For information about the test itself go to **http://www.education.uiowa.edu/itp/itbs/**.

Parents can administer the test if they meet certain qualifications. A good resource for purchasing the test and for checking on the requirements to administer it is BJU Press at **http://www.bjupress.com/services/testing/**.

Key Points

- ☐ Before starting high school, determine if there are any gaps in your child's knowledge and whether there is a need for refresher courses.
- ☐ Review the checklist of skills students should master before starting high school.
- ☐ Consider standardized testing to check elementary-level knowledge and high-school readiness.
- ☐ Check with your state for high school course requirements, and check with colleges your child is interested in for their admission requirements.
- ☐ Use ACT/SAT preparation resources to get an idea of general knowledge students should have upon entering college.
- ☐ Check with specific colleges for other required admission tests, skills, or documentation.

CHAPTER 5

Can I Teach More Than the Required Courses?

THE CONTENT OF YOUR PROGRAM SHOULD BE primarily, but not exclusively, driven by academics with an emphasis on building the learning skills necessary to succeed in college and life. However, children can learn much from non-academic classes and extracurricular activities too.

We tried to create a balance for our children between a rigorous program of study and participating in fun elective courses or other activities that didn't require academic-type study. Our daughter took several art courses and also completed various physical fitness courses. Our son participated in organized sports and semi-structured physical education classes. We required both children to take home economics courses to learn to cook, sew, and do the laundry. In addition, both were involved in community service projects each year.

We added extracurricular activities to our program to help the children learn that having a variety of interests helps them make friends, become involved in the community, and learn there is more to life than just studying all the time. However, we always emphasized the importance of academics and especially learning how to learn. As we expected, when our children applied to various colleges, the schools were not concerned with their extracurricular activities, but with their academic courses. So there are a few things you may want to consider before including too many electives and extracurricular activities in your curriculum.

Electives and College Admission Requirements

Theoretically, if a high school student completes multiple courses each year, she could complete high school in less than four years—perhaps in as little as two years. However, you should seriously consider why you would want your child to do so.

Unless there is an overwhelming reason why your child should complete high school and try to enroll in college or to enter the workforce at around age 16, you may want to give your child the last two years of high school to continue to mature personally and academically. You may also want to keep in mind that admission guidelines for many colleges and universities also include the age of the applicant to avoid enrolling students who are not socially or developmentally ready for higher education. You may want to spread out your child's high school curriculum over a four-year period for her benefit.

Beyond the academic courses required for admission, any other course that a student takes in high school will probably be considered extra by colleges. So if your child studies religion, music, art, physical education, or if she actively pursues a hobby or other interest as part of her educational program, the result may be a well-rounded child, but these courses and activities may not directly apply toward the academic admission requirements. If you have the minimum academic requirements for college admission well covered, then it's great for your child to take extra classes or participate in sports, employment, volunteer work, apprenticeships, and other activities that contribute to a more well-rounded individual rather than one who is focused exclusively on academics. Sometimes a school's decision between two equally qualified students is based on one student exceeding the minimum requirements of high school. Colleges want students who are going to be academically successful, but they also want students who will participate in school activities and who will represent the school well after graduation.

Colleges want students who are going to be academically successful.

Pros and Cons of College Courses during High School

Sometimes high school students may also take courses at a local community college or university. These courses may be used to fulfill high school requirements such as foreign language, science, or advanced math. In addition, students can also earn college credits.

It is not unheard of for homeschooled students to graduate from high school with enough college credits for an associate's (two-year) degree—or to be close to earning one. When students take college courses to earn high school credits and college credits simultaneously, this is sometimes referred to as "double-dipping" because the credits earned apply at both levels.

Double-dipping is not illegal or unethical. However, you should keep in mind a few things about this practice. First, some larger colleges and universities do not allow high school students to use courses to fulfill high school credits, though many community colleges are not concerned about this.

Second, taking courses at a college to fulfill high school credits does not mean that a student will automatically earn an associate's degree. Two-year degrees are usually in specific areas of study, which means that simply completing courses in English, science, mathematics, foreign language, and social studies (high school courses) may apply toward general credit requirements. More specialized classes in a chosen subject area must also be completed to earn a degree.

Third, earning college credits or even a two-year degree doesn't always mean a student will have fewer courses to complete for a four-year degree. For a bachelor's degree (a four-year degree), students are required to complete a certain number of general credits in addition to discipline-specific credits required to earn the degree. While some of the two-year college credits a student earned during high school may transfer to a four-year school, many may not. Of those credits that do transfer, only some may correspond directly to the courses the four-year school requires.

If your child does take college courses during high school, remember to document all of this information on your high school transcripts. Make sure all of the high school credits required for admission to a college are accounted for on transcripts. If high school credits were fulfilled through college courses, you will have to supply not only high school transcripts, but also *official* college transcripts in the admission application or packet.

Other Admission Requirements

Something else you may want to keep in mind is that even though colleges and universities have general admission requirements, there may be additional requirements for specific schools, programs, or departments *within* a college or university. For example, the school of music may require a certain level of musical experience, knowledge, or performance ability with an instrument or even require auditions before a student can be admitted. Depending on circumstances, students can often gain general enrollment to a college first and then apply for admission to a specific program at a later time.

If in doubt about what a college wants, you should call and ask. It is important to speak to an experienced enrollment counselor, preferably one that has some experience with homeschoolers. You may have to educate the counselor about homeschooling, in which case it pays to be positive, professional, and patient.

Get specific information about what the school needs from you to prove what your child accomplished during high school. Also keep in mind that admission requirements change from time to time, so it's a good idea to stay in touch with the school. It never hurts for the school to get to know you and your child prior to applying for admission.

It's also a good strategy to consider more than one college or university, because it may be possible that your child won't be accepted to his first choice school. Be aware of the admission requirements of all the schools in which your child is interested and work toward that end. Don't focus all your efforts on just one school.

Although your child is applying to gain admission to a school, you and your child are ultimately the customers because you'll be paying the bill one way or another. The school and its personnel are there to serve you, so take advantage of any services and assistance they offer to get you through the admission process.

The key to gaining admission to a college is to keep accurate records that "speak" the same language as that particular school. These records help prove to an enrollment counselor that your child successfully completed the required high school courses and is eligible for admission. We will address the subject of transcripts in more detail in Chapter 26.

Key Points

- ❒ Review the pros and cons of taking college courses during high school.
- ❒ Talk to counselors at specific colleges to verify any non-academic admission requirements.

CHAPTER 6

Is There More to High School Than Academics?

WHEN I CONDUCT HOMESCHOOLING WORKSHOPS, I ask participants if they can write a list of *everything* they were taught in grades K–12. I always get a number of blank stares and many more nervous ones because trying to recall all that information is a daunting task, to say the least, and the older we get the more daunting it seems!

Identifying what you were taught about a particular subject in a particular grade—this task might be a little easier, but it still would be overwhelming because you were taught a great deal of information in each subject every year you attended school. Similarly, if we asked you to recount the major events of the American Revolution—in chronological order—you probably couldn't. Don't worry! Most people can't remember all those dates, places, and names. We know we can't, although we probably did for a short time in order to pass a test or two in school.

If we asked you to name all of the elements of the Periodic Table, or to define what a predicate nominative is, or to conjugate any of the verbs of the foreign language you studied, or to recall a few mathematical theorems, could you do it? Could you pass the ACT test if you took it today? A year from now, five years from now, or even ten years from now, what will your children be able to recall based on what they were taught? They probably will be able to do about as well as you could now. Why?

In school students learn facts, dates, and other miscellaneous information to prove they are ready to be promoted to the next grade, which keeps parents very happy. However, this type of retention is usually short term because being *taught* something and *learning* something are two very different things.

> **Being *taught* something and *learning* something are two very different things.**

Teaching Skills and Concepts

If children can't recall specific information beyond the short term, what's the point of teaching them anything? What should be taught instead? These are very good questions. There are two key words you should keep in mind as we answer those questions in this chapter: skills and concepts.

If we asked you to recite the multiplication table, write a complete sentence, or follow written directions to bake a cake, you probably could. Throughout your years in school you learned a series of concepts and skills that continue to help you in your daily life. For example, at an early age many students learn how to memorize. This skill later helps with remembering basic mathematics concepts and the skills of adding and subtracting. In turn, those concepts and skills help students memorize and use the multiplication table, which later helps with learning how to perform long division and even more complex subjects such as algebra, geometry, and chemistry. In short, the information being taught is constantly re-inforced through learning and practicing skills associated with the information.

Assuming normal development, the brain retains most of what is learned in school, but it can't always be recalled on demand. This is because most students actively learn information just long enough to pass a test, write a paper, or answer a question in class. The needed information is then stored away in the brain somewhere as accumulated, but not readily accessible, knowledge.

What most students *really* learn in school are the basic skills and concepts that continue to be useful throughout life. These skills are associated with literacy. Every subject finished, every passage read, and every task or lesson completed primarily reinforces the basic skills of reading, writing, and problem solving.

Developing College-Level Skills at Home

Like many homeschoolers, we often field questions from non-homeschooling friends, family, and strangers about whether or not we are giving our children the skills they need to succeed in college and life. We hear questions such as, "Are you planning to homeschool all the way through high school?" "What about preparing your children for college?" "Can you do that at home?" We imagine that at one time or another most homeschoolers ask themselves these same questions. To be honest, it is important to help children develop their learning skills throughout their education rather than waiting until high school to begin.

Having taught college for several years, I have worked with a variety of students. The students have included individuals just out of high school, young people who have already tried college with varying degrees of success, and adult professionals in their twenties, thirties, forties, or fifties who either never attended college or never obtained degrees. A few students in each of these groups have excellent learning skills. However, even among the older students, the majority has under-developed skills, and a few have very poor skills.

The students who struggle with learning in college do so because they are forced to fight two battles simultaneously: 1) Learning the skills necessary to succeed in college and 2) Learning the information in the assigned material. Once they acquire college-level learning skills, learning the information in the assigned material is often much easier. Collectively, these skills are what we refer to as "academic discipline," and we've broken them into the following categories:

- Self-directed learning
- Critical thinking
- Self-discipline (which includes the skills below)
  - Time Management
  - Communicating
  - Demonstrating Responsibility

Although there are as many homeschooling approaches as there are homeschoolers, the skills required to succeed (not just survive) in college remain relatively constant. The chapters in Section II will help you understand these skills and will prepare you for later sections about creating lessons, activities, and learning experiences to help children develop these skills.

Emotions as Teaching Tools

Going back for a moment to our questions about what you remember from school, the information you *can* recall represents what you *actively* learned. Your strongest memories are associated with emotions. If we asked you to recall what you had to learn in school that was the most frustrating, rewarding, inspiring, or exciting, you could probably do it fairly easily because the learning experience had an emotion attached to it.

I recall writing a report about sharks in eighth grade. I was interested in them at the time, so my teacher let me write about them even though the assignment was about a completely different subject. When I finished the report, my teacher returned it with positive written comments. I don't even remember the grade I received, but I remember the report and feeling good about my teacher's feedback. I also still remember a few things about sharks because I was positively rewarded for my efforts.

Similarly, in high school my wife and I both had teachers whose praise and belief in our potential were motivational. Chandra developed a love of art and music in part due to her teachers' reactions to her talents. I, who at one point thought I might fail geometry, ended up passing the class because my teacher kept working with me and wouldn't let me fail. I was determined not to let down a teacher who displayed such faith in me.

Sometimes negative emotions can also help us retain information. I distinctly remember my father's reactions on two occasions to failing grades I received during elementary school—once on an assignment and another time on a test. It didn't take me long to figure out that I disliked displeasing my father, and I did not like feeling embarrassed about a grade for an assignment because I didn't give my best effort. I quickly learned new problem solving skills, such as how to organize my time and set priorities (homework first, then television). I never failed an assignment or test again—at least not for lack of effort.

Personalizing the Learning Experience

No matter what curriculum you use, it is important to provide your children with numerous opportunities to practice, develop, and refine their reading, writing, and problem-solving skills. Personalizing your child's learning experiences will help her retain more information in the long term.

What we mean by personalizing the experiences is to make learning fun whenever possible. People generally learn more when having fun—the emotion helps with remembering information and events. Also, if you have fun teaching, your children are likely to have more fun learning.

> **Personalizing experiences is to make learning fun.**

Our two oldest children took a variety of writing courses during high school. Rather than simply requiring them to read from a textbook and complete written assignments, we got creative and had the children produce newsletters to send to family and friends. The children used software to layout the newsletters, including clip art and photos, and the newsletters were filled with their short stories, poems, movie reviews, editorials, columns, and reports on various topics including sports, their siblings' activities, and the weather. We actually used this assignment several times throughout high school so the children could work together to produce the newsletters as well as create their own. They loved the results, and so did our friends and relatives. We also have fun stuff to keep in our memorabilia boxes to look back on in the years ahead.

Additionally, our children completed several "Great Books" classes during high school. I had them read certain books, like *Great Expectations* and *Moby Dick*, that I knew they were likely to encounter at least once during college. Some books they enjoyed more than others, of course. However, rather than requiring they read just *my* list of books, I also allowed them to choose some books from their own reading lists as long as I approved them first. Some of the titles they chose included *The Lord of the Rings* trilogy, *The Chronicles of Narnia*, and several books from the *Hornblower* series by C.S. Forester.

In educating our children, we tried to appeal to their individual interests whenever possible. Our daughter Holly loves art and took several art courses during high school. She produced two paintings based on two of Robert Frost's poems she and I loved. We then worked together to frame them nicely for Mother's Day for Chandra.

Our son Cameron has always been interested in sports. We customized lessons and a course so he could study the various sports during the winter Olympics, as well as study other sports he was interested in.

These are just a few examples of how we tried to make learning fun. If you can't make learning fun, then you should work toward at least making it rewarding. Certain information, such as multiplication tables, has to be acquired primarily through rote learning—

Rewarding effort and recognizing accomplishments helps to reinforce what is learned.

repetition that may not be much fun for some. However, rewarding effort and recognizing accomplishments helps to reinforce what is learned. When your child does learn something, especially something that is difficult, remember to reward your child—and yourself too.

We used various rewards ranging from verbal praise for high marks to special treats and outings. Ice cream, books, and art supplies were favorite options for Holly. Cameron enjoyed movies, staying up late, or extra spending money. Both enjoyed special outings by themselves with one of us for some one-on-one time.

We want to point out that we never used these things as bribes or incentives like the proverbial carrot on a stick. The children had to do well because it was expected of them. We wanted them to develop self-discipline with regard to their academics. We simply worked together to think of special rewards we could surprise them with after the fact.

Another reward option is to give your child more control over his academic choices. As your child grows older, after learning the basic skills of reading, writing, and problem solving, you have a tremendous opportunity to relax your control a little more. Older children, especially high school students, like to make choices and exercise some control over their lives. As a teacher you have the ability to present learning experiences for your older child in such a way that he can choose from a variety of acceptable options to complete the work for a subject.

Allowing your child the opportunity to "teach" you is a great way to reinforce skills and concepts and to determine just how much your child has learned. These can be informal sessions during which she explains a concept or subject to you, or they can be formal activities, such as a speech or presentation or some sort of academic project, such as a report, art project, paper, and so forth.

In the end, it doesn't matter so much what you *teach* your child as what they *learn*. In earlier chapters we've identified what subjects children should study academically, but how you design your program helps your child acquire the experiences and skills needed for college and beyond.

> **It doesn't matter so much what you *teach* your child as what they *learn*.**

Key Points

- ❏ Focus on teaching literacy and learning skills that your child will retain and use throughout her life.
- ❏ Personalize learning experiences—make them fun for your child when possible.
- ❏ Let your child choose from several options and exercise some control over her education.

CHAPTER 7

Is Higher Education Right for My Child?

WHEN OUR TWO OLDEST CHILDREN WERE OUR only children and we first started homeschooling, preparing them for college was one of the last things on our minds. We were just trying to get them (and us) through the preschool and kindergarten years. When the children were in grade school, we were concerned with their academic performance at each grade level. Our biggest concern was that we would make a mistake and fail to teach them some critical piece of information they would need down the line.

As the high school years quickly approached, Chandra began to have some serious doubts about being a high school teacher. It seemed that in the high school years we were playing for "keeps." What if the children couldn't pass the ACT or SAT? What if they wanted to get into college but couldn't due to academic reasons? What if they wanted to get a job but no one would hire them?

As it turned out, our oldest children did very well in high school. Both felt prepared for and were excited about going to college. Both successfully completed multiple community college courses. Both have jobs. And, while we can't take all the credit for their accomplishments, we do feel a sense of pride and satisfaction in knowing we are closely involved with helping our children make the best choices they can.

The high school years can be intimidating and overwhelming for children. They are on the brink of adulthood. And although they may not openly admit they want or need our help, or that they are glad we give it to them, we know they do.

Life Choices

At the beginning of the board game *The Game of Life*, players have to decide if they are going to go the career route or the college route. There is no room for hedging and saying, "I'll go to college for a little while and drop-out and go to work" or "I'll work and go to school part-time" or "I'll try college for a while and switch schools later or drop out if it doesn't work." These options aren't available in the board game—players have to make a firm choice right away.

If players play by the actual rules (and not "house" rules like we sometimes do), the choice of college or career limits some of the other options available. If players go the college route, they can eventually pick from any of the career cards. If players go the career route, their choices are immediately limited to careers that don't require a college degree. However, players who choose the work route may get a chance later in the game to attend night school, change careers, and gamble on the chance to improve their salaries, which is the situation of many working adult students I teach at the college level.

When we play *Life* with our children, it's interesting to hear their rationale for choosing college or the workforce. Sometimes they choose college so they can have more job choices later. However, when they consider the debt college attendance incurs, they are

Chandra's Perspective

We make ourselves available to the children regularly. One way that has worked particularly well for me involves my daily walk: I let the two oldest children take turns going with me so they have some one-on-one time. I've found it is during this time (and when we are alone in the car) that they use me as a sounding board for discussing thoughts about friends, work, school, life, and things that interest them like music, movies, or world events. I try to let them do most of the talking, but I give my input when appropriate and I think they are glad that I do—at least I hope so.

These discussion times are beneficial to me too. I not only learn more about what my children may want to do with their lives, but I learn more about them as well. Armed with this information, I am better able to guide them through their studies by relating the relevance and purpose of what they are learning to their goals in life. As a result, they tend to think I'm pretty cool because I "understand" them. I hope it's a long time before they figure out otherwise.

sometimes lured into the "make money early" (career) track. Sometimes they indicate that they've chosen the work route because in real life they are tired of school. Some children don't think college is for them because they don't think they are smart enough or have the skills to succeed in college.

In some ways, playing *Life* reminds us of the decisions our children will have to make—career or college. We wonder which option they will choose and what their rationale will be. We hope they will choose college, but if not, we hope they don't feel they lack either the intelligence or the skills necessary to succeed in higher education.

No matter what type of school your child attends, he will also have to decide whether to start a career or attend college after high school. There is the option of doing neither and just sitting on the couch all day, but it is doubtful many parents support that choice. You have a wonderful opportunity to help your high school student prepare to make an informed choice about attending college or starting a career after graduation.

Is Your Child "Intelligent" Enough for College?

As parents, we admit to being a little prejudiced concerning how talented and intelligent our children are, though we know they have their limitations with certain subjects. In order to best help our children, we need to put our prejudices aside and look at the situation objectively. And the truth is not every individual who wants to attend college is well-suited to do so. There are many individuals who are actually in college who probably shouldn't be, not necessarily because they aren't intelligent enough to be there, but because they aren't motivated enough to be there. Many students enroll in college because they think they should, only to drop out later.

Some students don't consider themselves "smart" enough for college. As a homeschooler, you might worry you aren't giving your child the instruction he needs to be "smart" enough for college. The truth is that researchers often disagree about what intelligence is. Some researchers and educators have concerns about the validity of so-called intelligence tests. Many fear they do more harm than good if they prevent an otherwise intelligent student from higher education simply because he didn't do well on an intelligence "test."

Despite concerns about intelligence tests, many colleges and universities continue to use them as a means of assessing incoming students and predicting their potential for future success. Variations of the IQ test, such as the ACT, SAT, and GRE tests, are still used by many colleges and universities as a requirement for admission, so you can use your child's scores on these tests to partially answer the question of whether or not your child is *intelligent* enough for higher education. However, standardized test scores are not necessarily an accurate measurement of intelligence. Rather, they are more a measurement of an individual's ability to *demonstrate the skills* associated with being successful in college—specifically, she must demonstrate problem-solving skills for subjects such as mathematics, science, and

"Intelligence" may not be simply a measure of accumulated knowledge, but the development of skills for accumulating and applying knowledge effectively.

language. As a result, "intelligence" as it applies to educational progression may not be simply a measure of accumulated knowledge, but the development of skills for accumulating and applying knowledge effectively.

So, the question isn't really just a matter of your child being intelligent enough for college, but does he have the skills necessary to be successful in college? Some newer theories seem to indicate that *emotional* intelligence may play a bigger part in a person's long-term happiness and success than her intelligence quotient. For further information about this, you may find Daniel Goleman's (1995) book *Emotional Intelligence: Why it Can Matter More than IQ* to be of interest.

To be successful in higher education, your child will need to acquire the skills that college entrance exams attempt to measure not just for the purpose of passing the test, but for the way learning is acquired at the college level. With college as a goal, your child's high school curriculum should include developing these skills in addition to learning the required academic subjects. In Section II we will explore four skills that we consider critical to success in higher education, as well as throughout life.

Another consideration for whether or not your child is ready for college is whether or not he *wants* to go to college. Some individuals simply aren't ready to go to college at the end of high school, not due to reasons associated with intelligence or skills, but due to personal maturity, interest levels, and motivation. Some students simply aren't motivated enough to succeed in college right after high school. Some may never be motivated enough for college, while others may find the motivation at some point later in life. Many of the adult students I work with didn't complete college "when they were supposed to" and now motivations such as wanting a higher paying job, obtaining a specific job, changing careers, or needing to keep their present jobs motivate them to return to school. They often perform much better as a result.

High school graduates who choose not to go to college may have specific goals in mind for their lives. They may want to take a break from school, be more independent for a while, pursue a business opportunity, or "find" themselves by taking the time to decide what to do in life, or what they want to be when they grow up. Some want to travel, serve in the missions, enter the military, or simply try different careers before going to college. Some may just not want to go to college at all, as they have other aspirations but don't verbalize them for fear of upsetting their parents who have their hearts set on them going to college. Some fear wasting time and money wandering around in college taking classes without knowing what value they provide.

Sometimes children don't even know what career or education options are available to them because their parents don't discuss these topics with them. When you are homeschooling your children, it is easy to get caught up in the day-to-day routine and forget about the "big" picture of preparing your child for life after high school. Even though you may devote considerable thought and effort to preparing your child for college, she may not choose to go that route—at least not right away. We recommend you spend time throughout high school discussing the future with your child to determine her wants and needs and to help her work toward achieving her goals.

One of my adult students, a young man in his late twenties, had dropped out of or was expelled from three different schools before I started working with him. After high school he had gone to a state university, and because there was so much freedom away from home, he fell into the party routine. He did poorly academically, since he often failed to go to class and submit his assignments on time or at all. Now he was no longer a child and realized how he had wasted his time and money drinking through college instead of getting an education. He told me how the people he thought were his friends had really just kept him from succeeding in life and how he had to get his college degree to get out of his dead-end job.

Another of my students was in his thirties when we met. He needed a college degree to get a promotion at work or to find a better job elsewhere. With three young children at home and the typical financial responsibilities of an adult, he understood the value of a college education. However, now he was juggling his responsibilities at home, a full-time job, and his studies. He often remarked how he wished he had been more motivated to go to school when "he should have," but he knew he just wasn't motivated then like he was now.

I also have had many women as students who, for one reason or another, didn't get their college degrees after high school. Some pursued jobs or careers while others had married. Many had children. Some were no longer married and now their college degree was important if they were to get a good paying job to provide for their children and themselves on their own. They, too, juggled jobs, family, and school to earn a degree.

Although my story is different, I can relate to these students because of my personal experiences. As I was growing up, I was always encouraged to go to college even though my parents never had that chance. I was never pressured into one career field or another, but I was always told that a good education would be the best option in life and so I never thought otherwise. However, I wish I had had a little more counseling about career options so I knew what specific courses to take in college. My parents simply didn't have the expertise in this area, and my high school and undergraduate school didn't do much for me in that regard. Of course, in all fairness, I may just have been too stubborn to listen to any advice back then.

Initially, I had wanted to be a teacher but was talked out of that by people who told me there weren't any jobs and the pay was poor in that field. So my career interests changed with every class I took ranging from lawyer, writer, psychologist, priest, and actor, to name a few.

By the time I reached my senior year in college I was very close to earning three or four different degrees if I wanted to stay another year or two. However, I was anxious to get out, and so, in the end, I completed college in four years and earned a degree in communications. While I never had a job specifically in "communications," that degree opened many doors to various jobs requiring communication skills, such as teaching. More importantly, the degree enabled me to attend graduate school years later where I earned a master's degree in adult and continuing education—the first step on the road to becoming what I really wanted to be when I grew up: a college professor.

Chandra and I want to support our children about whatever life choices they make after completing high school. We encourage them to go to college and often talk to them about going straight through to a master's program if they are so motivated. But if any of our girls decide to be a wife and mother instead, we'll support that wholeheartedly too. If our boys decide to pursue careers instead of college, we'll support those choices as well and we'll do both with the confidence that they've had a solid education through high school and have made their decisions based on the best information available to them about college, careers, and life.

It is very important to talk with your child about careers and college so they are prepared to make the decisions best for them. I personally encourage everyone to pursue a degree because I know many of the higher paying jobs require not only an undergraduate degree, but a graduate one as well. However, there is no need to rush through college taking courses of little interest. I recommend that students take some of the basic required courses while also taking courses in different fields that interest them the most. Sometimes students change their minds about what they want to do based on classes they take in college, such as thinking they want to become accountants but deciding to become actors instead.

No matter what path your child decides to take—college or career—the skills we've described are important. In the next section we provide you with ideas for using your homeschooling program to help your child develop the skills she needs to be successful in higher education and life.

Chandra's Perspective

Like many young students, I had gone to college without really knowing what I wanted to study or what I wanted to do in life—at least as far as what society seemed to indicate were the options available to me. You see, I always wanted to be a wife and mother, but unfortunately those vocations aren't always valued by some parents or by society, and so I spent a couple years of college just going through the motions.

Fortunately, I met Dave in college. When we met and decided to marry, Dave was closer to finishing college than I was, since he was a couple of years ahead of me. However, he was very supportive of my continuing until I completed my degree, but I really didn't have the interest in school to want to achieve that goal. So, I decided to drop out of college. I just didn't find it as rewarding as I wanted it to be, and the truth is I really didn't know in what subject I wanted a degree, so it seemed like a waste of time and money.

A few weeks before our wedding, I found another option for my education. Dave had always said he'd support whatever decision I wanted to make, and he did exactly that when I told him I wanted to attend a local business college. I enrolled in the administrative assistant program because it seemed very interesting and also practical. To me the education I would receive seemed immediately applicable in a work environment, and I think that was one of the things that most appealed to me.

Being motivated about what you study is really the key to being successful. I graduated at the top of my class and was able to secure a good paying job right after I completed the program. Throughout the years that training continued to be Invaluable as I secured various part-time or full-time jobs when we needed some extra income.

I think about going back for a degree every now and then, partially because I want to achieve that goal, but also because I think about needing a college degree should I ever be in a position to have to be the primary breadwinner for our family, which I hope never happens. Yet, every time I look at a college catalog, nothing interests me to the point that I find myself thinking, "That's it!" Certain courses in various programs may sound interesting, but nothing has really inspired me to decide on a particular degree. So, I've taken a course or two throughout the years and perhaps, one day, I'll find something I like.

Yet, to be very honest, no degree or career outside the home would ever make me as happy as I have been in my role for the last twenty-plus years—a wife and mother; those are what I always wanted to be in life. I know that's politically incorrect in today's society, but I don't care! And when I think about it, perhaps that's why no college degree program has really seemed all that interesting— they don't have college degrees in being a wife or in motherhood. If they did, I'd get my Ph.D. in it. If they gave college credit for life experiences, I think I'd have my doctorate degree without ever stepping foot in a classroom.

Key Points

☐ Prepare your child for tests such as the ACT and SAT. These tests measure skills associated with college success (not intelligence) and can be prepared for by teaching learning and test-taking skills.

☐ Remember the big picture of homeschooling— you're helping your child prepare for life. Talk with your child to determine his wants and goals, then work together to achieve them.

SECTION II

ACADEMIC DISCIPLINE— BUILDING SKILLS FOR SUCCESS IN HIGHER EDUCATION (AND IN LIFE)

CHAPTER 8

Self-directed Learning

THE TERM "DISCIPLINE" IS OFTEN THOUGHT OF in conjunction with "punishing" children for some action or inaction. Yet, the true meaning of discipline is to build self-control, develop efficiency, and to follow rules of orderly conduct. When we "discipline" our children for behavioral issues, we are really teaching them to control themselves and to behave in accordance with the rules of society—particularly our house rules.

The true meaning of discipline is to build self-control, develop efficiency, and to follow rules of orderly conduct.

As parents, we often have to "discipline" our children reactively—after the fact, such as when we find out they cut each other's hair or pushed someone out of the swing. Yet, we also teach our children self-discipline proactively by teaching appropriate behaviors for various situations, such as looking both ways before crossing the street, reviewing our expectations of using manners before we visit someone's home, or just teaching them to flush and wash their hands.

In much the same way, children need to be taught academic discipline, which is really just teaching them to have self-control as learners, to develop efficient and effective learning skills, and to behave or perform as skilled learners. As homeschooling educators, we are not only responsible for teaching subject-matter, but are also responsible for helping our children develop academic discipline—the skills that will help them succeed in higher education and life.

As teachers, it's our job to be consistent in our high expectations for our children's academic work and our low tolerances for poor work. We need to teach basic learning skills, to be specific in our directions, to set appropriate rewards and consequences for our children's academic work, and to follow through. By doing all of this, we help children prepare for the expectations their college professors and employers will have of them. In this chapter we break academic discipline down into the following skills: self-directed learning, critical thinking, time management, communicating, and demonstrating responsibility.

Self-directed Learning

In some ways teaching your child to be a self-directed learner is much like teaching him to be self-sufficient around the house. Whether you have one child or several, helping them become self-sufficient makes life easier for everyone in your home.

Whenever Chandra and I found ourselves struggling to meet everyone's needs, we would take a step back to look at how we could improve the situation. As far as homeschooling went, sometimes the best thing we could do was to get ourselves organized and to do some "pre-teaching" to head off distractions and problems.

For example, to prevent frequent requests for snacks or drinks while Chandra was trying to teach the older children, she set specific times for snacks and taught the younger children to read the clock. She instructed them not to ask for a snack before a certain time, thus helping them develop self-control while also teaching them how to tell time in the process. The same went for lunchtime. If they needed drinks, she made it easy for them to get their own by making cups and a step stool to the kitchen faucet easily accessible. Through this and similar experiences, our children learned self-sufficiency, which is part of being a self-directed learner.

Even with our teenagers, being organized and doing some "pre-teaching" has been helpful. It didn't take us long to teach them to go on to the next problem or to start working on a different subject rather than waste time doing nothing while waiting for Chandra when she was busy doing something or working with someone else. It took slightly longer for us to realize we didn't have to have all of the answers to their questions, nor did we have to devote large amounts of time to helping our high school students find every answer. Once we started making them responsible for finding the answers (or devoting enough time and energy to making sure they couldn't find answers themselves before they asked for help), life got much easier. More importantly, they began developing the self-sufficiency that would help them become self-directed learners.

Active vs. Passive Learning

Some students associate learning with being entertained. To them, obtaining knowledge should be something they can do passively, much like watching television, which is one of the primary reasons many students experience difficulties learning in college. These students believe that just by attending class the instructor will *make* them learn. It's almost as if some students expect the wise professor to open the tops of their heads and pour the knowledge in. When these students have to put forth anything beyond a minimal level of effort to learn, they quickly become bored, lose interest, and fail to pay attention. Subsequently, they often blame their professors for their own failure to learn.

Many college students are incapable of paying attention through a lecture or a discussion for more than a few minutes at a time. I've had so many adult college students who came to class expecting to be entertained with videos, games, or other "fun" activities. One of my colleagues once related a story about two graduate-level students who walked out on their first class when they discovered they would have to write papers; they had expected to only have to take multiple-choice tests.

Students such as these typically lack the attention span and self-control to be active learners, which is often a direct reflection on their personal habits, such as watching too much television, playing video games extensively, or surfing the Internet—all short-term, give-me-information-type activities. They don't enjoy learning—rather, to them learning is a task they have to perform to pass a class and earn a degree.

Many students don't even want to "earn" a degree or do anything to pass a class. It continues to amaze me how many students fail to turn in assignments, do not proactively seek help, and won't (or can't) use resources to find information. These problems occur at all levels of education, even with graduate-level students. It's almost as if these people have learned that if they wait long enough, someone will make an exception for them or baby-sit them through their lessons or let them slide by.

In all levels of education, but in college especially, students should

Students should be *active* rather than passive learners.

be *active* rather than passive learners—they should want to learn and enjoy learning. They should want to decide what to learn and always go beyond the basic requirements of every class because they want to learn more. These types of students are active participants in their education.

When students are young, they need a teacher or parent to help decide what is important for them to learn. Elementary and secondary school teachers usually decide which topics students will study and to what depth and breadth. In college, students also have to learn the required material as defined by the instructor, but as students become more effective and active learners, they often have their own learning goals to supplement what the instructor has planned. Having your child help plan classes or lessons, or to just identify some things she would like to learn in a class, encourage the development of self-directed learning skills.

Of course, students still need an "expert" to help them learn about certain subjects like algebra or chemistry, but they should be able to direct their own learning to some degree in many subjects. As students progress as learners, they may only need someone to guide them, provide critical answers or resources, share experiences, and test their understanding of what was learned.

The goal of self-directed learning is to help your child develop both a desire and an ability to obtain knowledge. Self-directed learners are *active* learners—they seek to learn new information and find ways to put it to use rather than just having it forced on them as it is in our media-driven age.

Self-directed Learning Resources

The easiest way to help your child become a self-directed learner is to create a learning environment in which she is primarily responsible for finding answers to questions or problems. With so much knowledge readily available in today's world, there really is no reason any student should answer a question with, "I don't know." A more acceptable response should be, "I don't know, but I can find out." To find out, your child needs to learn to use resources.

The earlier you teach your child to find his own answers, the better. However, you can help her become an active learner at any age by using some very simple learning resources—a dictionary, a thesaurus, and a comprehensive source of knowledge, such as the library, a set of encyclopedias, or the Internet.

One of the most important resources every student should own is a good dictionary—a physical book, not an electronic version on the computer. Of course, every student should also learn how to use this vital tool to the point she is proficient with it.

A dictionary provides a wealth of information. For those who don't spell well, a dictionary is a resource beyond compare. Many students today rely heavily on spelling and grammar checks on their computers. However, after years of grading college papers, I can tell you that these electronic tools are unreliable and students who live by them often "die" by them.

Dictionaries help students with so much more than just how to spell words. What other resource can teach a word's pronunciation, meaning, origins, parts of speech, and variations? If your child has difficulty with spelling, make it a requirement for him to grab his dictionary and *learn*.

In the college classroom I am always glad when students ask questions—even about the meaning of a word that I used. However, too many students come to class and ask how to define or pronounce a word that is in their reading materials. I used to respond, "Why didn't you just look it up in your dictionary?" I stopped asking that question because so many college students don't even own a dictionary. Students should always have to look up the meanings of unfamiliar words and use the dictionary to learn how to correctly spell any words marked as misspelled on their assignments.

The second most important learning resource every student should own is a good thesaurus—again, a book rather than an electronic version. A thesaurus is invaluable for students who want to write well— and *every* student should learn to write well. Not every student can be a Pulitzer winner, but they should know how to use words in the correct context, and they should be able to use a variety of words when they write so they don't repeat the same ones too frequently throughout their papers.

The last resource can be one of any number of comprehensive-knowledge resources, such as the library, an encyclopedia, or the Internet. There isn't much that can't be found on the Internet, which is why some parents (homeschoolers or not) prefer not to have their children use this resource for school— for fear of what their children might find. Although there are inherent dangers with the Internet, including potential to view inappropriate sites and exposure to computer viruses, there are ways to minimize or prevent these risks while allowing children to appropriately use this resource.

Despite how easily available information is on the Internet, every student should learn to utilize the library as well. If your library doesn't have an extensive collection, it may have a sharing agreement with other libraries, which will allow you to borrow more books and materials than what is available locally. Most libraries have a variety of resources, including complete sets of encyclopedias, and learning to use them is a great way to teach your child to find the information he needs—thus helping him to build self-directed learning skills.

Every student should learn to utilize the library.

I am dismayed at how many students don't know how to even begin working on a research paper—of any length. I have had many students over the years who don't know where to go to find the information they need. These students don't know how to use a library—online or in person. Often those who have access to the Internet rely exclusively on Internet searches, accepting any information they find without considering the credibility of the source. It never occurs to them to read books, to use the library's databases of academic articles, or to look at more than one source of information.

Open-ended Questions

What would happen if you asked your child, "Was George Washington an effective president?" Your child could answer either "yes," "no," or worse yet, "I don't know." This is a close-ended question and answer.

The answer may change if you asked instead, "In what ways was George Washington effective and ineffective as president?" Your child can't easily answer "yes" or "no" to that question. She might try answering, "I don't know," to which you can reply, "Well, find out." Subsequently, your child would have to use resources to find the answers to your question. This is an example of an open-ended question, which cannot usually be answered with a one-word or short answer. You can also use open-ended questions in conversations with your child to teach her to engage in conversations more extensively than simple, one-word utterances that some teens seem to love so much.

Too often children are taught to think only in close-ended terms and as such they never learn to go beyond the basic requirements of any assignment. I've even known college professors who continue to teach in this manner, having their students answer the questions at the end of the chapter or engage in mindless tasks like outlining a chapter rather than challenging them with assignments that require more extensive thinking skills, like those required to answer essay or open-ended questions.

The more often you use open-ended questions in your lessons, the more you will help your child become a self-directed learner. We'll talk more about how to do this in Section IV when we discuss assignments, subjects, and schedules in detail.

Learning from Mistakes

One of the courses I have taught over the years requires students to write a thesis paper. I learned years ago that just because a student is in college doesn't mean he can write well.

In these courses I have been required to teach a particular type of writing format, the skills of conducting research, and how to write a thesis paper. I wasn't required to teach spelling and grammar skills per se. However, because so many students lack these skills, I spent the time creating numerous handouts and devoting several class periods to grammar and writing skills. I also spent a great deal of time proofreading and editing students' papers prior to the date when the papers were due in order to give the students specific help with the skills they were lacking.

It is always amazing how many students kept making the same mistakes no matter what resources I provided them or how many times I edited their papers. One graduate student failed her thesis paper because she couldn't understand what was wrong with her paper enough to make the necessary corrections, despite the fact that I provided her with numerous resources and five detailed edits of the paper. Another student simply failed to complete his degree because he never got organized enough to write his research paper. These sorts of problems may occur for several reasons:

1. Students don't use the resources that would have helped them become better writers.
2. Students don't take the time to communicate with their instructor to find out what they did wrong and to understand their instructor's feedback.
3. Students don't manage their time well enough to put in the level of effort required to write well or to complete their work.
4. Students fail to apply the knowledge that comes from making mistakes; rather, they just keep making the same mistakes—they expect the professor to do everything for them.
5. Students don't have enough self-respect to care about how unintelligent they appear to be in front of their instructor.
6. Students simply aren't taught any better or aren't consistently required to do any better in elementary school and high school.

Another common cause of students not being responsible for learning is that they aren't trained to think. The computer, video games, television, and a host of other electronic devices are wonderful tools and fun sources of entertainment. However, students who spend too much time engaging in mindless activities, such as video games, are at risk for developing short-attention spans and learning problems later in life. I once had a student fail an important course because he couldn't pay attention in class or to his studies long enough to get the information he needed. When I asked him how he typically spent his time, he told me how he had recently got up one Saturday morning when his wife went to work and thought he'd spend a few minutes playing video games before studying. She found him in the same place on the floor in front of the television playing the same games when she arrived home ten hours later. He had not once opened his books.

It is imperative that your high schooler learns to use a dictionary and develops good study habits now when she is young, because it is much more difficult to teach adult college students these skills. Old habits are very difficult to break.

It is imperative that your high schooler develops good study habits now.

It is vital that you spend time reviewing mistakes on your child's work with her and then make sure she learns how to correct them and then does so. Even when you review your child's errors with her, it is important to stress that the goal is to avoid repeating the same errors next time. One possible solution is to have her make a checklist of past mistakes to use as a reference when starting a new assignment. It is then her job to double-check her work prior to handing it in to ensure the mistakes have been corrected.

Unfortunately, many students don't know how to learn effectively—primarily because they don't take responsibility for learning. Again, part of this problem can be attributed to how they are taught. Lectures, fact-based tests, and assignments that fail to challenge students to think beyond the basics of the subject matter too often result in students who are only passive learners. These students may have a very difficult time in the fast-paced college learning environment where professors have high expectations and low tolerance for students who turn in poor work because they don't even know where to find some of the answers on their own.

Key Points

❐ Focus on *active* learning— help your child do something with new knowledge other than simply answering questions on tests or within the textbook.

❏ Create a learning environment in which your child is largely responsible for finding answers to questions or problems.

❏ Teach your child to use resources—especially a dictionary, thesaurus, and comprehensive source of knowledge such as the library, a set of encyclopedias, or the Internet.

❏ Use open-ended questions rather than yes or no questions when checking your child's knowledge or discussing school work.

❏ Have your child identify and correct mistakes in his own work.

CHAPTER 9

Critical Thinking

A LARGE PART OF AN EDUCATOR'S RESPONSIBILITY is to help students acquire critical thinking skills. As educators, homeschooling parents share in this responsibility.

Critical thinking really boils down to reflecting on new information in relation to what you already know or believe. Students partially learn critical thinking through formal schooling, especially as they prepare for the transition from high school to higher education or to the workplace. Lectures, discussions, and reading and writing assignments help students learn new information and then think critically about it in the context of their past or present beliefs and assumptions about the world. As students are challenged in college and life with new ways of thinking, they may discard old beliefs, create new beliefs, or strengthen their original beliefs as a result (Mezirow, 1997).

The goal of education should be to have students learn to think for themselves

Ultimately, the goal of education should be to have students learn to think for themselves rather than to follow

93

blindly whatever anyone tells them, which is a critical skill for the real world. In the world of education, whether at the high school or college level, students who learn to think for themselves are often better learners because they take greater responsibility for determining what, how, when, where, and why they want to learn, which is the skill we just discussed: "self-directed learning."

Critical thinking means so much more than trying to remember new information like one would in order to pass a spelling test or a history quiz. Critical thinking means putting new knowledge into a useful context by relating it to existing knowledge. The key concept is that students *think* about what they are learning in a way that it becomes meaningful and hopefully useful to them to some degree.

Activities for Developing Critical Thinking

For young children new information is just that, *new*. As a child develops, associations between pieces of information also develop. New information for adult learners can be a tremendous resource for problem solving because they can add to the knowledge they already have acquired from formal learning, life experiences, and even emotional reactions to their experiences (Mezirow, 1997).

For instance, when children hear a campaign speech given by a presidential candidate, they may not fully understand the entire context behind what the candidate says. They may judge his credibility and competency by how he looks, how he acts, and whether they think what he says *sounds* good. They may also blindly believe any campaign promise they hear because they have no reason to believe someone running for the presidency would deceive them. Adults usually have experience that teaches them to be a little less trusting.

Young children lack life experience. Because they are still developing emotionally and mentally, they also lack the ability to understand themselves. As children become teenagers, they gradually become more self-reflective as a result of their natural development and their experiences with life (Cornford, 1999).

As children become teenagers, they gradually become more self-reflective.

Formal activities, such as those we will discuss later in this chapter, can help your child develop critical thinking skills, but you can also provide many other fun ways to develop this skill both directly and indirectly. What we mean by indirectly is by helping your child learn and practice other learning skills that teach him how to think, how to analyze information, and how to see the "big picture."

For example, in both our elementary and high school programs we reserved Friday afternoons for what we called "hands-on learning lab." During this time we used a variety of activities, including using learning tools, playing board games, teaching younger siblings, and creating learning materials. There are innumerable ways to do this same sort of thing with your children. Some of the more memorable activities we used to help the children develop critical thinking skills (often without realizing it) include the following:

- Building marble mazes
- Putting together jigsaw puzzles
- Creating electronic devices
- Quizzing each other with flash cards
- Experimenting with science equipments
- Creating poems with word magnets
- Counting money using coins of various denominations
- Learning about art and architecture with different types of blocks and building materials

- Playing various board games, like chess, checkers, *Stratego, Scrabble, Mancala, Mastermind,* or any other wonderful games that cause individuals to "think"
- Teaching other siblings how to play these same sorts of games
- Creating foreign language flash cards with the English translation on the bottom of the card for siblings. The cards were pasted around the house identifying common objects in each room. One of our teens was studying French and the other was studying Spanish, so the younger children got a trilingual lesson.
- Solving crossword puzzles or word searches
- Working alone or with a sibling to cook dinner or bake a dessert
- Reading something from the paper or a book and then having to explain it to us
- Engaging in debates about topics and purposefully having to analyze a position contrary to their own

We also work on building critical thinking skills while riding in the car with our teenagers. We'd talk about how everyone else was driving (usually badly) and we'd discuss what to do in certain situations when they became drivers. Sometimes we'd see the ways other teens were acting or how they dressed, which would then lead to a discussion about appropriate behavior. We'd also discuss how to deal with peer pressure—especially when driving a car.

Sometimes when the teenagers are alone with Chandra in the car, they talk about college, careers, and life. Chandra interjects her thoughts here and there, usually in the form of a question, to make the children clarify their thoughts or consider something they probably hadn't thought of before. All of these experiences provided opportunities for our children to develop and apply critical thinking skills.

The Value of Learning Journals

There are many different types of learning activities you can use to help your child build critical thinking skills. One activity some teachers and college professors use is a learning journal. Not to be confused with diaries or personal journals, learning journals can be an excellent academic exercise for students at the high school level. These journals are not just summaries of what was learned nor are they records of what was learned and when. Rather, a learning journal is a record of a student's thoughts and reflections *about* what she has learned—particularly in relation to her existing experiences and knowledge.

In their learning journals students can write down questions that occur to them while they read to which they may later want to find answers. They can write themselves notes to learn more about an author or to find other books written by an author. Students can make note of something to which the author referred such as a different subject or another book. They may want to simply note their reactions to what they've learned.

Students can also use learning journals to record their progress in a subject. It can be a great motivator for students to look back through their journals and remember that they were having trouble at the beginning of the class, but as time went on, they became quite successful in it.

In the college classes I teach, I like students to note the progress they've made, whether it's how many classes they've completed and how many are left to go, or what they learned that they didn't know before. Sometimes I ask students to recount how nervous and overwhelmed they were when they first started a class and how they were able to get past these concerns to succeed with a particular course.

While taking tests and answering questions in

textbooks are good exercises for helping students remember what they've learned, summarizing what they've learned in their own words is often more enlightening and rewarding. I like students to identify how at least one thing they read relates to something in their life or something else they knew or believed. Perhaps the new information challenged a prior belief or assumption they had or they learned something entirely new to them.

I also like students to write top-ten lists of the things they learned that they felt were most important in a particular lesson or course. When students write the main points of their lesson or the most important things they learned, they not only recall the information, but they have to sort out and prioritize what they've learned. They can go one step further and explain why they chose to include these points in their journals.

Learning journals can take any form. Students can buy nicely bound hardback journals with blank pages or they can use a spiral notebook or even loose-leaf paper. They can also type their journals and maintain an electronic file they can print out when finished.

As a teacher, it's important for you to give some guidelines about what your child should write in her journal and with what frequency she is expected to write. However, the key point here is that you should provide guidelines so there is a starting place but leave some flexibility so she can customize her journal to the method that works best for her.

Often just getting started writing is the tough part for some children. Generally speaking, it's a good idea to require your child to complete about one journal entry each week. An entry might be just a few words or several paragraphs—it's up to both of you. It's a good idea to date the entries to keep track of both effort and progress. However, journals don't have to be part of every lesson or every subject. Students can burn out if they have to write a journal for everything, so use them to help you child with the subject or assignment for which a journal would be most effective.

Journals are usually graded assignments, but grading them can be a very subjective matter that can squelch the value of the assignment. It is important to encourage and guide your children to make their journals worthwhile by letting them know they won't be judged on their opinions or reflections. Rather, the objective grading portion of the assignment can be on criteria such as completing the assignment, neatness, spelling, grammar, and overall effort. Reminding your children that these are learning journals and not diaries can help save everyone from undue stress and concern—especially when it comes down to grading.

We've listed just a few suggestions below of what types of entries could be included in a learning journal, but we encourage you to develop your own ideas:

- Describe what you learned that was the most interesting or surprising to you and explain why.
- Provide examples of real-life experiences you have had with this subject matter.
- Identify any current events related to what you learned and explain how they are connected.
- Explain how someone might misinterpret the information you learned.
- Explain what you would have changed about this course (assignment) if you could.
- Describe something you want to learn more about.
- Explain what you disliked most about the course, book, or subject.
- Explain what you learned that was new to you or made you think differently about something you already knew.
- If you had to tell someone about what you

learned in this course, what would you tell them?

■ What are the top ten things you learned and explain why they made your top-ten list?

Learning journals are appropriate for most subjects. Many subjects can be examined from a purely academic point of view or by looking at the moral and ethical implications of the subject matter, if appropriate. In either instance the goal of a learning journal is to help your child think critically about what she's learned so she learns more as a result. For all homeschooled students, any and all writing assignments will help prepare them for college and the expectation that students *think for themselves*.

Demonstrating Knowledge

When students *do* something with what they've learned, teachers can identify what knowledge the students *obtained* and how they've *thought* about it. In most college classes, students demonstrate their knowledge by writing papers. The ability to write well is an important skill for a college student to have.

Sometimes students complete individual or group projects, give demonstrations, conduct experiments, or participate in class discussions to show their professors they can actually *do* something with what they've learned. To successfully complete tasks such as these, students must be able to think logically and in an organized manner, be creative, speak well, get along with others in a group setting, and convey their thoughts to others both verbally and visually.

Many students struggle with poetry and yet reading and analyzing poetry is an excellent way to develop critical thinking skills. For example, the first time students read the Robert Frost poem "Stopping by Woods on a Snowy Evening," they may not think more than, "That's a nice poem." They might even think, "I don't get it." To avoid this problem at home, you can set up a series of tasks, such as the few listed below, to help your child think critically about and understand the poem better.

1. Read a biography of Frost to understand more about the poet himself.
2. Explain why you think Frost used the words "miles to go before I sleep." What might you have meant if you had written these words?
3. Read a book about poetry that describes imagery, metaphors, and expressing ideas through poetry versus prose.
4. Compare and contrast Frost's poem to other poems and other styles of poetry you've read. Or compare and contrast Frost's style in this poem to his other poems or to the style of other poets.
5. Read an analysis of the poem.
6. Discuss the poem with a parent, sibling, or another student. Compare and contrast what you both think about it.
7. Draw a picture of the poem and explain it.
8. Write the rest of the story. What happened before the poem? What happened afterward?
9. Write a fictional biographical sketch of the speaker of the poem.
10. Write the story behind the poem from the horse's point of view.

There are many ways to develop critical thinking skills through poetry and other subjects. Many times students fail to go beyond surface learning because they fail to think. They may read a poem and correctly answer the required test questions, but they haven't really learned anything because they don't *think critically* about it.

One of the best ways to develop critical thinking skills in any subject is to encourage children to ask open-ended questions, particularly "why" and "how," and then let them find the answers to their own questions. Questions help students learn to find connections between things—an important part of critical thinking. Also by asking questions, students challenge their existing knowledge to either replace old and faulty information, blend old and new information together, or reinforce existing knowledge by rejecting new information.

Poetry is only one example of a subject you can use to help your child develop critical thinking skills. Religion and philosophy are also excellent choices, but any academic subject can be used. Of course, as we described earlier in this chapter, many informal activities are useful as well.

Sometimes failing to think critically is due to a lack of personal or intellectual maturity. Sometimes students only want to pass a class, and they put forth just enough effort to achieve that goal. More often than not, students simply lack experience using critical thinking skills. You can help your child develop these skills through the activities we've suggested or come up with your own.

Key Points

✕ Look for everyday opportunities to develop critical thinking skills: board games, teaching siblings, one-on-one conversations.

✕ Encourage critical thinking in the context of past or present beliefs and assumptions about the world.

✕ Use learning journals for writing assignments

Subject-Specific Ideas for Developing
Critical Thinking Skills

SOCIAL SCIENCES

- Don't settle for just names and dates—focus on causes, effects, and motivations for historical events.
- Learn more about the people of history through biographies, autobiographies, and other books beyond textbooks.
- Find out what was happening in other parts of the country and world during the same time period as the one being studied.
- Learn how people and events influenced other people and events. Trace events forward and backward in time to see the connections.

NATURAL SCIENCE

- Find out why things happen.
- Create hypotheses and test them by conducting experiments.
- Spend time making observations and just wondering about the world.

LANGUAGE (English or Foreign)

- Play with the language to see what effects small changes can create on meaning.
- Explore languages by reading and writing poetry, literature, creative writing, letters, and essays.
- Create your own language.

MATHEMATICS

- Find real-life examples and activities that relate to the formulas, theorems, and problems being studied.
- Learn about number-related discoveries that are being made by scientists and mathematicians.
- Investigate the relation that subjects such as music or architecture have to mathematics.

CHAPTER 10

Self-discipline

WE'VE COVERED TWO OF THE MOST IMPORTANT skills students should have at least started to develop, if not have developed well before going off to college: critical thinking and self-directed learning. These two skills are essential in becoming academically disciplined, or in other words, being a college-level learner.

However, there is much more to being a college-level learner than just being able to think critically and engage in self-directed learning. Another essential ingredient in preparing for college is self-discipline.

Some people seem to be naturally self-disciplined, while others never seem to be. From an educational viewpoint, I believe that self-discipline is predominately a learned behavior that begins in the home as parents work with their children at a very early age to understand what behavior is acceptable or not, and more importantly, why the behavior is acceptable or not. When the behavior is unacceptable, there must be consequences. The child must learn that to avoid negative consequences, he must avoid the problem behavior in the first place. This requires self-discipline.

Consequences are not necessarily physical. Of course, some people believe that spankings are an ideal way to deter behaviors in young children, and we don't want to debate that issue. However, we do want to say that for the teenager preparing for college, physical punishment related to academic performance wouldn't make sense at all. Ideally, consequences should be logically related to the behavior, such as having to re-do an assignment that wasn't done well the first time. It is important to remember that the idea is to instruct the child about what she can do to avoid problems, help her learn to be successful, and teach her to have control over her mind and body—specifically as it relates to learning.

Unfortunately, not every parent sees self-discipline as something that can be developed in young children over time. Many feel like children are either naturally "good" or "not so good." For example, a while back Chandra was with our four youngest children at swimming lessons when another mother came up to her and complimented our children's behavior. She said something to the effect of, "Your children are so well behaved. They are very quiet. That must be their temperament. It must be nice to have easy children."

Chandra thanked her for the compliment and tried to nicely tell the woman that the children weren't necessarily "easy" and we did have our challenges with them, but the children typically behaved well because of our expectations for their behavior. These ideas seemed lost on the woman. Instead, she struck up a similar conversation with another mother with whom she seemed to have a much more rewarding conversation because the other mother indicated that her one son was so challenging to handle that she and her husband decided not to have any more children. The two women had a long conversation commiserating with one another about raising and "disciplining" children.

Observing these parents and others over the years, Chandra and I have seen how often parents fail to encourage self-discipline in their children. In fact, they often facilitate the development of behaviors completely opposite of those associated with self-discipline as they allow their children to misbehave, whine, fuss, demand, or do whatever they would like to do without any consequences whatsoever.

Discipline is often equated with punishment, but that's not necessarily correct. A *disciple* is one who follows someone else and is often seen in the context of following a teacher or mentor in order to learn from him or her. Thus, the student benefits from the teacher's instruction in order to acquire the knowledge and skills related to the instructor's academic discipline. As parents, our job is to teach our children (our disciples) in order to prepare them for adult life and ultimately for being contributing members of society rather than feeding off society in an unhealthy way.

As parents, our job is to teach our children (our disciples) in order to prepare them for adult life.

For those children who decide not to go on to college, the time up through high school is vital for learning to be disciplined enough to take on an active role in society through work, parenting, military service, religious service, or whatever life choices the student makes after high school. For the children who go on to college, they too will be involved with society through their pursuit of additional academic knowledge. In either case, the children will find it helpful if you work with them to develop at least three more skills during the high school years that will aid them in becoming more self-disciplined: time management, communication, and responsibility.

Time Management

As with self-discipline, some people just seem to be born organized and with the ability to manage time well. For many, managing time is something that has to be learned and even then it may be a constant struggle to be on time, submit things on time, and complete multiple projects that are due at about the same time.

I've had students who tell me they are always late to everything, but when they realize that I start deducting points from their attendance grade for being late to class, generally they learn to get there on time. As with parenting and the need to be consistent in the consequences for problem behaviors, an instructor must be consistent as well. Recently I had a student miss the first day of a new course. I didn't know the student personally, so I asked if anyone in the class knew him, which a couple of people did. One of his peers came up after class to tell me he was going to call "John" to tell him he'd better get to class each week because he could tell that in my class John couldn't be late or skip class and get away with it. It really is a matter of expectations being clearly defined and consistently applied.

In higher education good time management is vital for all students pursuing any level of degree—bachelor's, master's, or Ph.D. Unfortunately, some students don't learn about time management until it is too late. I vividly remember my first weeks of college—various professors had assigned 200–300 pages of reading, some had assigned papers, and others were giving quizzes, all due by the end of the second week! I thought, "What's wrong with these professors? Don't they know I have a ton of homework in each of my other classes, not to mention a need for some sort of social life?"

The truth is professors don't care about other professors and their classes. Each was only concerned with what I needed to learn in his or her individual course. I quickly learned that it didn't pay to fall behind.

Professors who teach multiple classes with hundreds of students each semester have no time to worry about whether one student completed a reading assignment or why another's paper wasn't completed on time. College professors don't call students to see if they are doing their homework. If they see students at the movies or in a restaurant, they don't stop and ask if they completed their reading assignment before going out with friends.

Professors don't take time to verify excuses about sick relatives, homework-hungry pets, or computer malfunctions. More often than not, they will just quietly enter a failing grade in the grade book with a shake of the head. It's not that professors don't want their students to succeed; they just assume that if the students really want to learn—and ultimately to graduate—they'll put in the effort it takes to succeed. It is vital to teach time-management skills in your homeschool program *before* your child is ready to attend college.

For teens, sometimes time management can be taught through natural consequences, such as, "If you didn't finish what had to be done on time, then you don't get a certain privilege." While Chandra and I have been blessed with good children, they are far from perfect. More than once they have had to miss a television show or fun activity in order to complete or redo an assignment. The bigger lesson was that their education is important and that's where they should focus their attention. This will be especially critical once they're in college.

We could write an entire book about time management. However, students really only need to understand a few simple principles about time management and then they must be disciplined enough to practice them. High school students who learn these principles will have a much easier time managing their time effectively in college and life. So, below we've offered some tips to students that may be helpful in learning to manage time. It's as simple as 1, 2, 3 and a, b, c.

1. **Get organized and stay organized.**
   This applies to students and to parents. Parents who are organized display appropriate behaviors to their children and act as role models as well.
   a. Have a place for everything and keep everything in its place. More time is wasted working in a messy environment than ever will be lost in a clean and organized one.
   b. Make a to-do list regularly and use it to help you know what to do and when (a syllabus acts as an academic to-do list for a particular course).
   c. Be consistent about where and how you write down information about assignments. We recommend you use one calendar and have an organized filing system rather than "piling" stuff up on your desk or work space.

2. **Keep track of all assignments and know when they are due.**
   We highly recommend parents take the time to prepare a syllabus for each course so their child can read and refer to it regularly.
   a. Know exactly what has to be done to complete an assignment. Set up a to-do list and prioritize all assignments. Don't spend so much time on one assignment that you forget the others.
   b. Read assignment instructions often and ask questions early—not just the day before the assignment is due, or worse, after it was due. Budget more than enough time for each assignment. This leaves time to check it for mistakes. If it's a paper, proofread it several times.

If it's a project, make sure not to forget any requirements.

c. Prioritize what has to be done and work hard to not procrastinate when working on assignments. Plan ahead and when possible work ahead since you never know if an assignment will take you longer than anticipated or if life will get in the way of your plans to study (or for parents, to plan lessons or to grade) "later."

3. Hold yourself accountable.

Parents should also hold their children accountable for getting their work done well and on time with consequences in addition to poor grades for substandard work.

a. Stick to deadlines assigned by the instructor. Don't plan to make excuses for yourself. Don't even expect that your professor will give you extra time to get the work done or that you can earn extra points later to make up for the ones you lose by turning in your work late. Saying that you didn't know what to do or that you didn't have what you needed to get the job done just isn't acceptable. Know what you have to do, have the materials and supplies you need to complete an assignment, and have it all ready before you start your work.

b. Don't waste your time and then try to crunch in your work later, which typically leads to poorly completed work. If you want to watch a favorite show on television, consider taping it and watching it when you have more time. If you want to go out with friends, make sure you have time to get your work completed first. If you want to play video games, reward yourself with that privilege AFTER you get your work done and done well.

c. Work where you won't be distracted easily. Turn off the stereo, television, video games, or anything else that will keep you from concentrating. If music helps drown out the background noise, then use it accordingly. Find the time and place that works best for studying.

It's important to know that successful students learn not to put off until tomorrow what should be done today. Many college students earn academic probation during the first year or two of college simply because they underestimate the time required to complete their assignments. A little preparation during the high-school years can prevent a lot of difficulty once your student is on his own.

Here are some other tips for parents about how to develop a student's time management skills:

1. Have high expectations and low tolerances for time- and academic-related behaviors.

2. Provide support, encouragement, and instruction, but don't feel like you always have to provide the answers or modify the deadlines—a college professor probably won't.

3. Refer your child to sources of information or have her use resources to find the information she needs rather than give her the answers just to save time.

4. Set deadlines for your child's work and stick to them. A little pressure can be an effective motivator.

5. Don't let her off the hook easily if she misses a deadline—provide a consequence in addition to a low grade, if applicable. For example, she may have to re-do the work again without receiving a higher grade. Or the first and second grades assigned to the work will be averaged, so the "F" that was earned the first time and the "A" earned the second time become a "C." If she had done the work correctly the first time, she could have had that "A," but she ended up with a "C" (although it probably

would have been an "F" in college).

6. Assign more than one assignment due on the same day so your child learns to multi-task effectively.
7. Don't excuse your child from her chores or other responsibilities just to get schoolwork done. She must learn to manage all of her time well just like adults must.
8. Teach her to prioritize her responsibilities and free time so she does the most important things first, thus learning to work both harder and smarter before "playing."
9. Grade objectively, fairly, and consistently to teach the same message of quality and effectiveness each time.
10. Provide follow-up instruction about what she did well and what she could have done better with regard to not only the assignment, but the time spent getting the assignment done.

Communicating

There is much we could discuss about the subject of communication, but we are going to focus on a couple of aspects of communication as they relate to time management and self-discipline specifically. Children who learn how to communicate to their instructors about their assignments gain valuable information and lessons as a result.

One of the nice things about homeschooling is that parents and children have the freedom to spend more time on learning than may be possible in other types of schools. However, there is a downside to this freedom if children never learn to adhere to deadlines—something they will face throughout college and life.

To help prepare our children for the consequences of missing a deadline similar to what they might face in college, we set specific due dates for assignments—particularly larger projects. While we had scheduled dates for each subject that showed the children which chapters needed to be read and which tests and exercises needed to be completed and by when, there was always some flexibility so they could work ahead or play catch up as circumstances, such as illnesses, warranted.

Typically, major projects were due at the midpoint in the semester and again at the end of the semesters. Since the children had multiple weeks to complete these projects, we gave them the freedom to choose how and when to work on the projects, as long as they were completed on time. Of course, with freedom comes responsibility. Once the children knew what work had to be completed and our criteria for what had to be included in their projects, we gave them three instructions:

With freedom comes responsibility.

1) Ask us questions as needed, 2) Notify us early if you have any problems that may cause you to miss the deadline so we can address them right away, 3) Don't miss the deadline.

It took only once, each, for the children to miss a deadline and to earn a failing grade on a project for this lesson to sink in. Once the deadline had passed, we discussed with the children the effect of a failing grade on their grade point average for the course. They were shocked to see how their other high marks earned in the course were quickly reduced to a much lower overall grade.

We discussed that when college professors allow students to make up work or do "extra credit," it makes much more work for the professors. We could have easily ended the lesson there and made the final grade stand and not allow the children to submit the work at all—like many college professors might. However, we felt that the lesson had been learned and that an even greater lesson could be taught. In order to make up the lower grade, all of their personal privileges were revoked until the overdue projects were completed. When they finally submitted their projects, the grade they earned was averaged with the "F" for a grade that was much lower than what it might have been had they submitted the work on time in the first place. To make up the missing points, additional work had to be completed to raise their overall average in that course. In the end, the children spent more time fixing the problem than if they had simply communicated with us early and taken responsibility for their work in the first place. We never had trouble with deadlines after that.

College Professors' Expectations

Professors appreciate and respect students who take the time to ask questions or to ask for help when they need it. We refer to students who ask intelligent questions to clarify assignments and expectations rather than to repeat information given during a skipped class. We are also referring to students who ask for help after making genuine effort on an assignment rather than students who are trying to get an easy answer.

Professors appreciate and respect students who take the time to ask questions.

Similarly, students can demonstrate responsibility for learning and a desire to be successful in a number of ways. First, they show up to every class and are often there early. When these students are in class, they are ready to learn. They've read and thought about assignments in advance. They actively participate in group discussions, ask questions, and are prepared to answer questions.

When responsible students know they are going to miss a class or when something unexpected forces them to miss a class, they contact the professor ahead of time to request information and to discuss make-up assignments. These students also turn in their assignments when due regardless of absence from class. I am always much more willing to be flexible about an assignment due date when a student gives advance notice.

Many times college students fail to show even basic levels of responsibility. These types of students often come to class without pens, pencils, paper, or even books. Often they lose or don't complete their homework, they get confused about or forget assignment dates, and sometimes they don't even bother studying for tests. They often beg for more time, make-up work, or special arrangements that no one else gets. Students who *don't* demonstrate responsibility do excel at one thing—making excuses.

While college professors try hard to be objective in their interactions with every student, there are some behaviors they often find rude and unacceptable, such as missing class, arriving late or leaving early, and submitting poorly completed homework. Most professors do their best to be professional and polite to students no matter how they behave, but this does not necessarily mean they approve of their students' behavior. When circumstances require a student to ask for extra assistance, the student's behavior during the year will affect how flexible and helpful a professor is willing to be.

Responsibility

College is vastly different from homeschooling and everything may seem unfamiliar at first. However, there are behaviors that should be the same in both settings. We emphasize the following behaviors in our homeschool program since we believe these involve demonstrating responsibility for one's own behaviors— a self-discipline skill:

1. Always be polite and respectful.

Rudeness should not be tolerated, as it demonstrates a lack of self-discipline.

2. Take the time to ask questions.
A student who asks questions demonstrates he really wants to learn.

3. Ask for help when needed.
Asking for help is not a weakness, but rather a demonstration of being responsible and the desire to learn and be successful.

4. Ask intelligent questions that help clarify assignments and expectations.
Asking questions to which the answers have already been provided in a syllabus, handout, or somewhere else often depicts laziness and lack of effort rather than responsibility and self-discipline.

5. Be ready to learn every day.
Think of learning as your job and "show up" each day ready to work.

6. Have your materials ready.
Being organized indicates responsibility.

7. Complete your reading assignments and give them some thought before starting to work on the written portion of the assignment.
We like the old axiom of measure twice, cut once for this one. In other words, know what to do so you can get the job done right the first time.

8. Participate in discussions.
You can bet that some classes in college are going to require you to engage in discussions with peers and your professor, so this is a good

time to practice speaking with someone about topics beyond what you might talk to your friends about.

9. **Be prepared to answer questions.**
It isn't enough just to complete an assignment and not expect to be able to talk about it if asked a question, so anticipate questions and prepare answers ahead of time. You should really know your subject.

10. **Remember deadlines and adhere to them.**
This one just smacks of responsibility, doesn't it?

11. **If you are going to be late with an assignment, discuss it with the instructors ahead of time.**
Expect the professor to not accept an excuse, but a reasonable reason for being late on an assignment, such as an illness or family issue just might be accepted; yet, it's not a guarantee! Just having to talk about it gives you practice for hearing "No late work will be accepted."

12. **Be prepared to sacrifice your personal time to get work done when necessary.**
School is your work and just like you have to go to work every day as an adult and save your free time until after the work day is over, the same goes for your school work. This is a good habit to get into before college.

13. **Don't turn in incomplete or poorly completed work.**
Nothing speaks more loudly about your character than incomplete or poorly completed work. It just screams "irresponsibility" and "lack of self-discipline."

14. Complete every job to the best of your ability.
This goes along with number thirteen, but it also stands alone as an example of the difference between a "C"—meaning "average work" and an "A"—meaning "outstanding work."

15. Don't do just the minimum work—go beyond and try to impress the instructors.
In the work world, to get a raise or a promotion or more responsibility, you'll have to work hard to impress the boss. In a school setting, your instructor is your boss and you should work hard to impress her to earn a high grade.

Chandra's Perspective

Instilling a sense of responsibility in our children for their own education was really a combination of factors. First, Dave and I designed our home environment to be one in which the children were expected to behave, be polite and respectful, do daily and weekly chores, and give their very best to everything they did. Over the years this environment established a sense of self-discipline in the children. We were, and still are, often complimented on our children's behavior. I think this is due to the fact that we always had high, but reasonable, expectations of the children and low tolerances for the types of problematic behavior we see so many parents put up with today.

The children also had to be flexible. After the morning routine of breakfast and chores, they talked to me about when would be the best time for me to "teach" them in their math classes. I would figure out what I needed to get done that day for my own routine, as well as what I needed to do to teach or take care of the younger children, and then set up a time to work with Holly and Cameron on their courses. Math was the primary subject I had to "teach" them, but I would also help them throughout the day with other subjects. If they got stuck on something and I was busy doing other things, they weren't allowed to just sit and do nothing or waste their time waiting for me. They simply put that work aside and went on to other things until we had time to work together.

Another big factor that helped the children develop self-discipline was that we never purchased any sort of video game system for the children and we limited their television viewing time. When the oldest children were very young, we noticed a rapid decline in their behavior whenever they watched too much television or played on the computer, even with educational games, for any length of time at all. Dave and I decided to steer the children away from activities that seemed to be mental distractions. We encouraged them to read, play games, and use their imaginations using the various toys we bought them. The lack of television and video games helped increase their focus, concentration, and in general just settled their behavior.

Lastly, we taught the children to take pride in their work. If they did it poorly the first time, they had to re-do it on their own time. As they grew older we tried to shift the focus away from just getting good grades and pleasing us to doing good work as a matter of personal honor, pride, and representing themselves in that work. I think we succeeded in doing that.

Key Points

- ❑ Create guidelines for demonstrating responsibility and effectively communicating in your home and homeschool program and expect your child to follow them.
- ❑ Hold your child accountable for deadlines.
- ❑ Create opportunities for your child to practice these essential skills.
- ❑ Teach and reinforce these skills.
- ❑ Help your child get organized and stay organized.
- ❑ Set assignment deadlines.
- ❑ Make it your child's responsibility to keep careful track of all assignments and know when they are due.

❏ Be clear about exactly what has to be done to complete an assignment.

❏ Have your child set up a to-do list, prioritize all assignments, and budget *more than enough* time for each one.

❏ Help your child prioritize needs and wants, such as whether to watch a favorite television show or complete homework.

❏ As a teacher and parent, have high expectations—expect effective time management and teach the necessary skills.

HOMESCHOOL TEACHING APPROACHES— WHAT WORKS AND WHAT DOESN'T TO PREPARE YOUR CHILD FOR HIGHER EDUCATION

CHAPTER 11

Teacher-directed Homeschool Methods

THERE ARE A VARIETY OF EDUCATIONAL METHODS and philosophies to chose from when teaching your children at home—usually with an almost unlimited amount of support material available to help implement your selected approach. This choice is highly personal based on factors such as your personal and educational beliefs, budget, comfort level teaching certain subjects, previous learning and teaching experiences, exposure to educational theories, and your child's needs and interests.

Some parents believe in an extremely structured learning environment using textbooks and stringent guidelines similar to a public, private, or parochial school setting. Other parents go the opposite direction and allow their children to explore their own interests in an unstructured environment using a variety of educational tools and materials. Many homeschooling parents employ an eclectic approach to teaching and learning, using a combination of several different methods.

Educational methods can be divided into two broad categories: *teacher-directed* and *student-directed*. Teaching methods in each category have their own strengths and weaknesses, particularly in regards to helping high school students develop the skills for higher education that we discussed in the last section. In this section we will review the strengths and weaknesses of various methods and offer our suggestions for finding the style that is right for you and your child. Three homeschooling methods we do not address are charter schools, online and distance education programs (Web-based or correspondence-based), and part-time enrollment in a private or public school (dual-enrollment). Using charter, public, or private schools for even part of the homeschooling program definitely involves teacher-directed methods rather than student-directed methods. Distance and online learning programs may be either student-directed or teacher-directed or both. These are all considered to be valid methods for homeschooling. However, we will not review them in this chapter because they involve a teacher other than the parent.

Teacher-directed vs. Student-directed Approaches

To some degree, any method of teaching children, especially at home, is teacher-directed because parents retain a certain amount of control over what their children do. Simply choosing a method of instruction such as unschooling reflects the initial influence of a parent over the learning environment and a choice of instruction that a child must follow. Implementing a child-directed learning method also requires parents to help their children gain access to materials and resources. However, there are key differences between teacher-directed and child-directed methods.

Teacher-directed methods are usually viewed as pedagogical in nature. The teacher has primary responsibility for and control over determining what will be learned, when, and how (Hiemstra and Sisco, 1990). Similarly, teacher-directed methods are often related to the study of specific subjects. Instructors use more traditional methods of teaching that may include textbooks, lectures, and related cognitive techniques, as well as methods of reward and punishment or correction (Marshak, 1983).

Student-directed teaching methods are focused more on what the student wants to learn, when, and how. Using one of these methods, the parent serves more as a guide or facilitator rather than a subject expert. Student-directed learning may involve working on realistic problems or projects rather than studying theoretical concepts associated with traditional paper, pencil, or textbook-type methods of instruction (Marshak, 1983).

Initially, the student-directed method may appear to be more conducive to helping students develop skills needed for college. While this conclusion has some validity, teacher-directed methods may also help children develop essential skills for higher education.

So which approach is best? To answer that, this chapter, as well as chapters twelve and thirteen, will review the strengths and weaknesses of various methods and offer our suggestions for finding the style that is right for you and your child. The remainder of this section discusses the information and tools you will need to prepare and teach your high school program.

Teacher-directed Homeschool Methods

Teacher-directed methods of homeschooling include the traditional approaches of textbook and scope and sequence, the classical and principle methods, and unit studies that include thematic and place-based approaches. Each of these methods, especially in a homeschool environment, can be adapted to allow students to learn on their own or with minimal interaction with their parents. However, they are considered to be primarily teacher-directed because the parent determines how, what, and when the child will learn.

In the following pages we will briefly describe these methods and review their benefits and drawbacks. We then evaluate the overall effectiveness of teacher-directed methods in developing critical thinking and self-directed learning skills. Our purpose in this chapter is to give you a general overview of these teacher-directed methods. Then in Chapter 13 we will present in greater detail a way for you to take what we feel is the best from all these methods and develop a plan for teaching your student.

The Traditional Approach

The traditional approach to homeschooling usually involves textbooks and direct instruction from a parent in the form of lectures, discussions, written work, and other teacher-prescribed assignments or activities. The scope and sequence of what the student will learn during a school year is usually determined by the breadth and depth of the subject matter, as well as what was taught the preceding year and what will be taught the following year. Often each subject is broken down into a series of topics organized sequentially in order to build a level of knowledge or skill for subsequent topics or grades (Bluedorn and Bluedorn, 1994).

A variation of the traditional scope and sequence approach was developed by E.D. Hirsch, Jr., who created a Core Knowledge program. Hirsch believed American children should acquire certain "pieces" of knowledge at each grade level. The pieces of knowledge he chose focused on topics, themes, and skills that should be common to our culture in the United States. In this theory, if children grow up with a common knowledge base, they'll have a similar frame of reference from which to continue learning as they develop into adults. Hirsch's associates produced a series of books for each grade level, K–6, using th—e core knowledge approach. There are even schools dedicated to using his approach. (For more information visit http://www.coreknowledge.org/CK/schools/index.htm.)

Benefits

Some families may thrive in a traditional environment since the structure and routine typically provides an opportunity to develop self-discipline in children. New homeschooling parents often utilize this approach since it is often the approach with which they are most familiar. The use of structured lessons and textbooks developed by educators also helps to relieve, if not eliminate, some of the initial worries parents may have about how to teach their children, how to teach certain subjects, or how to be certain they are teaching the correct topics in sufficient depth and in an appropriate manner. As a result, new home-schoolers frequently use traditional methods, but as they become more comfortable with educating their children, many parents soon begin to explore other approaches.

New homeschoolers frequently use traditional methods, but many parents soon begin to explore other approaches.

Drawbacks

Traditional methods may be too similar to public school programs with structured schedules and activities, as well as testing and grading techniques.

Such methods may be inappropriate for some homeschooled children who don't perform well in highly structured or rigid learning environments, or who have physical, mental, emotional, or learning needs that may not be met in a traditional school approach. Similarly, parents whose children don't perform well on tests or quizzes may find that these approaches seem to set the child up for failure if the child is unable to recall and regurgitate information in the manner that is typically consistent with standard testing practices. Further, parents and their children who utilize methods exactly like a traditional school often experience frustration, burnout, or boredom (Ishizuka, 2000).

Recommendation

The traditional approach is extremely pedagogical and therefore most appropriate for younger children who need to learn basic skills and establish a foundation of knowledge in order to be successful in subsequent grades. For older elementary-aged children and teenagers, a traditional approach is appropriate for certain subjects such as mathematics, science, and foreign languages where information needs to be presented in a particular order.

The traditional approach may also be appropriate for other subjects—especially those in which your child needs direct instruction or tutoring (Ishizuka, 2000). However, in high school, an exclusive use of the traditional approach may limit your student's ability to develop self-directed learning and critical thinking skills.

Although Hirsch's theory is interesting, we can't say we subscribe to it in its entirety. However, we do find his books to be an excellent resource for planning lessons and determining the scope and sequence of the subjects we teach. Our children also like to read his books on their own.

The Classical and Principle Approaches

The classical approach to teaching involves three focus areas: grammar, logic, and rhetoric, which together form the Trivium. The Trivium is considered to be the first three of seven categories that comprise the liberal arts (Bluedorn and Bluedorn, 1994). The remaining four are music, arithmetic, geometry, and astronomy.

In the truest sense of the Trivium, grammar includes Latin and Greek, logic includes understanding life and words by examining fallacies and symbolism, and rhetoric includes the skills of composition, speaking, and debate (Bluedorn and Bluedorn, 1994). In a home school, grammar may include the study of Latin and Greek, but also may focus on the formation and use of the English language and studying books about Western Civilization. Similarly, logic may include the development of thinking and processing skills through mathematics and language. Rhetoric remains constant, using writing, speaking, and debate to reinforce grammar and logic skills (Bluedorn and Bluedorn, 1994).

The principle approach is similar to the classical approach in its emphasis on reasoning and communication skills. The difference is that the basis of learning is the Bible rather than classic civilization. The Biblical Trivium focuses on knowledge, understanding, and wisdom, which are based on Christian principles. This approach emphasizes the student's ability to communicate and defend those principles as a result of his education (Bluedorn and Bluedorn, 2002).

Benefits

Whether patterned after the classical approach or taught in a different style, the principle approach focuses on the development of moral character based on Christian principles that permeate the homeschooling program and the student's life (Ishizuka, 2000). While they may not take the classical format, traditional materials published by companies such as A Beka and Bob Jones University Press still use Christian principles and a biblical basis for each subject. Although many biblical Trivium approaches follow Protestant teachings, Catholic versions also exist.

For homeschoolers, one benefit of the classical and principle approaches is the focus on and reinforcement of the family's moral and religious beliefs. Another benefit is the development of independent thinking skills, as well as written and verbal communication skills.

Drawbacks

A potential disadvantage of these approaches is a limited focus of subject matter (Ishizuka, 2000). The biblical approach limits the curriculum to a religious viewpoint, which may not be suitable for some families. The classical approach may be inappropriate for parents or children who want to explore other subjects or employ other approaches to learning more suitable for the child's learning style and interests. Also, given its specific focus, this approach may not enable a high school student to practice a variety of learning skills that are going to be needed to succeed in college or life.

Recommendation

The classical and principle approaches, when properly employed, can provide your child with a thorough education and a solid set of study skills—especially given the nature of the subjects to be taught. Because these approaches often focus on character development, students usually develop at least the skills of critical thinking and demonstrating responsibility. Extra care should be taken to make sure your student covers enough subjects to meet college admission requirements.

The Unit Studies Approach

The unit studies approach is often referred to by other terms such as interest-directed, thematic, and place-based studies. These approaches usually involve the student studying a topic of interest through a variety of activities associated with different subjects such as science, art, mathematics, literature, and language (Bluedorn and Bluedorn, 1994). Activities used to study a topic may include field trips, projects, model building, pursuit of hobbies, use of the Internet, interaction with subject-matter experts, reading books, or completing assignments such as written and oral reports (Ishizuka, 2000). The unit studies approach can be considered both teacher-directed and student-directed because it typically requires the teacher to prepare many materials in advance, then allows the student to work independently.

Benefits

The unit study approach has the advantage of providing a variety of methods through which students can explore a given topic. Another advantage is that parents can customize the curriculum based on their children's perceived interests.

Drawbacks

A potential drawback to the approach is that parents may feel compelled to explore a topic using every approach, every time. Also, the amount of time it takes to research and develop activities based on a central theme may be overwhelming and result in students losing interest in a topic prior to studying it.

Recommendation

The unit studies approach is often associated with teaching younger children because it is fairly teacher-intensive—at least with regard to planning and preparation time. However, at the high school level, a modified unit studies approach can be successfully employed to help create courses of interest to your student while simultaneously developing all of the skills we identified as essential for college. In Section V you'll see we use a similar approach for some of our high school classes.

Evaluating Teacher-directed Homeschool Methods

Teacher-directed methods may help you develop a solid teacher-student relationship with your children. In a traditional school, students like to please their teachers and be rewarded with high grades (Thompson and Thornton, 2002). In a homeschool setting, where the teacher is also the parent, the need to please the teacher may be even more pronounced.

Even though you may not assign grades to your child's work, positive feedback from you may help motivate your child. This positive feedback is especially helpful for younger students. It encourages discipline that will later help them become critical thinkers and self-directed learners.

If you are going to use a teacher-directed program, you may have to take special pains to incorporate the teaching of critical thinking skills. If you use a textbook or a scope and sequence format, you are tied to the publisher's materials, which may not be oriented toward the teaching of critical thinking and likely won't encourage self-directed learning. If you use a unit study, classical, or principle approach, you'll be working from your own materials and can weave critical thinking and self-directed learning into your lessons. Since teaching critical thinking skills is important, it is vital you develop lessons and activities that help achieve that goal while maintaining your child's interest.

Although teacher-directed programs are less likely to help students become independent learners, they do help students acquire and hone basic learning skills and do give you direct guidance over your child's education. You can customize the program to meet your child's overall learning needs, including teaching the essential skills of critical thinking and self-directed learning.

Teaching method	Chief advantages	Chief disadvantages
Traditional	Very structured— easy to stay organized, to know what to do and when, and requires very little creative effort from you to develop lessons Appropriate for younger ? children in most every subject and for entry-level subjects for older children Comfortable— typical to type of learning environment you probably experienced when you were in school	Perhaps too structured—can feel too rigid and too much like "school" Can contribute to burnout for child and parent Too limited in depth and breadth of learning Expense of materials

Teaching method	Chief advantages	Chief disadvantages
Classical or Principle	A variety of materials including teacher texts and grading tools are readily available from different publishers Easy to include all subjects required for college admission Focuses on development of moral character as well as academic learning Can reinforce your family's values When properly utilized it can develop strong study skills	Perhaps too structured—can feel too rigid and too much like "school" Can contribute to burnout for child and parent Too limited in depth and breadth of learning May not be enough of the subjects required for college admission

Teaching method	Chief advantages	Chief disadvantages
Unit Studies	Customized learning Diverse learning approaches Perhaps most useful with younger grades	Time-intensive preparation Can contribute to burnout for child and parent May be too much in depth or too broad in learning
Teacher-directed Methods	Helps develop and hone basic learning skills Teacher has strong control over curriculum	Perhaps too structured Limits development of self-directed learning May require extensive customization to meet college admission requirements depending on approach used

CHAPTER 12

Student-directed Homeschool Methods

STUDENT-DIRECTED METHODS OF HOMESCHOOLING include Charlotte Mason, Montessori, Waldorf,
unschooling (including purpose-led and delayed approaches), and unit studies that include thematic and
place-based approaches. These methods of teaching
children are similar to andragogical adult programs
in that the student is believed to have a strong motivation to learn and a need or interest in controlling
what is learned, when, and how. Andragogical theory
assumes the student either already has the skills
necessary for self-directed learning or that he is ready
to obtain these skills (Gaddis, 1999).

In this chapter we will describe each student-
directed method and review their benefits and drawbacks. We then collectively evaluate the methods for
their effectiveness in developing critical thinking and
self-directed learning skills in homeschooled children. We remind you that we categorized unit studies as both teacher-directed and student-directed and
covered it in the previous chapter.

Again, don't think you need to learn the details of each of these methods. In Chapter 15 we will take what we feel are the best features of each method and help you develop a program for teaching your child.

Charlotte Mason

Charlotte Mason was a nineteenth-century British educator who developed a method of instruction also known as Living Books. Mason opposed traditional methods of instruction, including the use of textbooks, because she believed such approaches limited the student's ability to learn and think creatively (Ishizuka, 2000).

Mason focused on helping students develop strong skills in reading, writing, and arithmetic, as well as exposing students to literature and the arts. She believed children should *experience* the world about them to gain an understanding of others by participating in nature walks, visits to museums, and reading quality books including autobiographies and diaries.

As part of the learning process, Mason advocated that children also teach fellow students (Ishizuka, 2000). Reading, writing, and speaking about a particular subject are educationally sound methods for helping children develop critical thinking skills.

Benefits

The Mason method teaches children to be self-disciplined through the performance of daily routines and planned activities that help them practice concentration, honesty, self-control, and other socially acceptable behaviors (Bluedorn and Bluedorn, 1994). These habits help develop self-directed learning skills as well. In the homeschooling environment, Mason's method of instruction may be less expensive to implement than a traditional program with scope and sequence textbooks because materials could be borrowed from libraries, museums, and other community resources to supplement the student's learning experiences.

Drawbacks

This method supposes that the parent is comfortable with student-directed learning, guiding the student through activities such as reading classical and autobiographical books and diaries, and teaching the student how to present information about what was learned. Because Mason's method focuses on literature, as well as the development of reading and writing skills, parents may feel at a loss for how to teach other subjects, such as mathematics.

Recommendation

Mason's approach is very appropriate for some high school subjects, such as literature, social studies, and even science when additional materials such as biographies, autobiographics, case studies, journals, and similar materials exist. In the past the field of mathematics seemed to lack "real books," but many new discoveries are leading to exciting books and videos about how mathematics applies to real life.

Montessori

Dr. Maria Montessori's work with poor Italian children led educators to a great interest in using her teaching methods in the United States, especially in schools with young children. Montessori programs are designed to allow each child to work at her own pace on a variety of activities or interest-centers that are set up by the teacher.

In a traditional Montessori school, the instructor acts as a guide, teaching each child how to properly use the specialized materials and to care for the learning environment. The children may work individually or in small groups (Ishizuka, 2000).

Montessori's original school was highly structured and primarily teacher-directed—by Montessori herself—who had to work with children who had few, if any, basic learning skills (Martin, 2004). However, Montessori programs are now considered to be primarily student-directed in that the child can usually choose to work at any time with any materials in the learning environment once the instructor or guide demonstrates the correct use of the materials.

Benefits

Homeschooling parents, especially during the elementary years, may find the Montessori philosophy to be an advantage, since part of her philosophy was to teach children to care for their environment through chores and other activities. In addition, the Montessori method does much for teaching students how to think logically, work in an orderly fashion, work with mathematics, and explore the world around them. Parents may use the approach to teach their children with real-life activities that reinforce critical thinking skills.

Drawbacks

Homeschools are not likely to contain the highly specialized and expensive equipment associated with modern and complete Montessori schools, which may be a disadvantage. Another disadvantage is that Montessori's work is usually associated with younger children (Ishizuka, 2000). There have been attempts made to adapt her methods to high school, but these Montessori adaptations are sometimes in name only because they involve someone's interpretation of Montessori's philosophies, or they incorporate teaching methods more typically used for secondary-level students.

Recommendation

Unfortunately, there is no trademark or copyright on the name "Montessori" or on her philosophies and teaching approaches. There are a variety of accrediting bodies for certain types of Montessori schools—each with their own interpretation of her work and how it should be implemented. There has not been enough research done to support the idea that using Montessori methods exclusively at high school levels is sufficient for preparing students for higher education. What may be the best option for parents who believe in Montessori methods is to help their children remember Montessori's emphasis on the beauty and joy of learning.

Waldorf

Rudolf Steiner created the Waldorf approach in the early 1900s. Steiner's approach is similar to Montessori's in that it emphasizes a need for the child to learn through experiences in a well-developed environment. Practical skills such as sewing and woodworking help teach self-sufficiency, as well as critical thinking skills (Ishizuka, 2000).

Although Waldorf-schooling is considered to be student-directed because of its student-centered focus, it nevertheless contains a definite teacher-directed tone with specific instruction times for each subject and control over when reading is taught (not until second or third grade). Also, in true Waldorf schools the teacher is assigned to the same group of students and stays with them from the first grade through the eighth grade.

Benefits

Homeschooling parents may find that the Waldorf philosophy of not formally educating children until they are older relates well to their own beliefs about not forcing their children to learn until they are ready to do so. Another advantage for homeschoolers is that the Waldorf approach, like Montessori, incorporates activities such as gardening and care of the home or school environment (Ishizuka, 2000) along with a focus on the joy of learning through direct interactions with the world.

Drawbacks

Homeschoolers who prefer a student-directed approach may find that the Waldorf approach is in many ways too teacher-directed. True Waldorf schools have extremely specific approaches for determining what should be taught, when, and how, which homeschoolers may find somewhat limiting for developing self-directed learning skills. Like Montessori methods, Waldorf methods are based in great part on one person's philosophy of teaching and learning. Numerous reinterpretations over the years have sometimes been true to the original, and sometimes not.

Recommendation

As with the Montessori method, those who incorporate the Waldorf approach should consider whether or not it is sufficiently broad for developing the skills students need to succeed in higher education. If so, parents should also evaluate whether they have adequate knowledge and training in the method to implement it successfully at any level, but particularly during the high school years.

Unschooling

Unschooling, a term created by John Holt in the 1960s, is in many respects the epitome of student-directed learning in the homeschool environment. Holt is credited as being one of the founders of homeschooling for supporting some of the first homeschooling parents who wanted to keep their children from traditional school environments (Ishizuka, 2000). There is really no specific approach to unschooling, hence the term "un-schooling." There is no specific structure to be followed, no rules to employ, or plans to use with unschooling—unless the child and parent want to create and use them, but then it would be doubtful that they would really be unschooling any more.

Some wonder how this approach really works. In a true unschooling environment, the child chooses exactly what she wants to study, when, and for what length of time as her interests or curiosity dictate. The parent then provides the supplies or the means to obtain the materials the child may want to use to study a subject, or the child may have to do this on her own. Therefore, every day in every way is strictly up to the child—at least as far as learning goes.

Unschoolers sometimes believe there is no way to predict what knowledge a person will need in the future so there is no sense requiring a child to learn specific types or amounts of information. Theoretically, as the child grows older and even into adulthood, he will continue to learn and will review subjects or information about which he believes his knowledge to be insufficient.

Benefits

The unschooling approach lends itself to an older child working on long-term interests or projects. For parents who truly believe in student-directed learning, unschooling provides the best model without a potentially conflicting philosophy or method, such as may be the case with the Mason, Montessori, or Waldorf approaches.

Unschooling allows the parent and student to work together to develop a program of study that specifically addresses the child's interests and needs at any given time. As the child's interests or needs change, homeschoolers have the flexibility of not being locked into any long-term plans or expensive materials.

Drawbacks

There are many concerns about this approach. Some parents feel uncomfortable with a total lack of structure about what is to be learned and when, especially if college is the goal. The unschooling approach assumes a certain maturity on the part of the child to spend time learning and not engaging in activities such as playing video games and calling it learning. Parents may also be uncomfortable with facilitating the child's learning about any subject about which she wants to learn. Parents may also be unable or unwilling to provide whatever materials, resources, or activities the child needs to learn what interests her.

One might also wonder if the child will learn enough and develop the learning skills required to be successful in college. While many colleges require a certain amount of self-directed learning from their students, I personally don't know of any that simply allow a student to create his own degree by studying whatever he wishes, whenever he wishes. So, one criticism of the unschooling approach might be that it sets the child up for failure if he is unable to accept the structure and direction that typically accompanies higher education. The unschooling approach may also make it extremely challenging to produce the evidence (transcripts) a child needs for college admission.

Recommendation

We recommend you take the best of unschooling, letting your student investigate topics that interest her the most, and combine it with some traditional structure to help prepare your child for higher education, because very few colleges use any approaches close to unschooling. Chapter 22 offers project ideas that combine aspects of unschooling with more traditional methods of teaching and learning such as textbooks. This approach can help children enjoy learning while developing the college-level skills we suggest.

Evaluating Student-directed Homeschool Methods

Because student-directed methods help children to take a more active role in learning, students may learn more and retain more information than with other more passive methods of education (Hiemstra and Sisco, 1990). A further step toward the student-directed method is to have the student evaluate her own work, which can also be an effective learning strategy.

In a student-directed environment, perhaps more so than in a teacher-directed environment, the motivation to learn is more intrinsic—coming from within the student—rather than extrinsically imposed by the teacher through grades or other rewards. Students start to become intrinsically motivated when they decide they are learning for themselves—their goals, their plans, and their satisfaction—rather than only to satisfy others.

In many ways intrinsic motivation relates to the ideal of self-motivated students who direct their own learning experiences. Intrinsic motivation is also tied to students learning that school is not simply for getting a diploma but is rather part of the bigger picture: preparation for life and contribution to society (Yarbrough, 2002).

Your role as a teacher is not minimized in a student-directed environment—on the contrary, in many ways you have a more important role in helping your child learn successfully. For example, you can have great influence over the development of your child's self-confidence in her own learning skills.

A student's success or failure with handling the responsibility of learning may affect her confidence in her own abilities (self-efficacy). This in turn affects later success in developing critical thinking and self-directed learning skills (Alfassi, 2003). Self-efficacy enables students to persist at tasks longer, resulting in successful completion and ultimately in greater self-confidence. A high degree of self-efficacy develops a sense of optimism in students, helping them appropriately manage the challenges and stresses associated with college and life (Chemers, Hu, and Garcia, 2001).

The transfer of responsibility for learning from teacher to student may be entirely appropriate for adult students. In the case of homeschooling, this is usually more appropriate for high school students preparing for higher education than for elementary students. However, the responsibility a homeschooling student has for learning should be equal to his maturity and readiness to take on this responsibility rather than via an arbitrary measurement of age or grade.

Teaching method	Chief advantages	Chief disadvantages
Charlotte Mason	Very literature-focused Strong focus on self-discipline May be less expensive with materials obtained through library or other such sources	Too literature-focused Assumes parent is proficient with student-directed learning Assumes parent has read all of the materials to effectively facilitate discussions May be difficult to teach certain subjects, particularly mathematics, to the level required for college admission
Montessori	Highly focused on self-discipline, development of logic, mathematics, working in orderly fashion, and care of home and school environment	Expensive materials May be best known (and perhaps suited) for elementary children Too many split-off versions of original philosophy May not be useful for all high school subjects

Teaching method	Chief advantages	Chief disadvantages
Waldorf	Highly focused on student, self sufficiency, critical thinking, working in orderly fashion, and care of home and school environment	May be difficult to follow original theory May be too limited in approach May not be useful for all high school subjects
Unschooling	Not limited in approach Not rigid or overly structured Heavily focused on student's interests Highly focused on self-directed learning	May be too unstructured, requiring even more instructor preparation to anticipate child's daily choices Difficult to track progress sufficiently for college admission Difficult to ensure all subjects required for college admission covered sufficiently

Teaching method	Chief advantages	Chief disadvantages
Student-directed Methods	Focused on development of self-directed learning May develop intrinsic motivation for learning Makes parent's role as educator less authoritarian	Too focused on student Not enough structure Perhaps prone to having parents not be involved enough in their children's daily learning activities

CHAPTER 13

Developing Your Own Homeschool Method

In a teacher-directed environment the parent has responsibility for planning what is learned, how, and when; the student simply follows the parent's directions. In a student-directed environment the child's interests help determine the topics of study, and the parent's role is to guide the learning experiences and provide resources. This environment also requires parents and their children to cooperate to identify what will be learned and how. This form of education supports the development of critical thinking and self-directed learning skills. The student is involved not only with learning, but also with planning his education.

It is really up to you to find an approach that works for you and your child. No matter how you teach, this book can help you find the best way to supplement in areas where your approach may be lacking. Because every method has its strengths and weaknesses, we recommend an eclectic approach, combining some of the structure of teacher-directed methods with some of the freedom and responsibility of student-directed methods.

Eclectic Methods

An eclectic approach is any combination of methods that works for your family. The combination of methods may change from month-to-month, year-to-year, or even child-to-child within the same family. Many homeschooling families who have a great deal of experience with teaching their children at home use an eclectic approach because they have tried one or more methods with varying degrees of success. Eventually they combine the best aspects from each approach into a format that works for them. Eclectic approaches to homeschooling are also popular for teenagers, as they offer more freedom to meet the needs and interests of older students (Cohen, 2000).

Benefits

The primary advantage is that eclectic approaches may better meet the learning needs of a child than a single approach. Flexibility is another major advantage because parents are not limited to one program, one set of textbooks, one philosophy, or a single approach that may not fit the parent's teaching style or the child's learning preferences.

Drawbacks

Parents who prefer a more structured approach to learning may find that this method seems too unstructured or that it requires a great deal more planning than a traditional (purchased) program might. Similarly, parents who prefer to use a teacher-directed approach with their teenagers may find that an eclectic approach is more student-directed than they prefer.

Recommendation

The eclectic approach offers the greatest flexibility of all the methods. Though it may require constant planning and adjustment to find the right balance of approaches for your program, your child will benefit as you prepare him for higher education.

Our Experience with an Eclectic Approach

If your self-confidence as a teacher is limited or you are new to homeschooling, you may prefer the traditional, textbook approach. In the beginning of our program, Chandra felt much more comfortable knowing exactly what she had to do as a teacher and what the children had to do as students, so using textbooks was appealing. Of course, this was also a familiar method since we both used textbooks when we were in school.

Regarding some of the methods we discussed in Chapter 11, we've never explored the Trivium approach in our program and don't think it would work for us, but some parents have success with it. As far as unit studies are concerned, we doubt we would have the time to put together or follow a unit study plan with the number of children we have and their busy schedules. We have seen this approach used in preschool and it seemed to work pretty well—even with multiple children. However, the children were all about the same age and pretty much

Choosing a Teaching Approach

Sticking to one style of teaching or adhering to one teaching theory means limiting opportunities for developing all the skills required for success in higher education.

Eclectic teaching approaches may be better than any single approach to fit your child's learning style and your teaching style.

Don't feel bound to follow any one theory too closely if it doesn't help you effectively teach your child.

confined to one room and one schedule, which is probably what helped make it successful.

Looking back, we realize how much Chandra has had to go beyond her comfort zone as a teacher. Now our homeschooling program is more eclectic than anything. We use textbooks quite a bit, but we also have both the younger and older children engage in other learning activities that are just as valuable as their book lessons. We like using "real books," so we incorporate some of Mason's methods. We focus on the beauty of learning, care of our home environment, and how knowledge is applied in the real world, so you might say we incorporate a little bit of Montessori and Waldorf philosophies into our program too. Because we allow the children to sometimes pick topics they want to study in greater depth and because we often assign projects, we incorporate unschooling and unit studies approaches as well.

Using a variety of approaches is one of the reasons our oldest children are excellent learners today—they learned many different ways to learn. In addition, both we and our children feel "in control" each day and we are all happier as a result.

Key Points

- ❑ Review various homeschool teaching methods and evaluate whether or not they are useful in preparing your child for college.
- ❑ Don't feel bound to just one method of teaching or to the method that worked best when your child was in elementary school if it doesn't sufficiently prepare your child for college.

CHANDRA'S PERSPECTIVE

In our early years of homeschooling, our program was probably much more rigid than it is now. Part of the reason for that was I didn't have a lot of experience as a teacher or even as a mother at that point in time, so I wanted to do everything "right." I put a lot of pressure on myself for fear of doing something wrong and academically scarring the children for life.

In those days there weren't as many resources as there are now. Dave created everything from scratch and wrote out all the lessons and instructor notes—in long hand! Remember, this was the age between typewriters and computers. I wanted detailed instructions on what I was supposed to do, when, and how, and Dave provided them. It was very time consuming for him to write out what he probably would have just done naturally; then to explain it all to me took extra time too.

At first I was a stickler for the schedule. If we were going to do it right and I was going to be held accountable for the children's success (my expectations of myself rather than Dave's expectations of me), then by golly we were going to go by the book. It totally stressed me out, especially if we got off track due to illnesses or the children just not feeling like they wanted to work in their books that day. Eventually I learned how to balance the children's interests each day with the need to follow the schedule and to a specific amount of work done each day. It was really a matter of confidence in myself as a teacher that made all the difference; at first the children and I had a difficult time of separating mom from teacher and school day from home life. However, as we just kept working consistently through each day, we eventually got the hang of it. I was glad I had Dave to talk to about what went well or what didn't each day. I know of many homeschooling mothers who really go it on their own since their husbands are either not supportive or interested; some even actively display animosity toward their wives about the whole homeschooling issue.

Overall, I'd have to say that I learned to relax and enjoy the process and privilege of being able to teach the children at home. I feel blessed to spend so much more time with them each day than I would have if they were gone six to eight hours at school each day. I feel the children are closer to one another as a result of homeschooling and I feel closer to them as well. Now that the first two are off to college, I feel much more prepared for the high school years for the next four.

CHAPTER 14

Learning Styles

DURING MY MASTER'S AND DOCTORATE PROGRAMS, I had the opportunity to study various theories about learning styles. The information I studied was based on actual research conducted by educators, psychologists, and other experts in various fields. However, as I prepared to write this chapter, I conducted additional research via the Internet to see what information a homeschooling parent was likely to find while doing a search about learning styles. Even though there is some good information available on this subject on the Internet, there is a great deal of confusing, if not misleading, information out there as well.

I was dismayed by the number of sites that promised to identify a child's learning style and offered advice on what to do with that information. Many sites were simply advertisements for books, software, or online programs providing some basic information, but for which you had to pay in order to get actual results. We encourage you to be cautious about any site, book, or program that seems primarily geared toward trying to sell you something.

What are "Learning Styles"?

Learning styles is simply a term for how individuals learn. Some theories about learning styles have been evaluated and tested with varying results, but for every study that seems to prove a theory, there are typically just as many studies that seem to disprove it.

> **Learning styles is simply a term for how individuals learn.**

While there have been quite a few researchers to study and write about learning styles, one of the forerunners was David Kolb. In 1984 Kolb introduced his *experiential learning theory*. His theory was broken down into a series of parts, with the first two parts being how individuals take in or input information and then how they process that information.

Kolb then broke it down further by theorizing that the input of information is really an individual's personal preference for either abstract concepts or concrete examples, which he indicated were polar opposites on what might be visualized as a vertical line between the two. An individual's preferences would fall somewhere on that line.

Now imagine a horizontal line bisecting that vertical line right in the middle. Kolb then put two opposite ideas on either end of that line to indicate how a person prefers to *process* incoming information—through active experimentation or reflective observation. Active experimentation could be most closely described as hands-on learning, while reflective observation might be more passive as a person thinks about what is learned.

The vertical and horizontal lines of Kolb's theory create four quadrants, which he referred to as *Accommodators*, *Divergers*, *Assimilators*, and *Convergers*. Responding to a series of questions, an individual indicates a preference between choices for how he likes to *receive* information and then for how he likes to *use* that information. A scoring system allows one to plot scores on the vertical axis and the horizontal axis. Connecting the dots between the scores creates a visual representation of where the person's preferences for learning lie in one of the four quadrants.

Thus, the four types of learning styles Kolb defined are described as a combination of a preference for how information is inputted and processed. In his theory Accommodators are defined as people who like concrete examples for incoming information and who prefer to actively experiment (work hands-on) with that information. The Divergers are individuals who also like concrete examples for incoming information, but they would rather engage in reflective observation with that information. The opposite types of learners are the Assimilators, who like abstract concepts and reflective observation, and the Convergers, who like abstract concepts and active experimentation.

A similar theory, known as *Index of Learning Styles* (ILS), was created in 1991 by Richard M. Felder and Barbara A. Soloman. The index was adapted from an earlier work (1987) by Felder and his colleague, Linda K. Silverman. Like the Kolb theory, there are four learning styles or dimensions to the ILS theory—active/reflective, sensing/intuitive, visual/verbal, and sequential/global. Felder believed individuals switch from one type of learning to another based on the situation at hand. For example, a person might use active or hands-on learning in one situation and a reflecting, thinking type of learning in another. Similarly, Felder defined the sensing learners as liking to learn facts, while intuitive learners like discovering relationships between things. Visual learners like to see information in order to best learn from it, and verbal learners like information they can hear, such as a lecture or an explanation of information. Sequential learners follow logical steps from one thing to another, while global learners look for the big picture before getting involved with smaller details.

These are just two types of learning models that have been researched by experts in various fields. These two models or theories have been tested and evaluated by other experts with varying results. Why with varying results? Because as we noted earlier, no one theory or approach ever seems to describe and define every single person's learning style with 100% accuracy, which goes to prove how unique we all are.

Simplifying Learning Styles

So what does all of this mean to you? Well, let's first break down the idea of learning styles in order to better understand it.

As mentioned above, a learning style simply indicates one's preference for acquiring and then using information. To acquire information, we use our senses. In reality, we probably use some combination of all of our five senses in different learning situations, but the most predominant of the senses used for learning are our eyes, ears, and "touch." Researchers usually will refer to these senses in terms related to learning styles—visual, auditory, and kinesthetic. Sometimes these are referred to as *modalities*, or the *modes* with which a person acquires and uses information.

However, these terms are not entirely sufficient to explain how one learns. For example, reading is a visual method for acquiring learning, but some individuals don't like reading or reading doesn't satisfy their learning needs. Instead, they may prefer to "watch" a lecture or demonstration, or they may prefer to "read" diagrams, instructions, or pictures. Some may get more out of watching a video about the subject than by reading about it.

In many college classrooms the primary methods of instruction are auditory (listening to the instructor's lecture) and visual (reading the text and other materials on one's own). Depending on the course, students may also use kinesthetic learning by working hands-on in a lab or conducting field work. Even getting work experience, such as being a student-teacher as part of a credential program, might be considered kinesthetic learning, but it would also incorporate visual and auditory learning as well.

It's fun to watch college students engage in an activity in class to see what their learning styles are. I use Legos™ in many different college classes for various types of learning experiences. The students who are visual learners want to "see" the instructions and will constantly refer back to them during the exercise. The kinesthetic learners typically dive right in and start "playing." The auditory learners will ask questions to "hear" my explanations. Through observation, I can often deduce a person's primary preference for learning. Yet, it isn't always her only method for learning and indeed may only be the preferred method for that type of exercise. In a different setting or even in a different course (subject), the student may have a different learning preference.

As parents and educators, you should utilize a variety of learning experiences.

As parents and educators, you should utilize a variety of learning experiences in order to assess your child's preferred learning style in a particular situation. Remember that even though she may learn a certain way most of the time, she may not learn the same way in every subject.

Varying Teaching Techniques

Understanding what visual, auditory, and kinesthetic learning styles are can help you identify your child's preference for acquiring information in general and in certain subjects. Yet, that knowledge only gives you part of the picture about learning styles, as they only tell you about how a person might acquire information, but it doesn't tell you about how he may understand information.

Looking back at Kolb's and Felder's theories, their approaches further break down learning styles into types of information and what is done with them. For example, some people prefer *abstract* types of information or *concepts* about a subject, while others need more *concrete* information. In order to really understand and be able to use information, many students need to actively experiment with it through practice problems or some other type of kinesthetic activity. On the other hand, some students simply prefer to "think" about what they've learned.

In mathematics (and even science to a certain extent) information may be very concrete or it may be very abstract. Algebra with its x's and n's, geometry with its planes and lines, and physics with its force and acceleration are all *very* abstract, but some students just get it. Yet, other students need to have that same information made more concrete through hands-on activities, visual displays, or real-life examples. One physics professor told me he takes his students to the amusement park in order to experience the formulas they used in class while riding the roller coaster.

Other subjects, such as psychology, sociology, philosophy, theology, and even social studies, may also seem abstract. Some students can learn about civilizations like the Ancient Greeks and Romans; philosophers like Plato, Aristotle, and Locke; time periods like the Middle Ages and the Renaissance;

the history of religion; and things like the Hammurabi Code and the Magna Carta, and they can put it all together to understand how each of these things affected the formation of the United States, our Constitution, and our present-day society. These types of learners see the big picture and make connections between what, to some, seem like unrelated topics. Other learners need to have someone connect the dots visually or verbally before they can appreciate how interconnected history is.

Looking at the different subjects in your high school program, you should examine what type of information is abstract or conceptual and what is more concrete, factual, and detailed. You can also look at what may be your child's best method for learning this information and for you teaching it—visually, verbally, or kinesthetically—or some combination of the three.

You can then see if your child likes to "think" about information to better understand it or if she likes to have lots of practical exercises before really understanding what she learned. Therefore, you can determine if your child would benefit more from additional reading about a subject, discussing it with you or having you provide more explanations and examples, or giving her a chance to produce something (a project or paper) related to what was learned.

Examples from Our Program: Holly

Each of our children is unique. As such, we've needed to learn about each one's talents and styles as we've gone along. When our oldest children were younger, we adapted our program and teaching approaches to better meet their unique learning needs.

Our oldest daughter, Holly, is hearing impaired and for almost the first two years of her life she was completely without hearing. Since we didn't know she was hearing impaired, Holly developed a strong visual learning style. She may have been a visual-type learner anyway, yet her visual learning preference was much more profound as a result of her hearing loss.

By the time she was diagnosed, Holly was two years behind in her speech development. She had a one-word vocabulary: "hot," which she pronounced "ha." The only reason she had that word is she heard Chandra yell it one time as Holly was about to touch the hot oven door. Since Holly could only hear sounds in the range of jet engines and jackhammers, up close Chandra's voice must have been pretty loud as she tried to protect Holly from getting burned.

Chandra took Holly to speech therapy twice a week and then worked with her several times each day helping her learn not only how to speak, but how to hear with her hearing aids. Within a few months, Holly had made considerable progress but was still behind.

The original audiologist who diagnosed Holly's hearing loss suggested we put Holly into a deaf school where she could be taken care of by her own kind because she would never learn to read, write, or speak. Holly's new audiologists and speech therapists never gave up on her, even though they had their doubts about how much of the two-year deficit in expressive language Holly would be able to make up.

Toting our son along with her twice each week, Chandra took Holly to a speech therapist to help her learn how to hear and speak. On the other days Chandra balanced being the mother of an infant (Cameron was only an infant at the time) and her responsibilities as a stay-at-home wife with being Holly's therapist. At one point Holly made well over a year's worth of progress on her speech in less than six months.

Chandra's dedication is one of the main reasons Holly is the successful young woman in college that she is today. The other main reason is Holly's strong visual-learning orientation combined with being into everything (kinesthetic learning) and a big heap of stubbornness—she never gave up. Better yet, she simply refused to fail.

From very early on in Holly's life, we promoted her visual learning style with lots and lots of books. She read them all and we read them to her—many times. When we couldn't afford to buy books, we used the library. We arranged every activity we could to help Holly utilize her kinesthetic learning skills as well. We incorporated art, experiments, or some sort of activity with as many lessons as we could. And through it all, we talked—a lot—to help Holly develop her auditory learning skills.

Throughout the high school years, Holly read books and wrote papers, tapping into her visual learning style preference. She developed her own newsletters, made movies, wrote poems, gave oral presentations, and created experiments and science fair projects. She also involved herself in a variety of activities outside the home, including volunteer work at the library, church, and within the community.

When she scored a 28 on her ACT, we were surprised and not surprised at the same time. In some ways it was a validation that we had done something right, but even more so, it was a tribute to Holly's accomplishments and her ability to overcome one of the biggest challenges in her life.

Examples from Our Program: Cameron

Cameron snuck up on us in more ways than one. We were surprised and pleased when we found out he was coming into our lives. We would later look back on the timing of his birth as part of God's master plan because Cameron was so instrumental in Holly's language development. With only twenty months between them, they grew up very close.

Holly's education influenced him as well. Being carted off to his sister's speech therapy twice a week and watching Chandra work with her at home, Cameron was exposed to visual and hands-on learning from almost day one of his life. So, we weren't terribly surprised to see how much he loved books, too, but his ability to read hit us, quite literally, like a lightning bolt.

Both of the children were very young when we moved into our first house. Holly was not quite four years old and Cameron was just a little over two years old. Being a young, one-income family in a new home, we didn't have a lot of money to go places and do things for entertainment, so the television was our outlet in many ways. So when a lightning bolt blew out the television one stormy day, the four of us were more than saddened by the loss. Fortunately, we acquired a little extra money to buy a new television within a few weeks.

At that point in time, most new televisions were being outfitted with a wonderful new invention called "closed-captioning." It opened up a whole new world for Holly, but we didn't realize what it had done for Cameron until one day when he brought a book into the room and claimed he could read it. Children often imitate reading by telling the story the pictures show or repeating bits of it they have memorized from when it was read to them. Expecting this to be the case, we were floored when Cameron actually read the book. It turns out all of those hours watching television with the closed-captioning on had reinforced Cameron's visual-learning skills (reading) with his verbal-learning skills (listening to the words spoken during the shows).

As Cameron got older, there were definite differences in his learning styles in terms of what types of information he liked to acquire and how he could use it. Cameron was much more accepting of mathematics and its abstract concepts than Holly, who preferred to creatively solve advanced mathematics problems rather than doing them correctly "by the book."

To make sure we filled in any gaps about math, both Holly and Cameron took math classes at the community college before taking their ACT, and both scored very high in the math sections on that test. Holly took an algebra class her first semester of college and earned an "A." Cameron took enough math classes at the community college that he will not have to take any during college to fulfill the general credits.

As with Holly, we had Cameron complete a wide variety of projects appealing to each of the three modes of learning—visual, auditory, and kinesthetic. We also provided opportunities to deal with abstract and concrete examples in every subject as often as we could. While they often had the same courses throughout high school, we provided opportunities for them to study topics of particular interest within those courses. We also enrolled them in classes especially designed for their interests and learning styles. For example, while Holly wanted more classes in creative writing, Cameron chose to take a sports studies class where he conducted research about several types of sports and wrote papers about each. Additionally, although both were required to read selected books to prepare them for college, they also chose books to read that they enjoyed individually.

We mentioned Holly's ACT score earlier and, out of fairness, we mention here that Cameron scored 27 out of 36 on the ACT test. We are happy to say that like his sister, Cameron will be eligible for a scholarship to the school of his choice.

We believe Cameron's score demonstrates the success of our program and Holly's accomplishments were not coincidental. However, Chandra and I do not credit ourselves with their success. We simply feel we were there to help facilitate their innate abilities to succeed. Whether they succeeded or not was really their choice and we're proud they chose to succeed. While we helped them learn *how to learn* and to *enjoy* learning, they were the ones who devoted themselves to studying and learning throughout high school and prepared themselves well for the ACT. So, in the end, we feel like we all succeeded as a team.

What to Take Away from this Chapter

There are a few key points we'd like you take away from this chapter. First, you don't need to pay money to try to figure out your child's learning style— it's probably either a visual, auditory, or kinesthetic method that she employs, and sometimes it may be a combination of two or all three of those methods depending on the subject and the type of information to be learned. Observing your child and talking to her about how she likes to learn is more helpful to you than any learning styles "test."

Second, it is more important for you to adjust your teaching style to your child's learning style than the other way around. As an educator, your job is to help your student learn and be successful rather than to risk his failure by getting into a power struggle over "style." Devote the time and effort necessary to figure out how your child likes to learn and how he learns best and then work to teach him accordingly.

Third, incorporate activities into your program that allow your child to not only utilize and practice her preferred learning style, but that also allow her to practice a variety of learning styles. Rather than simply having your child read the text, answer questions at the end of the chapter, or write a paper, consider making things more interesting and educational with a variety of projects, which we discuss in more detail in an upcoming chapter as we provide multiple examples of ways you can allow your child to demonstrate what she learned.

Fourth, we recommend you don't get hung up on any one learning theory or the use of one or more terms to define your child's learning style. They are just labels that are used to denote a certain status as a learner or to pigeonhole someone into one type of learning style. Labeling your child's learning style may actually limit him by leading you to believe you have to focus on only one way of teaching, and he on only one way of learning. One learning style or method isn't necessarily any better than another. It is more important to understand how your child learns, both in general and with specific subjects, and to be flexible enough in your teaching to satisfy his learning needs.

Labeling your child's learning style may actually limit him.

Just as there are different methods of homeschooling, there are many learning styles theories that may work for you and your child. Being open to a variety of theories and utilizing the best elements from each allows your child to become a more well-rounded and effective learner than choosing to follow just one method or theory. Also, using different types of teaching approaches and learning styles will better prepare her for the various teaching approaches she will likely experience in college and in the real world.

Key Points

❑ You don't need to pay money to try to figure out your child's learning style. Observing your child and talking to her about how she likes to learn is more helpful to you than any learning styles "test."

❑ It is more important for you to adjust your teaching style to your child's learning style than the other way around.

❑ Don't get hung up on any one learning theory or the use of one or more terms to define your child's learning style.

❑ One learning style or method isn't necessarily any better than any other. It is more important to understand how your child learns, both in general and with specific subjects, and to be flexible enough in your teaching to satisfy his learning needs.

❑ Be open to a variety of theories. Utilizing the best elements from each allows your child to become a more well-rounded and effective learner than choosing to follow just one method or theory. Also, using different types of teaching approaches and learning styles will better prepare her for the various teaching approaches she will likely experience in college and the real world.

SECTION IV

CREATING YOUR HIGH SCHOOL PROGRAM

CHAPTER 15

Buying Curricula

BEFORE YOU CAN START TEACHING YOUR CHILD at home at any level, you have to make a decision about whether to buy a curriculum or to customize your own. In this chapter we will focus on buying curricula.

For some subjects, such as foreign language and mathematics, we purchase our curricula through homeschool publishers and other suppliers. Sometimes our children take corresponding courses at a community college. Since we lack enough expertise in these subjects to create our own curriculum, it is easier to buy ready-made materials.

For other subjects we customize our own curriculum by adapting materials we've purchased and being selective about how we use them. For example, we may not have the children read the chapters in the same order in which they were written, and we do not typically require the children to answer all of the questions at the end of each chapter. Sometimes we use textbooks as the primary source of information and then supplement them with other materials, such as books, videos, or computer programs.

Buying a complete curriculum has both advantages and disadvantages. One advantage is that using a complete curriculum saves time and effort when it comes to planning lessons, grading a child's work, reporting what will be covered for each subject each year to the state, and keeping records of what was taught for any given subject. However, there are other considerations that may influence what you purchase.

The first decision to make is whether to buy one curriculum from a single publisher or to purchase bits and pieces from multiple publishers. Next you have to decide whether to buy just the textbooks or all the supplementary materials the publisher produces. You may even consider whether or not to enroll your child in a distance education program or an online school, in which case you would use that publisher's materials.

We suggest you use caution in planning what to purchase. Learning materials are like paint; it is easy to buy much more than you will ever use and then you are left with items that you can't use and are difficult to throw away, a common dilemma for parents who are new to homeschooling. Parents who don't know what they need tend to buy everything.

Choosing Materials

Purchasing materials for one child is expensive enough, but materials for multiple children can really add up fast! Investing in reusable materials can pay off in the long run. You can buy your materials new from a publisher or bookstore

Investing in reusable materials can pay off in the long run.

that sells homeschooling curricula. You may also buy used materials from other homeschoolers or occasionally at yard sales or thrift shops. Sometimes you can save money by buying a used text from another parent and then just buying the corresponding workbook or test booklet from the publisher.

For used materials it is a good idea to check the copyright date as well as the content. Some books are classics that can be used forever, such as literature or spelling texts. Others, like those for science and history, may become outdated quickly. Also keep in mind that a publisher may have produced an updated version of an older text, which means if you use the old text with a new workbook or test book, the information may not correlate.

There is a seemingly endless quantity of products on the market today and the selections change from year to year. A list of suggested resources can be found at the back of this book. We also recommend you take the time to ask other homeschoolers for their suggestions, but remember these are personal opinions based on individual preferences and experiences. We have found that listening to these opinions is valuable, but it is vital to trust your own judgment.

When deciding which publisher's textbooks to purchase, consider the variety of materials they offer, such as student textbooks, test books, speed drills, lab manuals, teacher's manuals, lesson plans, learning aids, flash cards, posters, and other supplemental materials. Often it will be sufficient to purchase just some of the available materials. Determine which materials you want, as well as which materials you really need to get the job done.

If the information in textbooks is presented at a high rate of speed, meaning that advanced skills and concepts are presented in rapid succession or before the appropriate age to learn the information, you may want to look for other materials instead. For example, check to see when the publisher introduces cursive writing or the multiplication tables. Publishers who introduce basic concepts and skills too soon for earlier grade levels may continue to rush new subject matter even in high school textbooks, which may leave you and your child feeling frustrated and disappointed.

What to Buy

In order to decide which materials you need to buy, first determine what you will need to fulfill your state's requirements and the requirements of the college your child wants to attend. Also consider which materials will fit both your child's learning interests and needs, as well as your abilities as a parent and teacher. When possible, examine the materials first to see how the information is presented and explained, how much practice is provided in the materials to reinforce concepts and skills, and the pace at which the information is presented. Often publishers have sales representatives who set up display booths during homeschooling events so you can preview actual materials rather than having to make educated guesses based on the catalog. If you order materials at one of these events or scheduled displays, sometimes you can get free shipping or a discount on the materials.

Choice of materials is largely a matter of personal preference. The more materials you have available, the more options you have to help with the process of teaching and learning. If you purchase just a textbook, you may limit the breadth of your child's lesson to reading the information, completing the activities, and answering the questions in the textbook. Yet, if you purchase all of the available supplemental materials, you may end up with more assignments and activities than your child can reasonably complete.

Chandra and I like texts written in an engaging manner with colorful pages, numerous opportunities for reviewing information, follow-up activities or practice exercises, and clear, concise explanations. Workbooks reinforce information presented in the text. Similarly, the review questions at the end of a chapter in a textbook can help you evaluate what your child has learned.

Lesson plans and teacher's materials show you how to use the materials appropriately and outline what to teach and when. Teacher materials provide answers to questions in the texts. However, be aware that in some subjects such as mathematics, and especially in the advanced grades, the teacher's manuals may provide the answers to only selected problems. If math is not a strong area for you, you may want to be certain the teacher's manual not only provides the answers, but also shows the steps used to obtain the answers.

We highly recommend buying materials that can be used repeatedly, such as flash cards. Flash cards are great for teaching a variety of information, as well as for speed drills, recognition practice, and oral reinforcement of knowledge. Flash cards can even be useful for high school to help reinforce math concepts, foreign language words, and so forth. Flash cards can be used to teach your child directly or she can use the flash cards to study alone. Consider laminating your flashcards to keep them clean and in good condition for years to come. Glossaries, appendices, and other supplemental material at the end of textbooks or workbooks are also excellent resources and can be placed into sheet protectors and kept in a three-ring binder.

What to Watch Out For

Sometimes there is a tendency for publishers of homeschooling materials to "accelerate" the learning process to promote the idea that homeschooled children learn faster than their public school counterparts. If your child needs more time and practice with certain skills or concepts than a textbook provides, you may have to set a schedule different than that recommended by the publisher.

Traditional schools usually present information at a rate that meets the needs of the average pupil or sometimes even the needs of the pupil who is struggling the most. This can be frustrating for other children who are ready to move more quickly through the information. Children should be able to progress through material at whatever pace suits them, as long as what they are learning is age appropriate and they are learning well.

> The ability to learn well means being able to understand the information, retain it, and then apply it.

The ability to learn well means being able to understand the information, retain it, and then apply it not only short-term, but long-term as well. It doesn't do a child any good to learn the multiplication table if he can't recall it later when learning long division.

When buying a curriculum for the new school year it is important the information, skills, and concepts in the materials build on what was taught the year before in that subject. Similarly, the materials should help set the stage for what will be taught the following year in the same subject.

Whether you purchase a single textbook or all the materials for a course, you are also buying the beliefs, opinions, and preferences of the person(s) who wrote or published the book. For example, depending on grade level and the time period covered in the material, an American history text from A Beka or Bob Jones University Press may include information about the Protestant Reformation and subjects such as The Great Awakening and the lives of various missionaries. In science texts from those same publishers, the books will attribute the wonders of creation to God.

While some may appreciate religious information and references to God, others may not. If the information or approach in the particular curriculum is a concern, you may want to look elsewhere for materials. Another option is to find a way to address your concerns when using the material, such as having your child skip certain sections of a book or using those sections as a teaching tool to learn about other viewpoints.

Other Types of Curricula You Can Buy

There are curricula options other than purchasing textbooks and supplemental materials. In our program we often use "real" books instead of textbooks—literature, biographies, histories, and other books are available for many subjects. Tutors and consultants are individuals who work one-on-one with a child or with groups of children in a classroom setting. Similar to tutors and consultants, distance education and online learning programs are available for homeschoolers.

Distance and Online Education

While there are several distance education and online programs for high school students, there are also many factors to consider when determining their appropriateness for educating your child. For the purposes of this book, we are going to review just a few of them.

In order to be successful with online and distance learning, students need to be self-motivated and self-disciplined. Distance education and online teachers do not typically supervise children to make sure they are getting their work done, so it is up to the student and parent to make sure he does whatever is necessary to make the learning experience worthwhile. Even adults who take online courses may struggle to keep up with their work due to a lack of self-motivation or self-discipline.

Parents may view online and distance learning as the ultimate solution for teaching their children—especially through high school. There are some benefits to this method, including having someone else, via technology, take the responsibility for teaching your child. However, there are also many potential disadvantages to consider, one of which is cost. The cost of tuition and materials (including a computer or shipping costs) can be rather high with some online and distance education programs. You can probably offer your child the same quality of education (or better) by using local resources for less money. If online courses seem the right choice for you but cost is an issue, perhaps taking just one or two courses online may be sufficient. Check with individual online schools to see if this is an option.

Another consideration for any of these courses is the teacher's qualifications. Is she state-certified or just experienced with teaching her own children? Is she qualified in specific subject areas and does she teach only those subject areas? Is she experienced with homeschooling? Is she experienced teaching via distance or online education—especially with homeschoolers? Will a student have many different teachers and will they all be equally qualified and experienced in the aforementioned areas? Even college professors with years of experience teaching in the classroom may not be effective when teaching online.

Similarly, teaching adults online is very different from teaching children online. Even if the method seems appropriate, you may want to carefully consider whether or not the lessons, materials, and assignments are appropriate for the child's age and developmental needs. Here are some things to consider:

1. Distance education and online learning rely heavily on written communication. Does your child communicate well in this manner? Also be alert to ensure that any communication your child has with an adult is appropriate.

2. How long does your child have in order to complete an assignment or a course? What type of response time will teachers provide your child? For example, when will your child know how well he performed on an assignment? In what form will that response be?
3. What quality of response will your child receive? Will the response include constructive feedback to help your child learn and develop his academic skills, or will it be generic praise with little value for providing your child with specific examples of what he did well and suggestions about what could be improved?
4. What are the standards against which your child will be evaluated? How will your child be graded?
5. Is there a logical progression of courses, information, skills, and concepts within the courses? Will they help your child get into college?
6. Do you have to pay by course or by a "term"? What is the cost if your child has to repeat a course or doesn't finish a course within the time limits?
7. How much time will your child have to spend in front of the computer if attending an online school?
8. How much research will be required and how will that get done?
9. What sorts of projects will your child complete and will they be educationally appropriate? Will your child continue to be motivated throughout the duration of the course?

These are a few questions to consider, and you may have others if you pursue this option for your child. Distance and online education have great potential, but they also have limitations as appropriate and effective options for children.

Tutors and Consultants

Personal tutors can be useful for helping you teach your children. Tutors usually specialize in certain subjects and may either use the materials you have purchased or that they have developed themselves. Personal tutors usually work one-on-one with children, helping them fill a gap in their knowledge about a subject or helping them build certain skills related to the subject.

Consultants work somewhat differently than tutors. For instance, parents who teach a subject at a co-op school to more than one child at a time can be considered consultants. Consultants, who may or may not be homeschooling parents, may offer classes for homeschoolers in a particular subject outside a co-op environment. Having your child attend classes at a community college may also fall into this category.

Consultants can also be hired to assist parents. For example, you might hire a consultant to help you better understand how to use the materials you've purchased or to work with you to develop a customized program of study for your child.

The one-on-one focus of consulting services is often beneficial, but the cost can be high. Before hiring tutors or consultants, you should consider whether or not they have actual expertise in the subject matter. Someone who has homeschooled her own children may provide excellent emotional support and be a wealth of general information but may not be an "expert" or really know how to teach children other than her own. You may also want to consider whether or not you could save money and accomplish as much yourself.

Similarly, an educational consultant is not the same as a psychologist, behavioral specialist, or someone who is specifically trained to help children with serious learning problems. Consultants cannot take the place of specialized professionals. Carefully consider what your child's needs are in comparison to the consultant's documented qualifications before making a decision.

A Note on Real Books

Sometimes parents like their children to read "real" books rather than textbooks—a major aspect of the Charlotte Mason approach. Real books include biographies, autobiographies, novels, primary source collections, or secondary sources written by experts on a particular subject. This is a sound educational method that has tremendous benefits not available in textbooks alone. However, consider how much time you will have to spend researching information to find books for each subject, the time and effort spent tracking the books down if they are not currently in print, and how much it will cost to buy the books once they are found.

Once you have selected real books, it is important to evaluate whether or not they provide your child with enough breadth and depth of information about a given subject—especially for fulfilling the educational requirements of the state and the college your child hopes to attend. You will also be on your own in evaluating what your child knows about the subject after reading a book, which means you will probably have to spend some time devising activities, exercises, or tests.

Creating and Customizing Your Own Curriculum

The real challenge of creating your own curriculum is deciding what materials you are going to use and how you will use them. When it comes to planning your school program, there are basically four options. The first option is to buy your textbooks and resource materials from any number of publishers (as discussed above) and simply follow the instructions, just as you would read a recipe.

The next option is to purchase materials and then customize them to your child's interest and learning abilities, as well as to your interests and teaching abilities. You may also choose to create a curriculum from scratch or utilize outside resources to teach your child, such as community college classes, tutors, and so on.

In addition to deciding whether or not to purchase a complete curriculum or to create or customize your own, you will also need to decide how involved you will be in the teaching process. Again, there are four options available to you:

1. Obtain materials your child can use to guide himself through the curriculum so that all you do is use the teacher's edition to grade his work. You don't really do any *teaching*, per se. Instead, your child basically teaches himself.

2. Plan to do at least some teaching yourself. If you aren't an expert in a particular subject matter or at least fairly well versed in it, you'll need not only the teacher's edition of the materials, but a published curriculum that guides you through every step in the teaching process.

3. Teach certain subjects based on your knowledge and expertise by developing your own curriculum, or buy materials and curriculum so you can significantly customize the course to suit the interests and abilities of both you and your child.

4. Find someone else to teach your child in one or more subjects, though if you hire someone to teach your child, you are buying the tutor's services and time. If your child takes college classes, you are in essence buying their curriculum and their textbooks and having some-

one else do the teaching.

Should you choose to customize materials purchased from a publisher, you may still need to create some of your own curriculum, or at least create plans for how to use the materials. For example, you could buy your child's books and materials from the publisher and perhaps the instructor's manuals, but you may or may not buy the lesson plans, teacher's instructions, and instructional-support materials (curriculum). These you have to create on your own, supplementing whatever you don't have.

You could decide not to go with any standard published materials and create everything from scratch. This means that either you have to create your own textbooks and supplementary materials for your child or find some other means of providing instruction. For example, instead of using a published Algebra textbook, you would have to create your own textbook and materials or utilize real-life experiences to make up for the lessons, activities, tests, and practice a child would normally gain from a textbook.

However, most parents are either not inclined to write their own textbooks or aren't expert enough to teach a subject in such a way that their child won't need any sort of instructional text. So, this means that you have to buy something from somewhere.

Again, you can buy materials from a homeschool publisher, a bookstore, online, or you can borrow such materials from a library. Yet, whatever materials you choose to use must be adequate for giving your child sufficient information for a particular subject in a manner appropriate not only for the subject, but for the child's grade level and learning abilities.

If you want to create some (or all) of your own curriculum for any subject, there is no magic formula that says do exactly *this* or *that* because each homeschool, each parent, and each child is different. Your interests, abilities, and knowledge as an instructor, as well as the interests, abilities, and needs of your child, will dictate what works best for you. However, for those who may be new to homeschooling or feel overwhelmed in selecting materials from the vast assortment available today, we do include a list of the resources and materials we have used in our home in Appendices B and C. We also make some specific recommendations according to subject in Chapter 18.

In the next few chapters we'll provide more detailed advice and instruction about how to create your own curriculum. We explain how to create objectives, schedules, assignments, and syllabi and how to grade your child's work once you've created or customized your own curriculum. We'll teach you the nuts and bolts about what to do and how to do it, including some tips about what materials to choose. Choosing the materials and deciding how best to use them is up to you.

Below is some additional advice we recommend you keep in mind as you read through the chapters about creating your own curriculum:

1. Remember your goal is to prepare your child for college and life.
2. Always keep in mind that there are specific subjects you *must* teach your child during high school to prepare her for college.
3. Determine which subjects your child is likely to learn best on her own and what you are competent and comfortable enough to teach to her.
4. Buy what you need to teach your child effectively, whether it's an entirely pre-packaged curriculum and materials or other resources you buy and mix or match from various vendors.
5. If you don't buy pre-packaged curriculum, you should either be an expert in the subject be-

ing taught or find other resources to help you.

6. Teach subjects that appeal to your strengths and knowledge as an instructor.

7. If you don't feel comfortable enough with any particular subject to develop your own curriculum, then don't. This doesn't mean you can't teach your child at home, it just means you should look at other options for helping your child learn about that particular subject, such as community college courses, tutors, and so on.

8. Certain subjects, such as mathematics, foreign languages, and even some science courses, have specific skills that must be taught sequentially and should really be taught by experts in those subject areas or with expertly designed materials you can effectively utilize. You can't customize a course in algebra, geometry, or trigonometry as easily as you could a creative writing course for English or a history course for social studies unless you are a mathematics expert.

Our Recommendations

Overall, we prefer customizing our own curriculum because we believe it enables us to better meet our children's needs than we could by using pre-designed curriculum alone. Creating curriculum from scratch can be tremendously rewarding, but it can also be very time consuming. Even mixing, matching, or adapting elements of purchased curricula can take time. However, we think the end result is worth it.

Remember, building your own curriculum doesn't have to mean creating it all from scratch. It can also mean adapting and supplementing purchased curriculum, organizing and structuring how the curriculum is implemented, determining how the school day will run, and more. We describe these activities in upcoming chapters.

We want to assure you that buying curricula is certainly a viable option. However, even if you buy all of your curricula, you still have to do some planning and implementing to make your program successful. We encourage you to read the next chapter in its entirety because the information is useful for both purchased and customized curricula.

Key Points

- ❏ Decide whether to buy from one publisher or multiple publishers.
- ❏ If you choose to purchase previously used materials, make sure the information is current.
- ❏ Decide which supplementary materials you need to purchase in addition to textbooks.
- ❏ Make sure your materials present information at an appropriate pace, level, and depth for your child's learning needs.
- ❏ Consider whether the content reflects religious or moral teachings compatible with your beliefs.
- ❏ Investigate distance education programs or online schools. Make sure any such programs are credible, cost-effective, and appropriate for your child.
- ❏ Consider whether you will have to supplement purchased materials with other learning materials, or if you will need to engage the assistance of a tutor or consultant.

ARE SOME CURRICULA TRYING TO RUSH LEARNING?

Over the years in our discussions with other parents and our review of different curricula from various publishers, we've concluded that some concepts and skills are a little rushed. Two areas that are particularly noteworthy are writing skills and mathematics.

Since we are most familiar with A Beka, we'll use a few

examples from their scope and sequence to explain our point. In A Beka, one of the objectives for three-year-olds is learning how to format (correctly write) vowels and consonants in upper and lower case. In what they call their K4 Kindergarten, cursive writing is introduced. In first grade A Beka has students writing complete sentences and short stories.

Now this isn't to say that some children can't perform these tasks at these ages, but some educational experts might be inclined to see this as rushing the curricula. At the younger ages some children may do just fine with these skills when they are introduced. However, others may have a difficult time holding writing utensils, recognizing letters, and writing in manuscript (printing), so focusing too heavily on the proper formatting of letters, writing in cursive, and writing in complete sentences may be too much for them.

A Beka also introduces mathematical concepts very rapidly. As an example, in the second grade children are introduced to multiplication facts zero through five and division facts one through five. Again, some children may handle these more advanced mathematical concepts well in second grade, while others may still be trying to master addition and subtraction. Others may even be working on recognizing numbers. Children learn differently and some subjects and concepts may be easier to understand than others.

In defense of A Beka, we've found their materials to be well written and the activities within their books are very well done. As you work through their texts or workbooks, you may not feel rushed at all. However, if you see your child struggling with new concepts, such as multiplication or division, then you should be more selective about which assignments to complete and when. You may also need to develop other practice exercises to reinforce concepts the child is still trying to master.

Similarly, if your child is having difficulty with writing or becomes easily frustrated or even afraid to try because he can't correctly format letters, then consider slowing down a little. A safer approach to writing is to make a variety of writing utensils and resources with letters readily available to your child. Reading to your child is an invaluable way to increase interest in writing. When your child starts to want to write letters, notes, and stories, that's usually a good sign she is ready to learn about the formation of letters.

Remember, the joy of homeschooling is that you can make your curriculum anything you want so you effectively meet your child's needs and abilities. Although the curriculum from the publisher is designed in a specific way, there are no rules that say you have to follow that way exactly.

What does this all have to do with students in high school? As we discussed in Chapter 7, even though your child may have successfully completed each subject during grade school, once your child begins high school you should assess if there are any gaps in his knowledge or any skills that need reinforcement.

Even if you plan to use the same curriculum for high school that you used for the elementary years, your child may have missed a few things along the way, some concepts or skills may be fuzzy, or perhaps there is simply an opportunity to revisit concepts or skills that haven't been used in some time. Below we offer a few ideas about how to evaluate your child as he moves from elementary to high school. The following examples refer to mathematics and writing. However, you can perform the same sort of check with other subjects as well:

1. Does he spell well or are some spelling rules confusing?

2. Does he use the correct verb tense for the subject?

3. Does he punctuate correctly?

4. Does he write in complete sentences?

5. When he writes, do his thoughts make sense and flow well from one sentence to another and one paragraph to the next?

6. Can he write coherently about one subject, clearly explaining what he's trying to say?

7. Is he able to quickly multiply numbers zero through twelve in his head?

8. Can he accurately perform long division?

9. Does he perform mathematical problems logically and sequentially, showing each step rather than guessing or jumping to the answer?

10. Is he able to figure things out using various approaches, including deductive reasoning?

Once your child actually begins his high school program, you'll want to make sure he has mastered each concept in each subject before moving on to something new. If the curriculum you choose doesn't offer enough practice problems for mathematics or enough practice exercises in writing, for example, you may have to supplement with other activities or materials to help your child learn what is required. Again, the beauty of homeschooling is that your child need not be forced to move forward in any subject before he is ready, but rather he can proceed at his own pace.

You child's success depends greatly on how involved you are in the teaching and learning process so you can keep track of his progress in each subject. There is no need to rush your child through high school. Instead, it's better to ensure your child thoroughly understands all that is required with regard to academics and to give him plenty of time for emotional, social, and physical development before college.

The Purpose of Educational Objectives

BEFORE IMPLEMENTING YOUR OWN CURRICULUM, the goals of each individual course and of your entire program should be considered. This chapter will help you better understand and define what you are trying to accomplish within each course in your high school program.

When creating educational objectives, focus on what your child should have learned by the *end* of the course, how he will demonstrate what was learned, and how you will describe the course to a college or university. There are four main reasons for educational objectives:

1. To define what *you* believe is important for your child to learn in a course.
2. To help you create assignments for a course.
3. To effectively evaluate what your child has actually learned, rather than what you assume she learned.

4. To help you create the documentation your child needs to get into college.

Scope and Sequence vs. Objectives

It is important not to get educational objectives confused with the scope and sequence concept we presented earlier. A scope and sequence is merely an overview list of the topics that will be taught in a course and generally in what order. However, just because you teach something doesn't guarantee your child will actually learn.

It is difficult to imagine the number of pages it would take to review every person, event, and invention or discovery in subjects like history or science. The sheer enormity of available information for each of those subjects is overwhelming. Subjects need to be defined and topics narrowed down when deciding what specifically will be taught and learned for any course, which is the purpose of a scope and sequence list. In other words, you can create your own scope and sequence for a course to determine all of the subjects to be covered and in what order they will be presented.

When you buy a textbook or curriculum, the author and publisher have already made decisions about what will or will not be included in the material (the scope) and in what order it will be taught (the sequence). These decisions are often based, at least in part, on "best educational practices"—meaning they have included at least the information that is likely to be in materials produced by other publishers for the same subject for the same grade.

If you buy a book or curriculum and determine that it contains information you don't consider important or you don't want your child to learn, you can easily have your child skip those sections. However, if the material does not include what you think is important, then you either have to create your own materials for that subject or supplement what you've purchased in some manner. In either case, educational objectives can be beneficial.

Educational objectives focus specifically on what a student must do to demonstrate what she learned in the course. For example, the scope and sequence of an elementary mathematics course may include multiplication tables zero through twelve. However, the scope and sequence does not indicate how you will test your child's knowledge and skills of multiplication facts.

An educational objective outlines how to evaluate your child's knowledge. For this example, you might decide, "The student will be able to recall multiplication tables zero through twelve in order to pass weekly multiplication tests with a grade of 90% or higher." This objective states specifically what your child will do to demonstrate his knowledge of multiplication and how you will measure his success rate.

If you buy curriculum, the publisher has already determined what your child should be tested on and how—whether it be through questions at the end of the chapter, a test booklet, or some other method. If you buy all of the materials the publisher offers, then all your educational objectives are most likely covered. However, if you customize purchased curriculum or create curriculum from scratch, you may want to create educational objectives as well. An understanding about the purpose and history of educational objectives may help you do so.

Educational Objectives and Bloom's Taxonomy

In 1956 Benjamin Bloom and his colleagues published a taxonomy (classification) of educational objectives. The taxonomy was designed to help educators classify different levels of learning, from simple to complex, and to specify how students might demonstrate what they've learned. Educators can use the taxonomy for the purpose of evaluating a student's academic performance.

Bloom's original taxonomy is arranged in six levels. Each level represents a level of learning and defines a method for determining the breadth or depth of knowledge a student has about the subject matter of a course or lesson. Entry-level or first-year courses usually use the lower levels of the taxonomy. As the depth and breadth of a subject matter increases, educators use the higher levels of the taxonomy to create appropriate educational objectives.

LEVEL 1: KNOWLEDGE—At the base of Bloom's Taxonomy is the level of Knowledge, which involves the student being able to demonstrate having acquired *knowledge of basic facts*, which can also be seen as one of the simplest levels of thinking. For example: "*Label* the anatomical parts of a frog."

- Most textbooks include questions at the end of a chapter or review questions at the end of a section. Usually these questions are geared toward determining what basic knowledge the students acquired from what they read. For example, "Identify the year in which the Declaration of Independence was signed."

- Most test questions that are based on a textbook are written at this base level to determine the extent of a student's knowledge about basic facts. In the example above, if this question had been on a test, a number of points would be assigned to the question. If the student answers the question correctly, he earns points. If the question is answered incorrectly, the student does not earn points; occasionally, teachers will allow students to earn partial points if part of the answer was correct.

LEVEL 2: COMPREHENSION—The Comprehension level involves students *understanding ideas or concepts* in addition to or instead of factual knowledge. For example, "*Explain* why the Pilgrims journeyed to the New World." Rather than recalling basic facts and merely listing the dates associated with the Pilgrims' journey to this country, the student must know the reasons for the journey and then understand (comprehend) them enough to explain them.

■ In some instances, textbooks and tests have Comprehension-level questions. More often than not, Knowledge-level questions are used because their answers are easier to list out in a teacher's edition of the text or test booklet than Comprehension-level answers.

While the first two levels of the taxonomy are considered the "lower levels" of learning, they are still extremely important—especially for creating objectives for first-year courses, as they provide the student an opportunity to learn basic information that will become the foundation for learning advanced information. In an earlier chapter we described types of learning skills college students should have, which included critical thinking skills. In the first two levels of Bloom's Taxonomy, you might see that the focus is on students *obtaining* knowledge and beginning to *think* about what they've learned. Progressing upward through the levels of the taxonomy, students begin to develop *critical thinking* skills as they apply the knowledge they've obtained.

LEVEL 3: APPLICATION—The third level of the taxonomy is Application. Once students have obtained knowledge, they should learn to apply it—especially to find solutions to problems. For example, "Use the scientific method to develop a hypothesis and test it." In this case the student must have some basic *knowledge* about the scientific method. She must also *comprehend* what a hypothesis is and how it can be tested. Then the student can use that knowledge to complete a task that requires her to *apply* both knowledge and comprehension.

LEVEL 4: ANALYSIS—The fourth level of the taxonomy is Analysis. Once students have knowledge of facts, comprehension of concepts, and the ability to apply both to solve a problem, they should learn to examine the components of a problem or a concept in relationship to the whole. For example, "Using one of the following industries: manufacturing, transportation, or communication, *categorize* the major inventions of the Industrial Revolution." In this case the student must use his knowledge about the identified industries of the Industrial Revolution enough to be able to analyze and group them in categories he creates.

In progressing to the final or highest levels of the taxonomy there is even more focus on what the student should be *doing* as a result of being able to *think* about what she knows. In other words, at the higher levels of learning, the student is assumed to have learned a great deal about a subject and to have demonstrated basic to mid-level skills already. Now the student must perform more complicated or comprehensive tasks to demonstrate her "mastery" of what has been learned.

LEVEL 5: SYNTHESIS—At the fifth level of the taxonomy, Synthesis, a student learns to *create* something new or to develop an original idea about something. For example, "*Compose* a poem for each of the types of poetry presented in the text." As a result, students must be able to identify the various types of poetry, understand how each type is written, and then pull all of that knowledge together to create poems of their own—that takes some thinking!

LEVEL 6: EVALUATION—The final level of the taxonomy is Evaluation. At this level students should be able to judge the *value* of ideas or products that they or someone else created in addition to judging the ideas or products themselves. Recalling the term "critical thinking" from an earlier chapter, it is possible to see how it might apply to this level. For example, "Critique your story in comparison to the standards of an effective story as discussed in the text."

The Benefits of Creating Objectives

Imagine you want to include a geography course in your child's ninth grade curriculum and you are going to create the course yourself. You should first define exactly what you want your child to learn and in what order—the scope and sequence—in order to determine what you need to teach, what materials to buy, and what lessons or assignments your child will have to complete. Here are some questions you might ask yourself:

- Do you want him to learn the names and definitions of every geographical landform?
- Do you want her to learn the locations of every continent, ocean, sea, country, and the capitals of every country?
- Do you want to focus on social geography instead of physical geography by having your child focus on locations of peoples and political boundaries?
- Do you want to focus on the geography of the United States? If so, do you want her to be able to name every mountain range, river, and desert?
- Or should your child be able to describe the

types and locations of the different climates in the United States?

Within each subject are an almost infinite number of potential topics. It would take an entire book to list what we think are the most important topics for every subject you could teach for each year of high school.

Once you have created the scope and sequence, you must then determine what parts of the course you will use to test your child's knowledge. While you might consider all the information in a course to be important, some information is much more important for your child to retain. For example, is it more important that your child understands the purpose behind Paul Revere's famous ride or that he remembers the name of Revere's horse?

Educational objectives help you define your goals regarding what is important for your child to learn about any given subject. Usually these goals include learning

> **Educational objectives help you define your goals regarding what is important for your child to learn.**

information, skills, and concepts that can be used in other courses. You can state these goals by using Bloom's Taxonomy to write educational objectives, making sure your courses help your child achieve the appropriate levels of learning. These objectives can then in turn be used to help you create assignments to evaluate how well your child demonstrated what he learned in a course. In addition, course objectives are useful for preparing course descriptions and transcripts that will be used when applying for college.

Can I Avoid Creating Objectives if I Buy Curricula?

You don't *have* to write objectives, period. If you buy curriculum, you probably don't need to worry about educational objectives at all—especially if you buy all of the publisher's materials: textbooks, tests, quizzes, answer keys, and so on. However, before you dismiss the notion of objectives entirely, consider how educational objectives may be helpful in the following situations:

1. If you buy curriculum, you will need to decide whether or not to complete every assignment provided by the publisher. Educational objectives may help you determine which assignments are or are not important.

2. If your child has trouble with one or more topics within a course, you may need to troubleshoot the problem by first understanding the point of the lesson, as explained in the educational objective, and then deciding how best to help your child learn the material.

3. When your child completes a course, you may want to test her knowledge. By comparing test results to the educational objective, you can determine what information she learned and retained.

4. Educational objectives explain the content of a course using clear and concise wording in order to prepare your child's transcripts and course descriptions for college.

Key Points

- Define what you believe is most important for your child to learn in each course.
- Learn about Bloom's Taxonomy and how objectives are created for college courses.

CHAPTER 17

How to Write
Educational Objectives

WHEN I FIRST STARTED TEACHING COLLEGE, I was given the task of revising and updating the two core courses I would be teaching. What that entailed was writing educational objectives for every single aspect of each course into what was called a "curriculum content guide." If the students were expected to learn something in a class, an objective stating *what* was to be learned, *how* the student would demonstrate what was learned, and *how* the instructor could objectively evaluate that demonstration had to be created. It was a labor-intensive process.

We don't recommend that level of detail for homeschool high school programs. Instead, we recommend you create at least a few objectives for an entire course by asking, "Overall, what do I want my child to learn in this course?"

What do I want my child to learn in this course?

How to Write Educational Objectives for High School Courses

To write educational objectives, you simply write statements indicating which observable and measurable actions (indicated by a verb) you want your child to be able to perform in order to demonstrate what he learned.

The following list of verbs is not meant to be comprehensive, but rather it is a sampling of verbs that might be used to create educational objectives. The verbs in bold may be more commonly used for "higher-level" learning or for more difficult tasks. It is not necessary to use all the verbs for every class.

Analyze	Interpret
Apply	Interview
Assess	Invent
Calculate	Investigate
Chart	**Judge**
Choose	Label
Cite	List
Classify	Measure
Compare	Modify
Compose	Name
Construct	Organize
Contrast	Paraphrase
Create	Plan
Criticize	Predict
Debate	Recall
Deduce	Recognize
Define	**Recommend**
Demonstrate	Record
Describe	Recount
Design	Relate
Determine	Repeat
Differentiate	Report
Discuss	Research
Distinguish	Restate

Dramatize	Revise
Draw	**Scrutinize**
Edit	Select
Evaluate	Show
Examine	Simulate
Explain	Solve
Formulate	Specify
Graph	State
Hypothesize	Summarize
Identify	Support
Illustrate	**Translate**
Implement	Write

We've created a few objectives for a sample high school course, included below. We did not write objectives for *everything* a student might do or learn about during the course. Instead, the following examples provide a clear understanding of what a student might have to do during or after the course to demonstrate she learned the *most important information* from the course. Notice the italicized words that specifically define what the student must do to demonstrate that learning has occurred. Also, notice some of the verbs are associated with basic learning skills and others are associated with higher levels of learning.

EXAMPLE #1:

COURSE: US Government
1. The student will be able to ***explain*** the history and significance of the US Constitution and the Bill of Rights.
2. The student will be able to *describe* the components of the three branches of our federal government and will be able to ***explain*** the roles and functionality of each.
3. The student will be able to ***explain*** the presidential election process.

4. The student will be able to **explain** how amendments are made to the US Constitution and be able to *describe* which amendments have been made to date.
5. The student will be able to *diagram* the process through which a bill becomes a federal law.

In this example only certain portions of the US government class are specified in the educational objectives. Are these the *only* things a student would learn in such a class? No. Depending on the materials used, the student might have read about the history behind the Constitutional Conventions, why James Madison is considered to be the "Father of the Constitution," and which delegates participated in the drafting of the Constitution. If the course materials started with the Declaration of Independence, the student might also have learned about the fates of the men who signed that historical document. Yet, none of these items were identified in the objectives.

Any of these concepts (and more) *could have* been included in the educational objectives. Is it more important to remember the specific fates of the signers of the Declaration of Independence or to be able to *describe* the components of the three branches of our federal government and be able to *explain* the roles and functionality of each? It's strictly a judgment call. You are the judge in determining which information is important enough to include in your objectives.

EXAMPLE #2:

COURSE: English/Research Paper
1. The student will be able to *research* information about a topic of choice.
2. The student will be able to *create* a topical outline for her research paper.
3. The student will be able to *write* a rough draft of the research paper.

4. The student will be able to *critique* her own rough draft paper to identify changes to be made.
5. The student will be able to *modify* her paper based on the teacher's edits.
6. The student will be able to *produce* a final draft of a ten-page research paper

In the example above there may have been any number of other topics covered in the course, such as how to use the library to find research materials and how to read the symbols proofreaders use when editing a paper. These and other topics could be turned into objectives. It's really up to you.

How do you best decide what topics should be made into objectives? To answer that, let's review the benefits of educational objectives we identified at the beginning of this chapter.

1. You can put into words the goals you have with regard to what information, skills, and concepts your child should learn for the overall course.
2. You can evaluate how well your child demonstrated what she learned in a course.
3. You can create assignments for the course.
4. You can prepare course descriptions and transcripts that will be used when applying for college.

The examples above show how you can accomplish the first item—putting into words the information, skills, and concepts you want your child to learn from each of the courses. In each course you now also have the means to evaluate what your child learned. For example, you can see whether or not your child can "*describe* the components of the three branches of our federal government and explain the roles and functionality of each" or if she can "*create* a topical outline for the research paper." Objectives suggest ways your child can demonstrate this knowledge via assignments (as we discuss in Chapter 20). The course objectives can also help you develop a description of the course that you can use for preparing your child's transcripts prior to applying for college.

To decide which topics to use when creating objectives, keep in mind that your objectives should help you realize these four benefits. Objectives should be clear, concrete, and measurable and should define what you decide are the most important aspects of the course.

Using Educational Objectives to Create Course Descriptions for Transcripts

Educational objectives are a way to "speak" to the college admission officer in a language she will easily understand. Since your child is trying to get into college from a non-standardized high school, the admission's officer needs to be able to compare your homeschool courses to the courses taught in traditional high schools to verify that your child has the same level of knowledge about each subject that students who have taken the same types of courses in a public, private, or parochial school have.

Using the example objectives, the course descriptions for the previous two examples might look something like these:

COURSE: US Government

DESCRIPTION: In this course the student studied the history of the US Constitution and the Bill of Rights in order to explain the significance of each document. The student learned about the components of the three branches of our federal government in order to explain the roles and functionality of each.

Particular emphasis was placed on learning about and being able to explain the presidential election process, how amendments are made to the US Constitution, and which amendments to the Constitution have been made to date. The student was also required to diagram the process through which a bill becomes a federal law. The student completed the following assignments in this course...

COURSE: English/Research Paper
DESCRIPTION: In this course the student was required to select a topic about which he would write a research paper of at least ten pages in length. The student was required to research information about a topic of choice and then to create a topical outline for his research paper. The student then developed a rough draft of the research paper and critiqued his own work to identify changes to be made. The student also was required to successfully modify his paper based on the teacher's edits and then successfully submit a final version of the paper.

Writing Educational Objectives

Now that you've had a chance to learn a little bit about objectives, we'll give you a chance to practice creating some. Below we've provided you with a course that might be found in a homeschool high school program. Use the knowledge you've gained so far to write some objectives for the course. Write the objectives as statements that indicate what it is you want your child to do to *demonstrate* what he has learned from the course.

Remember that students need to learn the basics before they can be expected to accomplish more advanced tasks, so try to create both lower learning and higher learning objectives utilizing the verbs listed earlier. Feel free to use verbs not on the list as well. Create as many objectives as you like. We've provided room for ten. There are no correct or incorrect answers.

COURSE: HOME ECONOMICS

    OBJECTIVES:

      1.

      2.

      3.

      4.

      5.

      6.

      7.

      8.

      9.

     10.

Now use the course objectives you've written to create a course description.

COURSE DESCRIPTION:

So that you can double-check your work, here is what we might have written as *some* of the objectives for the home economics course. All verbs are italicized; the higher level verbs are also in bold.

1. *Review* basic dry and liquid measurements with typical kitchen tools used for this purpose.
2. *List* the abbreviations for liquid and dry measurements found in cookbooks and recipes.
3. *Review* cookbooks or recipe cards to *select* one item in each of the following categories that you will create during the course:
Main dish
Cake
Pie
Muffins
Cupcakes
Bread
4. **Create** (bake) one of each item that you identified above.
5. *Utilize* cookbooks or recipe cards to **create** the following dishes as assigned during the

course:

Lasagna or spaghetti with sauce
Mashed potatoes (from scratch) or potato salad
Steamed mixed vegetables
Fruit salad

6. **Develop** one complete dinner menu for the family.
7. **Create** a shopping list based on the ingredients or items needed to cook the meal.
8. **Calculate** a price breakdown of the cost of the meal per person.
9. *Cook* and *serve* **(prepare)** the meal.
10. **Critique** the quality of your meal.

We focused only on the cooking portion of this home economics course. Obviously there could have been many more objectives. For instance, you may want your child to learn how to clean house, knit or crochet, prepare a household budget, wash and dry clothes, iron clothes, sew clothes from a pattern, or more. It is up to you to determine what is important for your child to learn and how she will demonstrate that learning.

The objectives you choose to include in the course can also be used to create assignments. The student may have to cook one or more meals, bake one or more types of side dishes, and so forth. The objectives can also be used to create a course description for your child's high school transcripts. Here is what we might have written as a description for a complete Home Economics course:

Home Economics 101 is a hands-on course in which the student engages in a variety of activities to learn some of the basic skills of meal preparation, baking, and household budgeting related to groceries. During the course the student prepares several main and side dishes, as well as plans and prepares an entire meal for the family. In addition, the student chooses one craft or sewing project to complete during the semester involving crochet, knitting, or sewing from a pattern. Other skills taught during the class involve washing, drying, and ironing clothes and cleaning/maintaining the household environment.

Why We Love Objectives

In our program I primarily create the courses and write the objectives. Yet, knowing how to write objectives has also helped Chandra as she facilitates the children's activities and lessons—especially when it comes to answering the question, "What's the point?" When the children ask why they have to learn something, we can honestly tell them more than "Because Dad says so."

Having a clear idea of the objectives of our courses has also helped us to feel more comfortable with homeschooling in general. We feel confident our children are getting the right information in their courses, their courses have a purpose, and we can objectively measure what they have learned.

Key Points

☐ Write objectives that describe what is most important for your child to learn in each course.

☐ Make sure all objectives are measurable.

☐ Include objectives both for lower levels of learning and higher levels of learning.

CHAPTER 18

Selecting Courses

IN ORDER TO HELP YOU DECIDE WHAT SUBJECTS to teach during each school year, it may be useful to look first at what courses your child has already completed and how many credits are still needed for various subjects. Then you can figure out which courses will help your child fulfill those credits.

In previous chapters we mentioned that the courses taught in most high schools reflect the minimum admission requirements for many colleges and universities. We'll repeat our list of courses and credits your homeschool program should include to meet these requirements:

- English (three to four credits with a heavy emphasis on developing reading and writing skills)
- Social Science (three to four credits with at least one course in American Government or American History)
- Natural Science (three to four credits with courses in Earth science, biology, and chemistry and at least one course with a hands-on lab)
- Mathematics (three to four credits including courses in Algebra, Algebra 2, and Geometry)

■ Foreign Languages (two to three credits of the same language with a language speaking and listening lab)

The requirements listed above are usually the minimum requirements for college admission. Students who can handle the workload can certainly complete additional courses in each subject area. For example, students may want to take two different foreign languages, but it is important to remember that usually at least two credits must be earned in the *same* language.

Parents should spend an adequate amount of time finding materials and resources that work best for them. Some parents may prefer using a standardized curriculum from a particular publisher while others may prefer to create their own. While we do mention some titles in this chapter, *Appendix C: Course-Specific Resources* provides a more detailed list of recommended texts and curricula for each subject. We offer advice about the specific subjects to be taught during high school and what program options are available to you in the following section.

> **Parents should spend an adequate amount of time finding materials and resources that work best for them.**

Course Options

When possible, high school students should be able to choose which courses they'd like to take to fulfill the credits for particular subjects. For example, for English credits you might give your child a choice among classes such as great books, journalism, creative writing, Shakespeare, or poetry. For social studies, your child might have a choice among world geography, world history, or ancient civilizations.

A report published in 2006 by the Department of Education indicates there are several important factors that affect whether or not a student will complete a bachelor's degree. The report indicates that a rigorous academic curriculum during high school helps prepare a student for college and actually promotes his chances to successfully complete an undergraduate degree. In fact, the intensity of the high school curriculum seemed to play a larger role in predicting and ensuring a student's success in college than did high school grades or scores on standardized testing (Adelman, 2006).

The same opportunity to choose their courses works well when it comes to electives too. Although children aren't always required to take electives during high school in order to get into college, electives can help balance out a rigid or heavily focused academic schedule.

Some of the electives you may want to offer include sports studies, physical education, volunteer work, film studies, typing, or computer applications. Electives can also be additional classes in any of the main subject areas, such as a creative writing course, which can also be applied to English credit requirements. The following sections review each of the required subjects for high school and offer suggestions about course options for you to consider.

English

For the subject of English, most colleges and universities want high schools to focus on developing reading and writing skills. To that end, courses that include specific instruction in English grammar and composition are a must, especially if your child struggles in those areas. Writing reports for non-English courses is another option for developing writing skills. Other types of English courses can also help a student practice writing skills while allowing the student to develop her interests. Some of these classes may include speech, journalism, creative writing, poetry, and even playwriting. If your child has had consistent instruction in grammar and composition, then the high school years can be spent reviewing the basics, fine tuning her skills, and offering multiple opportunities to practice what has been learned through comprehensive writing assignments.

Spelling

We highly recommend high school students continue to take spelling courses during high school. If spelling isn't an appealing topic or if the child's spelling skills are well developed, then we recommend courses that focus on the definition and use of vocabulary words, particularly those associated with advanced writing skills and learning in higher education. Additional time spent on prefixes, suffixes, and root words can help improve spelling and vocabulary skills. While we used A Beka's *Spelling and Vocabulary* series in our homeschool, most spelling resources published today would provide sufficient instruction.

Essays and Papers

In college, students will write two primary types of papers: opinion papers and expository papers. Opinion papers require the student to think logically and write well using proper grammar, punctuation, and spelling. Opinion papers are usually written in the first-person, and as a result, students often are more successful writing them than they are expository papers.

Expository papers require more effort from the student because they are usually written in the third-person (no personal pronouns, such as "I"), and students often have to incorporate expert knowledge and direct quotes in their papers. Term papers, thesis papers, and formal reports are often written in an expository manner.

In order to develop and practice expository writing skills, high school students should write many book reports, project papers, and thesis papers. You may also want to help your children learn to use one or more of the writing formats commonly used in many college and universities, such as APA (American Psychological Association) or MLA (Modern Language Association). Some of the titles we recommend using include *Publication Manual of the American Psychological Association, Fifth Edition; Mastering APA Style;* and *Concise Rules of APA Style.*

Reading and Writing Classes

Various English-related courses can include activities that strengthen reading and writing skills. For example, in a speech class students learn how to write different types of speeches. Reading and analysis skills can also be developed through reviewing well-known speeches. In a journalism class students learn to write news articles. You may have your child write and print newsletters rather than a newspaper. Reading newspapers and magazines also helps develop reading and writing skills. A creative writing course can encompass writing short stories, novels, poetry, or even plays.

From a reading standpoint, exposing your child to the world of great literature is one of the best things you can do. While many popular books are good for children to read, to make the most valuable use of reading time, your child should read the types of books that are used in English courses in traditional high schools and colleges. The resources that can be utilized in teaching reading and writing are too numerous to list here. These would, of course, include not only studies in literature, but also books designed to help children learn to develop their own styles of writing.

Not all books that are hailed as classics or labeled as great literature are interesting to or appropriate for children. We suggest you read the books you will include in your child's curriculum. If you don't have time to read the books, you may be able to find summaries of books online or via other sources (such as discoveryjourney.com) in order to determine if the content is appropriate for your child.

Even the books you may consider to be appropriate may not be easy or interesting for your child to read. More often than not, children have trouble relating to the work of writers like Charles Dickens if they don't have enough knowledge to understand the context of what the author has written. Study guides such as *Cliff's Notes* can be tremendous assets when helping children understand a "great" novel. Discussing the book with you or with a group of peers may go a long way toward helping your children understand what they've read.

Not all reading assignments need to include novels or even "classics." Consider having your children read diaries, biographies, autobiographies, or compilations of stories. Again, remember that writing book reports is a great way to develop writing skills.

Poetry

The study of poetry can be used to develop a student's reading skills and is an important subject for high school students. In addition to studying the structure of poetry, students often benefit from learning to enjoy the beauty and creativity of poetry, especially in contrast to prose. Although many students think poetry is just about love, nothing can be further from the truth. Poems encompass a variety of other subjects, such as patriotism, war, religion, morality, and nature. Reading and analyzing poetry is a great way to study world cultures too. While the list of poems that can be studied is endless, some texts we used in our home include Mary Oliver's *A Poetry Handbook*, Paul B. Janeczko's *How To Write Poetry*, and *The Best Loved Poems of the American People* published by Doubleday.

Plays

The study of plays, particularly the works of Shakespeare, should not be forgotten in high school. Reading and analyzing plays offers children a unique chance to learn not only about the written word, but about life and human nature. Plays and poetry help children better appreciate culture and the arts in general.

As with great books, there are a variety of resources children can use to help them understand poetry and plays. For Shakespeare's plays, we have found the side-by-side editions written by Alan Durband to be very useful because each part of the play is written in its original version on one page, and the opposite page has a modern English version of the same dialogue.

For both plays and poetry, it's helpful for students to read books that present some "behind-the-scenes" information to help put the material in context. For instance, when studying the works of one poet, your child might want to read a biography about the poet and the times in which he lived. For Shakespeare's plays, reading about the *Globe Theater* and the life of Shakespeare may be interesting, as well as helpful. Recommended titles include *The Essential Shakespeare Handbook* and *Shakespeare Made Easy*.

Social Sciences

The social sciences help children learn about their own country and culture, as well as about countries and cultures around the world. The social sciences include a variety of subjects, including recent and ancient history, geography, government, politics, civics, ethics, cultures, anthropology, psychology, and sociology.

For homeschooling students in the United States, the study of US history is very important in order to give them a sense of identity about their own culture and country. The history of the United States can be studied generally from its origins to the present day, or specific aspects of it can be studied in depth. For example, courses may be about the wars the United States has fought to obtain and keep its freedom. Or courses may focus on people and events in US history, such as its leaders, its discoveries, and its progress.

Every US student should study and understand the functions and organization of the federal government. No US government class would be complete without a study of the Declaration of Independence, the Constitution, the amendments to the Constitution, the election process, the functions of the

> Every US student should study and understand the functions and organization of the federal government.

three branches of the federal government, and politics in general. Recommended titles include *The Bill of Rights: A User's Guide*, *Why America Is Free*, and *A Brilliant Solution: Inventing the American Constitution*.

Often US history or government courses are limited to the federal level, but students may find it interesting to study the various states individually or even collectively by region. Students should study their own state history and state or local government.

Studying world history allows students to better understand their own country, government, culture, and society in comparison to those of other nations. As with a study of the US, students may choose to study world history in an overview course or from a more specific examination of periods in history, peoples, events, cultures, or even governments. Our son wanted to study decisive battles and wars in world history. So, we devised a course that focused not just on military strategies, but on the causes of conflicts and their effects on world history. We also utilized A Beka's *World History and Cultures* curriculum.

Through geography, students can learn about peoples, places, and nature, either within their own country or throughout the world. If students want to explore the topic of peoples in greater depth, they may also want to take courses in psychology, sociology, or even anthropology.

Natural Sciences

High school students are usually required to complete courses in earth science, biology, and chemistry. Physics is another common natural sciences course. Some colleges also require students to complete at least one lab in any one of their natural sciences courses. Remember the requirement of one lab is a minimum; students may enjoy and benefit from completing labs for each subject.

Each of the natural science subjects at the high school level is usually a comprehensive overview course that can easily keep a student busy for an entire school year. However, within each major subject there are many areas the student may want to study in greater depth. For example, within biology a student may have a particular interest in human biology, botany, or even zoology. In earth science a student may want to study geology or meteorology.

While each sub-area of the natural sciences can be developed into its own course, we recommend students still complete an overview course in order to be exposed to the general subject. Additional courses can focus on one or more of the topics within each major subject or you can devise assignments that will allow your child to complete the overview course and also explore particular topics in greater depth. In our home we often utilize resources from A Beka, including their *Physical Creation* and *Biology: God's Living Creating* series.

Mathematics

As with the natural sciences, there are specific courses that high school students must complete, such as Algebra 1, Geometry, and Algebra 2. Some colleges and universities may also require students to complete additional mathematics courses, such as trigonometry or advanced geometry, particularly for admission to a technical or engineering school within a university.

Because mathematics courses are usually very comprehensive and are designed to build knowledge and skills step-by-step, they cannot be divided into specific sub-courses as might be done for social sciences. However, you may want your child to complete additional mathematics courses beyond the requirements, such as calculus, statistics, business math, or consumer math. While we used A Beka curriculum as the basis for our mathematics instruction, we also utilized titles such as *Elementary Algebra for College Students* and Pearson Education's *Intermediate Algebra.*

Foreign Languages

As with mathematics courses, foreign language courses are designed to build knowledge and skills sequentially. Foreign language courses usually include grammar, composition, and pronunciation as specific topics. Within a foreign language course, students may also study the culture of the peoples who speak the language. Usually this study is part of the regular course. However, some parents may develop separate courses that allow students to immerse themselves in the culture.

Language labs are important in providing opportunities to practice speaking and hearing the language, and most college and universities want to know how a student fulfilled this element. Language labs may consist of audio tapes, visual recordings, computer software, conversations with native speakers of the language, visits to countries where the language is spoken, and participation in language clubs.

As far as texts are concerned, we preferred A Beka's foreign language series, but also utilized a variety of other resources, including computer programs (such as *Learn Spanish Now!* and *Learn French Now!*), bilingual dictionaries, and audio cassettes.

Electives

There are so many potential elective courses that it is impossible for us to cover each one in depth in this book. Instead, we will provide an overview of elective courses and then review their purpose and usefulness in a homeschool curriculum.

Elective courses may include the arts (music, dance, art, and theater), sports or physical education, volunteer or internship work tied to a specific course, or structured groups or clubs tied to a specific course (newspaper, yearbook, speech/drama, foreign language, and others). Some elective courses focus on developing skills or knowledge in one or more areas, such as typing, computer programming, computer applications, home economics, media communications, auto mechanics, photography, electronics, child care, first aid, and public speaking. Skills such as typing and basic computer skills are very important for students to have prior to college.

For elective credits students may also decide to complete additional courses in the basic academic areas: English, science, mathematics, social sciences, or foreign languages. For example, a student may decide to complete an elective course on meteorology in addition to a required general earth sciences course.

Electives offer several benefits. First, they provide balance to academic study schedules and often provide a different type of mental (or physical) stimulation, which high school students may find refreshing in many ways. Electives also allow students to pursue a variety of interests while earning credits for them.

Electives may provide homeschooled students more opportunities to engage in social interactions with their peers than can usually be done with academic courses. When students participate in elective courses, they may have opportunities to take on leadership positions, such as club president, which helps develop skills including communication, problem solving, and time management.

Some elective courses provide opportunities to exercise the theoretical knowledge students learn in a class. For example, a student may learn the basics of giving speeches in a speech class, but she will gain practical experience through giving a speech or presentation to club members.

Any elective courses you plan to use for your child's transcripts and college admission packets should have some structure and organization. Create a description of each course, a list of written objectives or a statement of purpose for the course, descriptions of assignments (if applicable), and the criteria used to determine your child's grade for the course. We cover all of these tasks in the next few chapters.

As we mentioned earlier, most elective courses may not count toward the academic admission requirements for most colleges and universities. However, the quantity and variety of a student's high school electives may play a factor in the admission process if the college or university wants students who are not only successful academically, but students who are also well rounded, involved in their communities, and have experience working as part of a group—particularly in a leadership capacity.

Remember elective classes are just that, *electives*. Sometimes electives can be extremely time and energy consuming, which may detract from the time and effort a child should be putting toward the required academic courses. You and your child should carefully consider which electives to include in your curriculum.

Course Recommendations

The choice of which courses should be included in a homeschool high school curriculum is strictly a personal matter. However, since Chandra and I are often asked which courses we use in our program, we have included a list of our suggestions here. We highly recommend high school students earn more than enough credits in each subject whenever possible. The courses listed below are one full year (one credit), unless noted as being a half-year (half credit) course. The total number of recommended credits is shown by subject.

English (Nine credits total)

- Grammar and Composition 1
- Grammar and Composition 2
- Ninth Grade Spelling
- Tenth Grade Spelling
- Vocabulary Words 1 and 2 (junior or senior year)
- Journalism 1 (half year)
- Creative Writing 1 (half year)
- Great Books 1
- Reading, Analyzing, and Writing Poetry 1 (half year)

- Shakespeare 1 (half year)
- College Thesis Paper Writing 1 (preferably with a focus on APA or MLA)

Social Sciences (Six credits)
- US History
- US Government
- US Geography
- World History
- World Geography
- Civics (with a heavy emphasis on volunteer work)

Natural Sciences (Four and a half credits)
- Earth Sciences (with full-year lab worth 1/2 credit)
- Biology—(with full-year lab worth 1/2 credit)
- Chemistry—(with full-year lab worth 1/2 credit)

Mathematics (Five credits) *
- Algebra 1
- Algebra 2
- Geometry
- Statistics (half year)
- Economics (half year)
- Business Math (half year)
- Consumer Math (half year)

*Depending on the student's interest and specific college requirements, both trigonometry and calculus might be considered.

Foreign Languages (Two credits)
- Spanish or French 1 with lab
- Spanish or French 2 with lab

Required Electives (Four credits)

- Typing 1 (half year)
- Basic Computer Applications (half year)
- ACT/SAT Prep and College Review (half year)
- Speech 1 (half year)
- Home Economics (Two to four years of half credit courses each year)
- Physical Education (Two to four years of half credit courses each year)

Optional Electives

- Arts 1 (single or combined overview course of art, music, and theater—half year)
- Great Books 2, 3, and 4 (half year)
- Creative Writing 2 (half year)
- Journalism 2 (half year)
- Shakespeare 2 (half year)
- Poetry 2 (half year)
- College Thesis Paper Writing 2 (half year)
- Course focusing on developing a student's abilities in an area of personal interest or talent—art, music, and so forth.

Figuring Credits

Once the courses are selected, you need to determine the length of each course—one semester (half a year) or two semesters (a full year). Again, if your child is planning to go to college, she will have to complete a specific number of high school credits in certain subjects.

Since homeschools are not usually set up with specific class times, credits and credit hours may not be figured the same as they would be in a traditional school system. Of course, depending on state requirements, you may have to account for a certain number of total educational hours per month, which may vary depending on your grade level. How those hours break down into credits may be entirely up to your discretion.

Usually one credit is equal to one full academic year of study. A full academic year is about nine months long and is broken down into two semesters—fall (September through December) and spring (January through May). Each semester is about twelve to fifteen weeks long depending on holidays and other breaks. One high school credit is worth about 150 study hours.

Homeschooling students can sometimes complete an entire year of study in less than an academic year because their programs have been set up so they can focus on one subject for extended periods of time rather than having to change classes like they would in a traditional school setting. However, there is no need for your child to hurry through high school. It is usually better to take the time to fully understand the subject matter of each course and to hone study skills needed for college.

The Basic Schedule

In our program we spread the courses out over the entire year—two semesters—in order to give our children adequate time to fully comprehend the material and complete multiple projects. We find little educational value in rushing the children through their studies.

For subjects such as science, foreign language, and spelling, we plan each course for a full year, spreading assignments and projects over a period of two semesters. However, for other subjects such as English or social studies, we often break the subjects into two or more separate courses to provide a wider variety of knowledge and experiences. For example, a single English course might be divided into one semester of journalism and one semester of creative writing—together they add up to one English credit. Below we've provided a sample schedule of courses (and their lengths) for one child for one year:

Sample Course Schedule

English—Three credits

- College-Prep Great Books (two semesters—one credit)
- College-Prep Shakespeare Studies (fall semester—1/2 credit)
- College-Prep Poetry Studies (spring semester—1/2 credit)
- Journalism 2 (fall semester—1/2 credit)
- Creative Writing 2 (spring semester—1/2 credit)

Math—One credit

- Applied Mathematics (fall semester—1/2 credit)
- Consumer Mathematics (spring scmcstcr—1/2 credit)

Science—One and a half credits

- Chemistry (two semesters—one credit)
- Chemistry Lab (two semesters—1/2 credit)

Social Science—One credit

- American Government I (one semester—1/2 credit)
- American Government II (one semester—1/2 credit)

Foreign Language—One credit

- Spanish (two semesters—one credit)

Electives—Two credits

- Home Economics (two semesters—one credit)

■ ACT/SAT Prep and College Study/Review (two semesters—one credit)

Extracurricular — (volunteer-related activities count toward volunteer hours)
■ Volunteer Work
■ Teacher Assistant
■ Physical Education Class
■ Bowling

Once you've decided which courses to offer and how long each one will be, it's time to prepare your yearly schedule, which we review in the next chapter.

Key Points

❏ Check with your state to assure your program adheres to homeschooling regulations.

❏ Determine which courses you need to meet state requirements and college-admission requirements.

❏ Plan which courses and credits will be covered each year so your child can complete them all in a timely manner.

❏ Include plans for when your child should take required tests for college admission, such as ACT or SAT.

❏ Examine various course options for completing required credits in each subject.

❏ Purchase or develop the necessary materials or find outside resources, such as community college courses.

CHAPTER 19

Creating and Following a Schedule

SOME PARENTS MIGHT CONTEST THE VALUE of a schedule because they prefer a less structured homeschool environment than exists in traditional schools. Whether or not you implement a schedule is a matter of personal preference, unless otherwise mandated by state regulations.

Setting up a general schedule for the year, as well as specific weekly and daily schedules, can help create a flexible structure that facilitates learning and develops organizational skills. In an upcoming chapter, we'll provide more detail about setting specific schedules for each course so your child can learn to organize her time to complete assignments—an essential skill for college students.

The School-Year Schedule

After choosing courses it's time to set up a general schedule for the school year. How you set up your school schedule depends a great deal on your personal preferences, as well as on your state's regulations.

The first step is to determine how many days or hours the state requires your homeschool to operate each year. Usually, by spreading the total number of required days or hours out over several months, a typical school year is about nine months long (September through May).

The next step is to determine when your child won't be "in school" due to holidays, vacations, and other breaks and then count the total number of days in the school year to ensure compliance with state regulations. If your state requires your child to attend school for a certain number of hours each year, you'll need to determine the length of each school day and multiply the total hours per day by the number of total school days you plan on in order to make sure you meet state regulations.

> **Benefits of Schedules**
>
> 1. Schedules act as guidelines while still allowing your homeschool environment to be flexible enough to meet the child's interests or needs.
>
> 2. Schedules establish routines that may help children develop time management skills.
>
> 3. Schedules also help children (and parents) get back on track following unexpected or prolonged breaks.
>
> 4. Schedules help free parents from constant inquiries such as, "What do I do now?"

For example, in Nebraska high school students must be in school 1,080 hours per year, but the number of days is not specified. If parents want their children to be "in school" six hours per day, the school year will be 180 days long. Counting just the weekdays, each month has approximately 20 school days, which makes the school year about nine months long altogether.

If you want to factor in two days off for Thanksgiving and two weeks off for Christmas vacation, you've extended the school year out another couple of weeks. Some families choose to have a spring break, which again extends the school year. In order to avoid extending the school year, you may prefer to increase the number of hours in a school day, if your state measures attendance requirements by hours and not days.

Often homeschools are able to start the school year just after Labor Day and end around Memorial Day. The first semester usually starts after Labor Day and ends at Christmas break. The second semester starts after the Christmas break and ends by Memorial Day. Based on how you set up the schedule for the school day, you may end up with a few "extra" hours—more hours than are required by the state, which provides some leeway for needed breaks or "absences" due to illnesses. Below is an example of a school year breakdown for a homeschooler in Nebraska.

Schedule for the Year:
August 30–May 27
6 hrs day x 183 days = 1,098 hours
(+18 hours or 3 days beyond
state's requirements)

Days Off:
9/6—Labor Day
11/25–11/26—Thanksgiving
12/20–12/31—Christmas

One thing you may find helpful is to provide your children with a week-by-week breakdown of the general schedule (see below), which can then be used to set assignment deadlines.

First Semester

WEEK	DATES	NOTES
Prep	8/30–9/3	
1	9/7–9/10	Off 9/6 Labor Day
2	9/13–9/17	
3	9/20–9/24	
4	9/27–10/1	
5	10/4–10/8	
6	10/11–10/15	
7	10/18–10/22	
8	10/25–10/29	
9	11/1–11/5	
10	11/8–11/12	
11	11/15–11/19	
12	11/22–11/24	Off 11/25–11/26 Thanksgiving
13	11/29–12/3	
14	12/6–12/10	
15	12/13–12/17	
	Off 12/20–12/31	Christmas Break

The Daily Schedule

Some parents prefer to have strict control over the daily routine and schedule while others find that allowing their children the freedom to structure their own daily school schedules gives the children a sense of empowerment. In the homeschool environment, the order in which children work on their assignments each day may not matter as much as it might in a more traditional school. It is more important that the

Second Semester

WEEK	DATES	NOTES
16	1/3–1/7	
17	1/10–1/14	
18	1/17–1/21	
19	1/24–1/28	
20	1/31–2/4	
21	2/7–2/11	
22	2/14–2/18	
23	2/21–2/25	
24	2/28–3/4	
25	3/7–3/11	
26	3/14–3/18	
27	3/21–3/25	
28	3/28–4/1	
29	4/4–4/8	
30	4/11–4/15	
31	4/18–4/22	
32	4/25–4/29	
33	5/2–5/6	
34	5/9–5/13	
35	5/16–5/20	
36	5/23–5/27	

work gets done by the deadlines set by the parents.

Children, especially high school students, may feel inspired by a particular assignment, or they may wish to get less appealing assignments out of the way. When this occurs, allowing them to concentrate all of their effort into that assignment for an entire day may be beneficial. Many parents structure their days around their immediate interests and motivation levels, so why shouldn't their children have that same opportunity?

The one aspect of the day that may require a schedule is the time you spend teaching your child, such as for mathematics or other subjects that require direct instruction. If there are younger children in the household, sometimes it is best to review lessons with the high school student early in the morning, later in the evening, or during nap time. Sometimes this schedule will need to vary on a daily basis due to illnesses, doctor's appointments, and so on. In our home we usually try to follow a daily/weekly schedule similar to the one shown below:

General Daily/Weekly Schedule

- 8–9 AM—Breakfast and chores.
- 9–10 AM—Daily review of work to be done, meet to discuss assignments, review homework, test grades, and so forth. Instruction in any subject can occur during this time, as well as throughout any part of the day.
- 10 AM–12 PM—This time is devoted primarily to independent work, such as reading and reviewing materials in preparation for assignments, completing workbooks, or taking tests.
  - Monday—Math
  - Tuesday—Science
  - Wednesday—Social Science
  - Thursday—English (writing)
  - Friday—Foreign Language
- 12–12:30 PM—Lunch
- 12:30–3:30 PM—This time is devoted primarily to independent work, such as working on projects or papers, or completing lab times for

science and foreign languages.

■ Evenings—Homework (if applicable, but this time isn't counted in the school day)

Key Points

❏ Check your state's requirements for hours/days your child must be in school.

❏ Develop an overall schedule for the year that is in compliance with your state's regulations. Include holidays, vacation days, and other necessary time off.

❏ Develop a general daily schedule. Allow flexibility to accommodate your family's needs.

CHAPTER 20

Creating Assignments

AFTER SETTING UP A SCHEDULE, THE NEXT STEP is to create assignments for each course and set due dates. Having to complete specific assignments by specific due dates not only helps your child develop time management skills, but it allows him to take responsibility for his own learning.

Creating Challenging Assignments

High school assignments don't have to be boring. However, all too often assignments created primarily from textbooks are just that.

Textbook assignments often confine children to the lowest levels of learning—the Knowledge and Comprehension levels according to Bloom's taxonomy. When children are confined to only the lowest levels of learning, they often turn into passive learning machines performing like automatons to crank out the answers to questions at the end of the chapter or on a test. Subsequently, students end up in a constant output mode with very little information, if any, going back in or staying in.

In order to use approaches that appeal to higher levels of learning, we moved away from using textbooks as the primary source of assignments for our high school courses. However, textbooks have many uses and shouldn't be discounted altogether.

Textbooks from any of the major publishers provide reliable information and can be excellent reference tools. We use them primarily as reading assignments for most subjects. Textbooks also can help define the breadth, if not depth, of the subject matter when creating course objectives.

> Textbook assignments often confine children to the lowest levels of learning. However, textbooks have many uses and shouldn't be discounted altogether.

We still use textbooks as the primary sources of information and assignments for mathematics and foreign languages. There are two reasons for this. First, to build basic skills in these subjects requires a different type of learning—rote learning or drill and practice learning. The exercises in the text are perfect for providing the sort of repetitive practice that helps children learn mathematics or the basics of a foreign language. Second, since these are not our strongest subjects as teachers, the textbooks provide information and assignments we couldn't possibly create on our own.

However, even for these two subjects, children reach a point when they will need to move beyond the textbooks for the subject matter to continue to be interesting and challenging. At that point it is important to provide "real-life" practice opportunities that will require your child to use his knowledge in a context beyond rote answers. Foreign language study and discussion groups or hands-on mathematic challenges are just two possibilities.

Reading Assignments

To help our children focus on specific topics within each subject to a greater depth, we use other materials in addition to textbooks. We prefer to purchase many different types of books all of our children can use, but it isn't always necessary to buy materials since many books are available from local libraries.

If you want your child to read about American history in general, a textbook is a good place to start. However, if you want your child to learn more about events such as World War II or the Civil Rights Movement, or if you want him to learn more about a specific person from American history, consider using primary and secondary sources. These include books such as biographies, autobiographies, diaries, historical novels, or historical accounts written by subject matter experts. Videos and DVDs are also good resources.

When you know what materials your child will have to read, you can determine if he should read the whole book or just part of it. We rarely have our own children read an entire textbook simply because many textbooks contain extraneous information that isn't necessarily useful.

More often than not, we will have our children read an entire "real" book. Since real books are more focused in subject matter than textbooks, the information throughout the books is often more pertinent. Once you determine which books your child will read and to what extent, add the books and the specific reading assignments for each book to the syllabus, which we'll discuss in the next chapter.

We don't usually specify a deadline for reading assignments. Instead, we give the children a timeframe within which they must complete both the reading assignments and a project. We then create due dates for papers and projects and let the children determine how best to get the work done in the time allotted.

Writing Assignments and Projects — Putting Knowledge to Work

After reading the required material, students should complete one or more assignments to demonstrate what was learned. Along with most college professors, we are in favor of students writing papers. Reading and writing skills are important for college preparation.

However, writing papers constantly can be just as dull and unrewarding as answering questions out of the textbook. It's a good idea to be creative when designing assignments for high school students. Also keep in mind that completed assignments can be used to help create a child's portfolio for

Be creative when designing assignments for high school students.

college applications, as we will discuss in an upcoming chapter.

The key elements to an effective assignment are having the student *learn, think,* and *do.* Learning and thinking can be the result of completing the reading assignments, but the assignment should also challenge the student to *do* something that will make him learn and think even more about the subject.

Every assignment should challenge a student to locate information and communicate what he has learned in some fashion. A major course paper is certainly one type of medium that fulfills these guidelines, but as we mentioned earlier, papers can become unproductive as teaching and learning tools after a while.

For this reason, we give our children a balance of "book work" and "project work." When we give them project work, we allow them to choose one or more topics to study and then provide them with a variety of options for demonstrating what they've learned.

For example, we had our daughter read through her textbook in her biology class. She also had to complete a variety of lab activities related to biology, which also tested her knowledge of what she had read. In addition, she completed the tests that corresponded to the reading assignments because taking tests in high school provides necessary practice for college. Most of these assignments appealed to the lower levels of learning—Knowledge and Comprehension.

Chandra and I read through her biology book too. It was broken down into three major topics: human biology, plant biology (botany), and animal biology (zoology). With a little thought, we figured out that each of those topics could be divided further. For example, sub-categories of human biology include reproduction, physiology, DNA, heredity, nutrition, and even the study of the immune systems from the viewpoint of illnesses, drugs, alcohol, and sexual diseases. Botany and zoology could also be divided into more specific subjects.

Since there were three major topics in the course material—human biology, botany, and zoology—we assigned three projects: one for each topic. We allowed our daughter to choose one or more of the areas within each topic that she wanted to learn more about. She had already acquired and "proven" her basic knowledge of the subject matter by completing reading assignments, lab work, and tests. The more focused projects helped her expand her knowledge about biology while simultaneously challenging her to engage in higher levels of learning.

For human biology she chose to complete a project on heredity and DNA. Choosing a topic she was interested in was exciting and motivating for her.

In the biology syllabus we gave our daughter some guidelines for her project. We then gave her a number of options for projects she could complete. These were the same options we offer for every course. Some options lend themselves more easily to certain subjects than others. However, in our courses we don't limit the children to any specific options. We tell them to make a logical choice that they think will effectively show us what they learned. If our daughter had decided to write a children's book about human DNA, we would have been interested to see the results because it is extremely challenging to be creative with factual data. She chose to produce a display and give an oral report instead, with great results.

Project options

Book Report
Research Paper
Oral Report
Critique or Editorial
Simulated Newspaper Story
Newsletter
Simulated Diary or Letter (written)
Interview or Simulated Interview
  (written or videotaped)
Simulated Autobiography
Biography
Poem or Poetry Collection
Creative Story
Children's book
PowerPoint Presentation
Spreadsheet
Timeline or Map
Diorama
Art Project—model, sculpture,
  painting, drawing, illustrations
Report Display
Photo Display
Experiment
Videotape
Music or Song
Scrapbook or Collection

Almost every project option requires the children to write to some degree. Book reports and papers require the most writing. If the children choose to give an oral report, or to create a map, diorama, timeline, or some other "non-writing" project, then we require them to write a short paper to go along with the project. Being able to clearly and concisely convey information in writing is an essential skill to have for college.

With Freedom Comes Responsibility

Having the freedom to choose the topic and delivery method for their project is exciting for high school students, and they often feel a sense of exhilaration at being "free" to do whatever they want. However, they also learn that freedom carries with it the burden of responsibility.

Because we give the children our expectations and grading guidelines for their projects rather than detailed instructions about how to complete a project like we did when they were in grade school, they work harder to make sure their projects are "right" and good enough to turn in for grading. In essence, we have raised the performance bar. Now, because our children have the burden of responsibility for deciding what to learn and how to demonstrate that knowledge rather than just checking off items from a list we provide, their work has, in many ways, never been better.

We still control the overall content for each course by creating objectives, determining the depth and breadth of the course, selecting the reading material, creating reading assignments, assigning book and lab work, issuing tests, and defining the topics for papers and projects. We also control the number of papers or projects to complete.

In this pedagogical manner, we make sure the children learn what they are supposed to learn for each subject in each grade. We also control the timeframe in which everything occurs by deciding whether each course is one or two semesters in length. These are normal tasks for any teacher or professor.

By giving the children some control over deciding what topics they want to study in greater depth and what projects they will complete, we are also appealing to the andragogical level of learning. This provides them with opportunities to practice using a variety of skills they will need for college.

Subject-Specific Schedules

A schedule for each subject gives the children a guideline for their reading assignments, test dates, lab work, and project deadlines. For courses that will last the entire year, we usually add two or three major projects to the curriculum; for semester courses, usually one project suffices.

We've provided two sample schedules for a full-year course (two semesters) and a half-year course (one semester). The full-year course is a combination of textbook work, lab work, tests, and projects. The half-year course involves work from only one textbook and the student is required to read the text, solve the problems in the text, and answer questions at the end of each chapter.

Consumer Math (half-year, one semester)

Weeks	Chapter
16–17	3
18–19	9
20–21	10
22–23	4
24–25	5
26–27	6
28–29	7
30–31	1
32–33	2 & 8
34–36	11 & 12

Biology (full-year—two semesters)

Biology Text Assignments
Weeks 1–10 (9/7–11/12)
- Read Unit 1—Chapters 1–5

- Test 1—Week 4
- Test 2—Week 8
- Labs (see schedule)
- Project #1 due 11/12

Weeks 11–24 (11/15–3/4)
- Read Unit 2—Chapters 6–12
- Test 3—Week 14
- Test 4—Week 18
- Test 5—Week 20
- Test 6—Week 22
- Labs (see schedule)
- Project #2 due 3/4

Weeks 25–36 (3/7–5/27)
- Read Unit 4—Chapters 16–21 and Chapters 22–24
- Test 10 and 11—Week 36
- Labs (see schedule)
- Project #3 due 5/20

Biology Lab Assignments
Weeks 1–10 (9/7–11/12)
- Labs 1–6

Weeks 11–24 (11/15–3/4)
- Lab 9
- Read lab 13
- Labs 16, 17, 18, 22

Weeks 25–36 (3/7–5/27)
- Labs 24 and 25

Biology Projects
- Botany—(Project due 11/12)
- Human Body, Anatomy or Physiology—(Project due 3/4)
- Zoology—(Project due 5/20)

Schedules and Flexibility

When all of the schedules and lessons have been written, we review them and make any modifications to the schedules for each course and for the overall program. We have the children then review the plans to look for any flaws in our logic.

Setting a yearly schedule and project due dates is one thing; setting up and carrying out a daily schedule is something entirely different. It would be untruthful to say that every day in a homeschool runs like clockwork. Actually, most days can be pretty well organized, but having school at home can also be filled with distractions ranging from ringing phones to taking sick siblings to the doctor to tracking down dogs that escaped from the yard. However, even in a traditional school, events such as assemblies, parties, and fire drills interfere with the school schedule.

Yet, dealing with distractions can also be a valuable learning experience for children. Homeschoolers are often used to completing their school work during the school day. However, having to do some work in the evening or on the weekends when it might interfere with their personal time is a great way to learn about the sacrifices that are part of going to college.

Chandra and I don't push our children to do too much "homework" after school hours. We prefer to impose upon them the responsibility for getting the job done during the school day. As part of preparing them for college, we ask our children to do the same thing that professors expect their college students to do—talk to us before the assignment deadline if they have questions or if they are falling behind and then take responsibility for getting the work done as soon as possible thereafter.

On another note, no matter how well parents plan the school year, there will almost always be some sort of change to the plan. Sometimes changes are necessary because we over-plan and the children have too much to do, so something has to be eliminated. However, we find it is better to have plenty to do and to cut back than not have enough to do and have to either add on work or worry that our children didn't learn enough.

Sometimes our children get engrossed in a project and want to spend more time on it, so we adjust the schedule accordingly. Sometimes the projects get completed faster than planned and the children finish a course more quickly than anticipated, so we allow them to spend more time on other courses instead.

To be honest, sometimes changes have to be made because everyone in the household catches the flu or some other extremely contagious "bug" and everyone ends up sick for a week or more. Other distractions can occur, such as relatives who decide to visit and want to be entertained for extended periods of time. No matter what the circumstances are, having a well-planned schedule allows parents to easily determine what has been accomplished, what still needs to be done, and to make adjustments as necessary. In the end, parents can stress about everything that happens or they can deal with life as it happens and make adjustments. Sometimes we do both, but we try to just do the latter.

Key Points

☐ Create assignments that challenge your child to reach higher levels of learning.
☐ Provide opportunities for real-life application, such as language discussion groups.
☐ Offer project options to encourage your child to apply new knowledge to a variety of situations.

❒ Consider requiring a written portion for every assignment, even for projects that do not necessarily involve writing.

❒ Provide subject-specific schedules that include due dates for assignments and tests.

CHAPTER 21

Evaluating and Grading
Your Child's Work

EVALUATING AND GRADING MAY SEEM LIKE drudgery.
However, grades serve at least three important purposes, especially in high school:
1. They help children understand how others
   judge their work so they can learn to judge it
   themselves prior to completing and submitting it.
2. They help children prepare for completing college-level course work and being judged accordingly.
3. The work that children complete during high
   school and the grades they earn for their work
   provide the basis for keeping transcript records
   and developing portfolios that may be used
   when applying to colleges and universities.

Evaluating and grading your child's progress can
be challenging and even intimidating. To make it
easier, we've categorized evaluations into fact-based
assessments and assessments of conceptual knowledge and skills. Both types of assessment are impor-

tant not only to check your child's educational progress, but to prepare him for the types of tests and projects he will be expected to complete in college. This chapter reviews each category, gives ideas for creating your own evaluations, and offers suggestions for assigning grades. We also provide some tips to assist you with the grading process.

Evaluating Factual Knowledge

In our program, when we want to evaluate our children's basic factual knowledge, we use tests, workbooks, and discussion questions or assignments from the textbooks. We could create our own evaluations, but it is much more time consuming to do so.

Evaluating factual knowledge is important for a variety of reasons. It is important to identify whether or not your child has obtained a basic knowledge of each subject, such as key terms and their definitions. Also, tests and other evaluations of base-level knowledge are easy to score objectively and define quantitatively (with numbers). Finally, evaluations given throughout the course help to identify whether or not your child is learning what needs to be learned. If your child is struggling with some aspect of a course, then corrective action can be taken sooner than if you had waited to give one big test at the end of the course.

It is usually easy to set up grading criteria for tests and other evaluations of factual knowledge. Typically a certain number of points is assigned to each correct answer and the total number of possible points adds up to 100%.

A grading scale like the one shown below can help you determine your child's grade for a test:

90–100 = A (Excellent)
80–89 = B (Good)
70–79 = C (Average)
60–69 = D (Below Average/Poor)
0–59 = F (Failing)

If your children do not score well on these types of evaluations, they may not be reading the material, either at all or well enough, or the evaluations aren't effective in identifying what the children really did learn or how it was learned. If you purchased tests, workbooks, and textbooks from the same publisher, chances are the evaluations are set up correctly. So, a low score may mean your child is having a hard time processing the information. It does not necessarily mean she has a learning problem.

As humans, we sometimes have trouble processing information because we get distracted, we aren't concentrating, or we just aren't trying very hard. Sometimes we have a hard time anticipating what information we should be retaining in order to be tested on it. Sometimes tests just make us nervous.

If your child earns low scores on these types of evaluations, first look at her past patterns of performance with similar evaluations. If the "trouble" is new, then you may want to check the materials and look at the way your child is trying to learn the information and troubleshoot from there.

If your child has had trouble in the past performing well on tests or other evaluations, you may have already sought the help of a professional experienced with helping children work through learning difficulties. If you haven't and you've tried everything at home to no avail, it may be time to consider obtaining professional assistance.

Evaluating Knowledge of Skills and Concepts (and Facts)

To move beyond the basic levels of learning and evaluate our children's knowledge of concepts related to a subject, we devise other "tests," usually in the form of projects. Projects help us evaluate our children's knowledge of facts and concepts and provide opportunities for the children to demonstrate their learning skills.

Usually projects are due at the end of a section in the course or at the end of the course itself. With this timing, projects usually provide an overall summary of what the children have learned.

Projects can be fun, especially for teenagers, because they have a chance to be creative and break away from the usual study "grind." Chapter 20 provided a list of some of the types of projects that we use. Keep in mind that writing assignments can be projects too.

Evaluating projects can be more subjective than grading a test of facts. We always provide evaluation criteria to guide the children in creating their projects and to provide some consistency in evaluation methods. However, using even this sort of grading breakdown leaves the door open to some level of subjectivity.

Project Evaluation Criteria

Thoroughness, attention to detail, and accuracy

Appearance, neatness, and creativity

Correct grammar and spelling

Amount of knowledge displayed through the ability to explain the subject and answer questions

Since learning to write well and communicate effectively through writing is very important in college, we have our children write papers in just about every course. Even when the children choose a non-writing type of project, we require a short paper.

Particularly with papers the children have written, but with other assignments as well, it is important to provide specific and constructive feedback. Tell your child what was good and why, as well as what could be improved, why it should be improved, and how to improve it.

One of the skills for college we identified earlier in the book is the ability to communicate well verbally. When children put together a display, an experiment, or some sort of visual project, it is a good idea for them also to prepare and deliver an oral presentation to tell about what they learned and about the project itself. We often videotape these presentations and let the children see how they look and sound when giving a presentation. Sometimes we discuss how to improve in this area as well.

For other types of projects, as well as for projects that require a presentation, we'll ask the children to be prepared to answer questions about the topic and the project. This question-and-answer period is great practice for question-and-answer sessions that occur during college courses. Learning to explain their thought processes, logic, and rationale is a great learning tool for children too.

Evaluation Criteria and Grading

Some parents don't like to assign scores to tests or grades to projects, while others have no problem with doing so. Some experts worry that homeschoolers all have 4.0 or "A" averages because they are taught at home and grades aren't *really* assigned like they are in other types of schools.

Although some parents worry that scores and grades can negatively affect a child's self-esteem, they don't have to be confidence destroyers. Scores and grades should be used to recognize and reinforce a child's efforts, as well as to help the child learn how she can grow and improve academically.

Scores and grades are also important for determining grade point averages that you may need to report to your state's education department. You may also need such information for your child's academic records for college admission.

Let your child know what her score equals in terms of letter grades. We use the same scale we described for evaluating tests, because it the same scoring system used by most colleges and universities.

For projects and papers we divide the assignment into "points" and assign a letter grade based on how well each requirement is met. It is still somewhat subjective when we decide how many points to take off for spelling, grammar, neatness, and so on. However, we try to be consistent and deduct two points for each error. It is up to our discretion about how many points to deduct for incomplete or poorly completed work.

Presenting projects in an interesting and appealing manner is part of each project. Students should know that college professors will grade their work subjectively too. College students who take the time to neatly type a paper and then bind it in some fashion give their professors the impression that they have taken a little more time with their work compared to a student who turns in work scribbled on the back of a piece of scrap paper. However, upon closer inspection, work that is beautifully presented can be full of mistakes and lacking in content.

When we see a spelling or grammatical error in a paper, we tend to look more closely to see if we find more. One typo is acceptable, two or three are understandable but regrettable, while four or more are unforgivable—at least in terms of our grading standards.

It may help you to find out what type of grading scale is used by the college or university your child wants to attend and use it. Usually this information is in the student catalog or even on the school's Web site.

More often than not, schools use a grade point average system, giving numerical value to each letter grade. A's are worth 4.0, B's are worth 3.0, C's are worth 2.0, D's are worth 1.0, and F's are worth 0. In between each letter grade is usually a partial point to indicate pluses or minuses for each letter grade, (that is, an A- versus a B+.)

Whether you use this system in your program or not is up to you. However, reviewing your child's grades with him and determining the overall grade point average is great preparation for the harsh reality of grades in higher education.

Defining Acceptable Levels of Performance

I believe it is an unacceptable teaching approach to give students the impression that trying to earn less than 100% on any assignment is acceptable. For example, sometimes teachers like to use rubrics (grading guidelines) that tell a student what he should do to earn an "A," what to do to earn a "B," and what to do to earn a "C." Of course, there is more work associated with going for the "A" than there is for the "B" and so on.

Why would you want a student to try to earn a "B" or a "C" rather than an "A"?

My question is always why would you tell a student what he can do to just "get by" on an assignment? Why would you want a student to try to earn a "B" or a "C" rather than an "A"? Why not encourage him to work hard enough to earn an "A," and then if the work simply isn't good enough or if it contains too many errors, deduct points accordingly and let the grades fall where they may?

When the children were very young, we worked to instill in them a strong work ethic to always try their best at whatever they did. If they didn't perform as well as they had hoped or even if they failed while trying their best, we never criticized their work.

In our high school program the children were always expected to try to earn an "A." When they made mistakes on assignments that caused them to fail to earn enough points for an "A," we carefully reviewed those mistakes and taught the children how to correct them and avoid them next time. We never allowed them to re-do work just to get a higher grade, but we did sometimes require them to re-do very poorly done work (that earned a "D" or an "F") to the level it should have been done in the first place to see the grade they could have earned compared to the one they did earn and were now stuck with. It was a powerful lesson! It was even more powerful when the children saw what one bad grade could do to their overall grade point average.

Allowing a student to do less than the best she can do promotes laziness. It sends the message that the teacher is fine with mediocre work being submitted. I've had students at the undergraduate level who had obviously been led to believe during high school that less than their best was good enough. I've also had graduate-level students—students who have an undergraduate degree already—who seemed to have this philosophy about school work too. It always made me wonder what their work/career performance levels were like.

> **Allowing a student to do less than the best she can do promotes laziness.**

Although some students don't try hard enough for any number of reasons, typically these reasons are really just excuses they've developed over time to rationalize that they prefer to be lazy in their work. Unfortunately, these behaviors are sometimes developed or even encouraged in their undergraduate programs by instructors who don't have sufficiently high expectations about the students' work. The instructors actually accept adequate work and often give such work high marks that should be reserved only for students who really perform "A" work.

For example, a professor I know told his students he didn't care about things like spelling, grammar, and punctuation in their papers. Unfortunately, when some of those students enrolled in my classes, they were more than shocked to earn "F's" on multiple assignments because they weren't putting forth enough effort to earn "A's." These students couldn't follow simple directions. They didn't use the resources they had been given. They failed to check their work before submitting it to identify errors and correct them. They also couldn't seem to understand that poor writing was not acceptable in a graduate-level program (it shouldn't be acceptable at any level, really) because these people would then go on to the work world with that same attitude about their work there. In short, they had been conditioned to perform poorly at everything they did.

I hold every student to a high standard of quality. I am also very understanding of honest mistakes, but I try to help students not to make mistakes by providing numerous and detailed handouts designed to help avoid unnecessary errors. Unlike the example stated above, most college professors expect quality work from their students and will grade assignments accordingly.

So what does this all mean to you and your homeschool program? It means you are preparing your child each year to go on to the next year and next level of her education. During high school you are also preparing her for college and the work world. The habits she develops in high school can mean success or failure when it comes to college-level studies and performance on the job.

It is important that you help your child understand exactly what your expectations are and what she must do to earn an "A" in a course. In the example below we've defined expectations for a biology project—specific requirements are in bold.

Course: Biology

Assignment: Biology Project

To earn an "A" on this project you must:

1. *Select* one of the following topics for which to complete a project: the major systems of human physiology, human anatomy, DNA, the effects of drugs/alcohol on the human body.

2. *Use* **a minimum of five resources in addition to your text** to gather information for the project.

3. *Develop* a visual and oral presentation in which you will explain the information you learned about your topic. Your presentation must be **between five to ten minutes long.** You must **utilize a presentation board** and **have a demonstration of some sort.**

4. *Write* a ten-page thesis paper to accompany the presentation. **Your paper must be typed, double-spaced, with one-inch margins on all sides. Your paper must have no more than two spelling or grammar errors. Your paper should have a cover page and a reference page.**

5. **Write a *self-critique* of your presentation** focusing on what you did well and what you could have done to improve it. Your self-critique should be **at least two typed pages long** and should **identify at least three items for improvement.**

6. **Two points will be deducted for any errors in your assignments. Additional points will be deducted for incomplete or poorly completed work.**

In the example above we've added some very specific performance criteria. By defining the acceptable level of performance, you create an objective standard by which you can evaluate your child's work in

Grading Tips

Clearly and specifically describe the criteria with which you will evaluate your child's work.

Identify what grade your child will earn based on the number of mistakes she made on the assignment or the level of effort she demonstrates.

Let your child know up front what has to be done to earn the highest grade possible on an assignment and in the course.

Don't have hidden expectations of what your child needs to do to earn the highest grade possible.

Don't tell your child what he will need to do to earn an A, B, and so on, as this encourages him to believe that not putting forth maximum effort is acceptable. Define the requirements for earning an "A" and expect your child to meet them.

order to assign a grade for the assignment and/or the course. You also have more specific information about your courses that you can provide a college admission counselor who may want to know what specifically your child had to do to earn all those A's.

It is perfectly acceptable to expect your child to work toward achieving 100% or an "A" as long as you have provided appropriate instruction and support along the way. It is also important to know when to accept that your child has performed to the best of her ability, even though a grade of 100% or an "A" wasn't attained.

We've always told our children that we expect them to do the best they can. If they do the best they can and earn a less-than-perfect grade, we don't have a problem with that. However, if they earn a grade lower than an A because they haven't tried hard enough, that's another matter altogether!

Key Points

☐ Use tests, workbooks, assignments, and text-book questions to evaluate factual knowledge.

☐ Provide specific evaluation criteria for projects and other more subjective assignments. In order to encourage your child to give her best effort, only define requirements for obtaining the maximum score.

☐ Teach your child to evaluate her own work (quality, accuracy, appearance) before submitting it.

CHAPTER 22

Developing a Syllabus

INFORMATION ABOUT ASSIGNMENTS, SCHEDULES, and grading should be contained in the syllabus so your child can easily refer to it throughout the year. When our children entered high school, we created a syllabus for each of their subjects. In colleges and universities, instructors usually create a syllabus for each course they teach. The syllabus outlines the purpose of the course and describes what both the instructor and students will do during the course—usually specifying that the student will do the work and the instructor will grade it.

Generally, a course is organized so learning takes place progressively, starting with introductory concepts and then moving toward more advanced concepts as defined by the course objectives. In the syllabus the course objectives are ultimately of the greatest importance for both the instructor and the students.

Instructors use objectives to develop lessons, create assignments, and design methods for evaluating the student's knowledge and abilities. Students may see course objectives and anything else in the syllabus as merely tasks to be accomplished—what they have to *do* rather than what they should *learn* (Dugdale, 1982). It is important for students to understand how to use a syllabus not only to complete the requirements of the course successfully, but to help identify what they should actually *learn* during the course.

More than likely, homeschooled students who go to college will also have professors who will create syllabi for their courses. By developing and using syllabi for their high school courses, you can help your children learn to get the most out of these important documents. You may also find that once you get used to writing syllabi, you'll wonder how you ever got along without them because they can be extremely effective tools for communicating goals and expectations, as well as for defining assignments and establishing timelines.

How to Create a Syllabus

A well-designed college course syllabus contains a variety of information about a course, including the instructor's background, her educational philosophies, lists of textbooks and other reading materials, reading assignments, papers or projects to be completed, methods of instruction, a course outline, course objectives, and grading procedures (Smith and Razzouk, 1993). In some instances the syllabus may indicate that the students have a choice of assignments to fulfill the requirements of the course. Sometimes students also have some say in how they will complete the assignments, although this is rare.

The first step for creating a syllabus for a homeschool course is to identify what subject is being taught so your children can better keep track of the work required for each course. You will also want to provide your child with the objectives for the course to help him to identify what's important to learn.

Of course, it's important to include all of the information about required papers or projects in the syllabus. You may want

Include all of the information about required papers or projects in the syllabus.

to specify which project options your child has, if any, as well as to define the due dates and any criteria that will be used for evaluating papers and projects. The next few pages show a complete sample syllabus for a homeschool course.

Sample Syllabus

Sample Syllabus: US Government I

Class Name: US Government (one semester—1/2 credit)

Class Description: In this class you will learn about the three parts of the US government and their roles and responsibilities. You will learn about the system of checks and balances that help regulate each of the three parts so no one part has too much power. You will learn about how the government was founded by reviewing the Declaration of Independence and the US Constitution.

Objectives:
- The student will be able to identify the roles and responsibilities of the three branches of the US government as defined in the US Constitution.
- The student will be able to describe the checks and balances that regulate the three branches of the government as defined in the US Constitution.
- The student will be able to analyze and evaluate the Bill of Rights and discuss its significance.

- The student will be able to discuss and debate the significance of the remaining amendments to the US Constitution.
- The student will complete and self-critique one or more projects related to the study of the US government.

Reading Assignments:
- *All The People*
- *Timetables of American History*
- *Why America is Free*
- *Scholastic Encyclopedia of the Presidents and Their Times*
- *Constitution of the United States and the Declaration of Independence* booklet
- *To the Best of My Ability*
- *Bill of Rights: A User's Guide*
- *Words that Built a Nation*
- *Brilliant Solution—Inventing the American Constitution*
- *American History I* (textbook)—pages... (if using a textbook)

Text and Test Assignments:
This course runs from September 7 to December 15. There are no tests. You may complete the reading assignments in any order you prefer. Your first project is due by November 1 and your second project is due on or before December 15

Written Assignments—Projects: Complete two projects as described below:

Project #1—Election Portfolio:
For this project you will take a bipartisan (objective) look at how we elect a president in the United States, including topics such as the process for electing a president as set forth in the US Constitution, the Electoral College, campaign issues and platforms,

and political parties—past and present.

Study the upcoming election to see if you can predict who will win. Research some controversial elections from the past to understand the roles of Congress and the Supreme Court for deciding who gets to be president. Review the lives and accomplishments of some of our most notable presidents.

Complete the worksheets in the assignment binder and add them to your portfolio in a section just for worksheets. Some of the assignments on the worksheets include:

- Identifying what the Constitution says about electing the president
- Defining the roles of Congress and the Supreme Court in determining who gets to be president
- Identifying and describing "controversial" elections from the past
- Reviewing the inaugural speeches of at least one past president and critiquing it
- Creating a biography for two of your favorite presidents
- Creating biographies of each candidate
- Identifying the platforms of the two major parties
- Completing a map of the US indicating the votes associated with the Electoral College
- Identifying your choice for president
- Predicting the winner and describing your rationale

Collect articles from newspapers, magazines, and the Internet related to the election process and the candidates.

Select certain headlines, portions of articles, entire articles, or pictures and sort them into the following categories: Democratic candidate, Republican candidate, other candidates, and the election process.

Create a montage by creatively arranging and displaying your selections on appropriately sized paper so they can be put in your portfolio into separate sections as indicated above.

Include your second project paper (as described below) in your portfolio.

Written Assignments—Projects (continued):
Project #2

Choose from the following list of topics for your second project and then use one or more of the project options from the list below that you think is the best method(s) for demonstrating what you've learned. Be prepared to give a short presentation about your project, and be prepared to answer questions about it.

If you select a project that is not a paper, please also include a two to three page paper describing your project and the results of your research. If you want to suggest a different topic or have a different idea for a project, please discuss your ideas with me.

Topic Options:
- The roles and responsibilities of each of the three parts of the US government
- The history and purpose of political parties in the United States
- The development and history of the US Constitution

Project Options:
- Research paper
- Simulated newspaper
- Collection of poems
- Creative story
- Children's book
- PowerPoint presentation
- Timeline

- Map or diorama
- Art Project—model, sculpture, painting, drawing, illustrations
- Report display
- Photo display
- Scrapbook
- Collection

Timeframe:

This course runs from September 7 to December 15. Your first project is due by November 1 and your second project is due on or before December 15.

Grading Criteria:

Your projects will be evaluated as follows using our usual evaluation criteria and grading scale:

- Thoroughness, attention to detail, and accuracy
- Appearance, neatness, and creativity
- Correct grammar and spelling
- Amount of knowledge displayed through ability to explain subject and answer questions

Practicing College-Level Skills

When we offer a syllabus, our children are responsible for carefully reading it to understand what they have to learn and how. It is up to them to use course materials and other resources to learn important facts, concepts, and skills. They are also required to complete a paper or project in order to effectively demonstrate what they learned that fulfills the criteria provided in the syllabus. They have to learn not only to manage their time to get everything done by the due dates in the syllabus for one course, but to prioritize their efforts in order to get everything done for *all* of their courses by the due dates in *all* of the syllabi.

We stagger the dates for different assignments for different subjects so the children don't get too overloaded. After all, we want to teach them, not burn them out.

As a result of using syllabi and giving our children more freedom and responsibility with regard to their education, we've been extremely pleased with the quality of their work. More importantly, we've been pleased with the amount of knowledge they've retained, which is more than they ever did when just answering questions out of the text.

What we describe in this section is a lot of work, not just for you, the parent, but for your child as well. But all of this preparatory work really has helped our program run smoothly and has enabled our children to be successful during high school (and elementary school).

We feel better about being organized for Chandra's sake because it makes her day and job easier as the one who runs our homeschool program from day to day. However, we also feel good knowing that our children shouldn't have any surprises when they go off to college because they've experienced some of the same structure, responsibility, and classroom practices at home that are typical in a college environment.

Key Points

- ❐ Develop a syllabus for each course.
- ❐ Include a course description, learning objectives, assignments and options (if any), due dates, instructions, and grading criteria.

SECTION V

PREPARING FOR THE END

CHAPTER 23

Keeping Records

WE'VE REVIEWED ALL OF THE PRACTICAL ASPECTS of running your high school program except one: keeping records. Some parents postpone thinking about record keeping until their children are trying to get into college and schools want transcripts and course descriptions. By that time many parents have forgotten what courses their children have completed, what materials they used, what activities they included, and what grades they earned.

This section covers the important task of record keeping. We review and offer examples of transcripts, proof of curriculum, and portfolios. We encourage you to keep careful records throughout your program and not attempt to compile them when you near the end.

Keeping records of a child's high school courses and academic performance serves two primary purposes:

1. Reporting the information to the state education department (if applicable)
2. Applying for admission to a college or university

Since each state has its own requirements about what records you need to keep for your homeschool program, we won't attempt to address that type of recordkeeping. However, while we focus only on records for college admission, this information may also be useful to you in fulfilling your state's reporting requirements.

What Records Do Colleges Want?

Since we couldn't possibly write about the recordkeeping preferences of every college and university, we are going to provide general guidelines for college requirements. However, as we've mentioned previously, it's a good idea to contact the schools your child hopes to attend and ask what format they prefer for homeschool transcripts and portfolios and what specific information they require. You don't want to provide too much or too little information or put the information into a format that would be frustrating for an admission counselor to sort through and try to understand. It's best to ask questions ahead of time and make the admission process as smooth as possible.

At the most basic level, colleges and universities want to be able to quickly and easily identify the courses a student completed during high school that fulfill the college's minimum admission requirements. Schools are also interested in your child's grade point average (GPA), which has to be high enough to meet minimum requirements. All of this information is included on high school transcripts.

It is important to know specifically what the college or university's course requirements are and to make sure the transcripts reflect them. For example, many schools require high school students to have three to four years of mathematics. Some schools further specify that students need to have completed at least one year each of algebra and geometry and the remaining two years should include courses somehow related to algebra. Certain schools may specify that students must also take trigonometry or calculus. When planning curricula and keeping records, keep in mind the requirements of your child's preferred colleges.

It is also helpful to know what the school's policies are for students who don't meet the minimum admission requirements. Colleges and universities realize that students from smaller schools and homeschools may not have had the same learning opportunities as students from larger schools, and they occasionally make allowances for this.

For example, many colleges require at least two years of courses in the same foreign language and want to know how the student fulfilled the speaking lab portion of the courses. Many smaller schools may not be able to provide foreign language courses or if they do, the lab portion may have been extremely limited. Colleges and universities often handle situations like this on a case-by-case basis or by setting a policy that allows students to fulfill the missing credits by taking the appropriate classes during the first year or two of college. However, it's better to get this information ahead of time while it can still be addressed in the high school program instead of waiting until your child applies for admission.

In addition to mathematics and foreign languages, many colleges and universities require three to four years of English courses with an emphasis on reading and writing, three to four years of natural sciences with at least one course that includes a lab, and three to four years of social sciences with at least one year of American government or American history. Again, individual schools may have more specific or more general requirements, so check ahead of time. Of course, it's difficult to gear your curriculum and records to appeal to every school, but usually there is a commonality between the requirements for various schools. You can deal with exceptions on a case-by-case basis.

Beyond the basic courses, some schools may have *preferred* or *required* criteria for the types of extra-curricular courses or school-related activities they want to see reflected in a student's transcripts. These criteria are likely to be different for each type of school, but may include physical fitness/education courses (especially for military academies); courses that require volunteer work, church activities, or community involvement projects (especially for religious or private colleges); or involvement with sports, clubs, or any sort of school-related activities where students have opportunities to work with others in a group setting and act in a leadership capacity.

Strong academic marks are always a credit to any high school student who is applying to college, but 4.0 grade point averages and perfect scores on the ACT and SAT aren't everything. Some colleges and universities emphasize diversity in their student populations. Well-rounded students with a variety of experiences *and* good grades help provide that diversity.

Beyond a list of courses and activities completed during high school, colleges and universities may require that students obtain at least minimum scores on the ACT or SAT tests to prove they are ready for college-level work. Although these scores are sent to colleges and universities via the testing service, you should know each school's requirement for which test must be taken, by what date, and the minimum score that must be obtained. At some schools, students' scores on these tests determine the scholarships they are eligible for. Some schools, such as the military academies, have their own admission tests students must complete.

Some colleges will accept a homeschool transcript as proof that a student completed high school, while others require that incoming students take the test to earn a GED (General Education Diploma) or the student take the SAT-II test. However, these requirements have been challenged on more than one occasion by the Home School Legal Defense Association (HSLDA). If a school indicates that a GED or completion of the SAT-II test is required for admission and this presents a problem for you, you may want to contact the school to see if there are other options. Sometimes high school transcripts, achieving a certain level score on the ACT or SAT test, or transferring from a two-year school can be substituted for the GED. Currently, the GED is not required for federal financial aid. If you run into difficulties in this regard, contact the HSLDA for assistance (www.hslda.org).

Key Points

- ☐ Contact schools your child is interested in to find out what types of records they require.
- ☐ Develop a plan for keeping detailed records of your child's academic work, including descriptions of courses, materials used, assignments completed, and grades earned for each subject to prepare transcripts or portfolios for college.

Recordkeeping for College Admission Requirements

Prepare transcripts and course descriptions

Acquire transcripts from community colleges, other schools attended

Complete required high school courses

Attain and document sufficient grade point average (GPA)

Attain sufficient placement test scores (ACT, SAT, others)

Record extracurricular activities

Complete GED or other testing, if required

CHAPTER 24

Creating Transcripts

A HIGH SCHOOL *DIPLOMA* IS SIMPLY A PIECE of paper. For colleges and universities, proof of graduation is the *transcript* that indicates which courses were completed, when, and what grade was earned. To make sure your transcripts are adequate, you'll need to include the right information.

Colleges and universities may require you to put transcripts into a specific format, such as a spreadsheet. Usually schools want to see a breakdown of courses in a semester-by-semester format. They may require that you send the transcripts via regular mail or the school may prefer an e-mailed copy. Some schools may request an official copy with the "school administrator's" signature and a notary stamp. Again, it's important to contact the school(s) to determine any requirements.

At a minimum, the following information should be easy to identify on your transcripts:

1. Student's full name (and probably social security number too)
2. Name of the "official" submitting the transcripts
3. School name, address, and phone number

4. Years of attendance—indicating each grade level by year(s)
5. Courses (by name) that were completed—by year, semester, or grade level based on the school's preferences
6. Grade earned for each course
7. Credits awarded for each course
8. Graduation date and statement of completion

If a child earned credits from another school, such as from a college or university, you will want to note these courses, credits, and grades on the transcript as well. You will probably also have to request *official* transcripts from the college your child attended, which will be then sent directly to the new college or university.

It may be necessary to break the transcript information down into semesters (fall and spring) if a school requires it. Additionally, some schools may want to see the following:

1. The total credits for each year
2. The GPA (grade point average) for each year
3. A running total of credits
4. The overall GPA

The goal is to make it easy for schools to get the information they need from your transcripts. Remember, school admission counselors have to review the information provided to complete paperwork for their records. It's for your child's benefit that you make it easy for counselors to get what they need from the transcripts—to this end, schools may have you "transfer" the transcript information to their preferred credit-summary form.

Sample Transcript Format

On the next few pages we've provided some sample formats you might want to use for your homeschool transcripts. Although we only listed one or two years, you should include all of your child's years in high school. We've provided different views of the course breakdown as examples—usually schools will want to see only one view to avoid confusion.

OFFICIAL TRANSCRIPTS—
DOE HOMESCHOOL HIGH SCHOOL

STUDENT'S NAME: John J. Doe
SOCIAL SECURITY NUMBER: 123-45-6789
SCHOOL NAME: Doe Homeschool
SCHOOL ADDRESS: 123 Main Street
SCHOOL PHONE NUMBER: 555-555-9876
SCHOOL CONTACT PERSON AND POSITION: Jane Doe, Principal
YEARS OF ATTENDANCE:
   9th grade: 1999–2000
   10th grade: 2000–2001
   11th grade: 2001–2002
   12th grade: 2002–2003
GRADUATION DATE: May 28, 2003

STATEMENT OF COMPLETION: John Doe successfully completed the requirements of Doe Homeschool and was awarded a high school diploma on May 28, 2003.

JOHN DOE—COURSES AND CREDITS
SORTED BY SUBJECT

ENGLISH CREDITS: 5
English Grammar—1 credit
English Literature—1 credit

American Literature I—1 credit
American Literature II—1 credit
Creative Writing and Poetry—1/2 credit
Journalism I—1/2 credit

MATHEMATICS CREDITS: 4
Algebra I—1 credit
Geometry—1 credit
Algebra II—1 credit
Trigonometry—1 credit

SOCIAL SCIENCE CREDITS: 4
American History—1 credit
World History—1 credit
American Government—1 credit
World Studies—1 credit

NATURAL SCIENCE CREDITS: 5
Physical Science—1 credit
Biology —1 credit
Biology Lab—1/2 credit
Chemistry—1 credit
Chemistry Lab—1/2 credit
Physics—1 credit

FOREIGN LANGUAGE CREDITS: 2
Spanish I—1 credit
Spanish II—1 credit

TOTAL CREDITS: 20

JOHN DOE COURSES AND CREDITS BY YEAR

YEAR	SUBJECT	COURSE	GRADE	CREDITS
9th	Foreign Lang	Spanish 1	A	1
9th	Mathemati-cs	Algebra 1	A	1
9th	English	English Grammar	A	1
9th	Social Studies	American History	A	1
9th	Science	Physical Science	A	1
			9th grade GPA: 4.0	9th grade credits: 5
			CUMULATIVE GPA: 4.0	TOTAL CREDITS: 5
YEAR	SUBJECT	COURSE	GRADE	CREDITS
10th	Foreign Lang	Spanish 2	B	1
10th	Mathemati-cs	Geometry	B	1
10th	English	English Literature	A	1
10th	Social Studies	World History	A	1
10th	Science	Biology	A	1
			10th grade GPA: 3.6	10th grade credits: 5
			CUMULATIVE GPA: 3.8	TOTAL CREDITS: 10

JOHN DOE COURSES AND CREDITS BY SEMESTER

SEMESTER	SUBJECT	COURSE	GRADE	CREDITS
9th Fall	Foreign Lang	Spanish 1	A	.5
9th Fall	Mathemati-cs	Algebra 1	A	.5
9th Fall	English	English Grammar	A	.5
9th Fall	Social Studies	American History	A	.5
9th Fall	Science	Physical Science	A	.5
9th Spring	Foreign Lang	Spanish 1	A	.5
9th Spring	Mathemati-cs	Algebra 1	A	.5
9th Spring	English	English Grammar	A	.5
9th Spring	Social Studies	American History	A	.5
9th Spring	Science	Physical Science	A	.5
			9th grade GPA:4.0	9th grade credits: 5
			CUMULATI-VE GPA: 4.0	TOTAL CREDITS: 5

Colleges and universities may need help understanding the scope and sequence of the courses a student completed.

Transcript Proof

Most public, private, and parochial high schools within a state follow a conventional standard for their curricula that is recognized or at least accepted at face value by many colleges and universities because the curricula is usually regulated by the state's educational department. When college or university counselors see Algebra I, American History, Journalism, or Spanish II (for example) listed on a transcript from a private, public, or parochial school, they assume the course has met the school's admission requirements. They don't require additional information to indicate what was taught for each subject or how the student earned the grade for each subject.

However, since homeschools are non-conventional in nature, colleges and universities may need help understanding the scope and sequence of the courses a student completed, as well as help with understanding how a student fulfilled the requirements of the course. This is when detailed record keeping benefits both you and your child.

Again, check with each school to determine what they want or need to be certain you are keeping the correct breadth and depth of records. In general, it is better to have more information available to provide a college or university rather than too little information. It is also easier to keep track of this information as your child progresses through high school rather than trying to remember all of it at the end of her senior year. The next chapter provides more information on course descriptions.

Key Points

- ❏ Prepare transcripts for college applications. Include all home-taught classes, as well as classes from other schools or community colleges.
- ❏ Consider including course descriptions in transcripts to help colleges understand the scope and sequence of each course.

CHAPTER 25

Writing Course Descriptions

IN CASE YOU NEED TO EXPLAIN YOUR CURRICULUM to a representative of a college or university, and you probably will, we recommend that for *each course* your child completed during high school, you prepare a course summary.

Each college or university will have its own requirements for what information you need to provide to supplement and explain the courses listed on your transcripts. The list below includes most of the basic information colleges are likely to request:

Course Title

■ Make sure the title agrees with the title on the transcript

Brief Description of the Course (paragraph form)

■ This is similar to what might appear in a course catalog. Keep it brief and easy to understand and make sure it corresponds to the school's admission requirements.

Text Information

- Include the full title of the text, the publisher's name and address, and the copyright date of the text.
- If additional materials beyond the textbook were used (test booklets, workbooks, audio/video tapes, lab books, or others), list that information as well.
- If you created your own curriculum, include the full titles of the books or resources your child used with the names of the authors, the publishers' names and addresses, and the copyright dates.

Course Scope and Sequence

- Create a listing of the major topics (only) included in the course that help define its depth and breadth. You may also want to include the course objectives to help define what your child was supposed to learn.
- If you used a standard curriculum, provide the publisher's description of the course or scope and sequence information. Clean copies of textbook tables of contents may help you recall this information and may be required by the college or university.
- If you created your own curriculum, a bulleted list of the scope and sequence or objectives is also important. Again, clean copies of the table of contents of each book may help identify this information and may be something the school wants to have.

Course Work Description

- Provide a brief overview description of the work your child completed to fulfill the requirements of the course. Such information may include the numbers and types of:

- Tests (number of tests and types—multiple choices, true/false, essay). Don't worry about the scores of each test; the course grade and GPA reflect this information.

- Projects (brief description of projects, hours spent on each, and learning outcomes)

- Papers (titles of papers, an abstract or brief description of the purpose and content of the paper,—and the length)

- Lab work (include an overview of type of lab, major project or experiments, and hours spent completing work)

- Real-life application of the course work—internships, volunteer or paid work, apprenticeships (include hours spent and duties performed)

Extracurricular Activities

You can keep a similar record of your child's extracurricular activities. The trick is to keep track of enough information to provide an admission counselor with a clear understanding of what your child did without overwhelming (or boring) him. It is important to include information about your child's leadership positions, skills obtained, and goals accomplished in every extracurricular activity.

We recommend using a combination of brief paragraph descriptions and bulleted lists for at least the following items:

- Sports played (number of years)
- Jobs held (number of years, paid and volunteer)

- ◼ Clubs or organizations (description of the organization, number of years a member, positions held and years, if applicable)
- ◼ Honors and awards received (include descriptions)
- ◼ Unique skills or training (be specific about skill level obtained)
  - ♦ These skills might include typing speed, ability to use software applications, training in the martial arts, musical training, hours flying planes, or other instances of training that help describe who the child is

Remember, these typed summaries can be used as a reference when you need to provide a college or university with high school transcripts, for an admission application, and for preparing a résumé or portfolio. Having this information already prepared will make these tasks easy.

Saving Your Information

Since information about the child's classes, activities, and accomplishments is very important, you want to make sure you protect it. Computers are useful tools, but they can fail without warning due to a virus or failure of computer components.

We recommend you print copies of your child's writing assignments and store the copies in a safe place. We also recommend you create at least one electronic backup copy of important files on a disk or CD and store it in a safe place as well. Whenever you update your primary computer file, be sure to update the backup copy, print an updated version, and destroy the old printed version or store it somewhere else to avoid confusion.

Sample Course Descriptions

On the next several pages are some examples of detailed course descriptions that colleges and universities might want to see. These are examples only and may not contain all the details a school may require, nor are they necessarily shown in the format a school may require. More examples are provided in Appendix C at the end of the book.

Course Title	English Grammar and Composition 9
Curriculum/ Approach	A Beka Homeschool Publishing—Scope and Sequence
Text/ Materials	*Grammar and Composition III Work Text for Grade 9* (A Beka)
Course Description	This course is a traditional approach to grammar and composition via workbook explanations and exercises. It is a continuation of a series from the 7th and 8th grades, as well as preparation for the same subject in the 10th grade.
Length/ Credits	Two semesters/one credit
Major Topics	Capitalization rules, punctuation rules, kinds of sentences and diagramming, eight parts of speech and their uses, diagramming eight parts of speech, sentence structure, manuscript form, writing process, the library, outlining, book reports, paragraphs, exposition, writing letters, character sketch and type sketch, the research paper, improving writing style.
Assignment/ Projects	Completing workbook assignments and exercises and writing a thesis paper.

Course Title	Great Books I
Curriculum/ Approach	Course designed by your name here focusing on reading, thinking, and writing skills.
Text/ Materials	*Treasure Island, The Incredible Journey, Around the World in 80 Days, The Time Machine, The Red-Headed League* (Sir Arthur Conan-Doyle), *Tom Sawyer, The Magician's Nephew* (C.S. Lewis), *The Lion, the Witch, and the Wardrobe* (C.S. Lewis)
Course Description	This course introduces students to the beauty of literature and the techniques used for writing prose.
Length/ Credits	Two semesters/one credit
Major Topics	Literature appreciation, character development, plot, theme, setting, and imagery.
Assignment/ Projects	Read each book, write a book report for each, and hold discussions with the instructor.

Course Title	Physical Education
Curriculum/ Approach	Hands-on participation in team activities facilitated by coach.
Text/ Materials	N/A
Course Description	This is a course in which the student can participate in an organized flag football league for three months, an organized physical education class that meets twice per month for two semesters, and a bowling league that meets once per month for two semesters.
Length/ Credits	One semester/1/2 credit
Major Topics	Sports, physical education, conditioning, team work, learning rules of the sport, and development of sport-specific skills.
Assignment/ Projects	Participate in flag football for three months, physical education class twice a month for both semesters, and bowling league once per month for both semesters.

Course Title	Algebra I
Curriculum/ Approach	A Beka Homeschool Publishing—Scope and Sequence
Text/ Materials	*Algebra I Student Text* (A Beka), *Algebra I Student Test Book* (A Beka)
Course Description	This course focuses on developing the student's mathematical skills through an understanding of algebra.
Length/ Credits	Two semesters/one credit
Major Topics	Linear equations in one variable, algebraic numbers, graphs, formulas, positive and negative numbers, fundamental operations, special products and factoring, fractions, ratio, proportion and variation, linear systems of equations, powers and roots, exponents and radicals, quadratic equations, numerical trigonometry.
Assignment/ Projects	Completing text exercises and unit tests.

Course Title	College Thesis Paper/APA Style
Curriculum/ Approach	Course designed and facilitated by *your name here* to teach students how to write a college-level thesis paper in APA style.
Text/ Materials	*Publication Manual of the American Psychological Association, Fifth Edition*
Course Description	This course is designed to provide the student with the opportunity to write a college-level thesis paper in APA style.
Length/ Credits	One semester/1/2 credit
Major Topics	Thesis paper writing, APA style
Assignment/ Projects	Research and complete a three to five page thesis paper using APA format.

Course Title	American History
Curriculum/ Approach	Course designed by *your name here* focusing on reading, thinking, and writing skills
Text/ Materials	*To the Best of My Ability: The American Presidents—James M. McPherson* (DK, 2001), *We Were There Too—Phillip Hoose* (DK, 2001), *Why America is Free—Kenneth E. Hamburger Ph.D* (Society of the Cincinnati, 1998), *Words that Built a Nation—Marilyn Miller* (Scholastic, 1999), *Huckleberry Finn, When the Legends Die, A Separate Peace, To Kill a Mockingbird, Diary of Anne Frank*
Course Description	This is an introductory course to US history and the events that shaped our country. Students are also able to read classical literature relating to events or time periods from US history. Finally, students are able to complete multiple projects of their own design through which they are able to study events, persons, or time periods from US history.
Length/ Credits	Two semesters/one credit
Major Topics	People, events, and time periods of US history
Assignment/ Projects	Complete reading assignments, write book reports, and complete four history projects relating to people, events, or time periods of US history.

Course Title	Biology and Lab
Curriculum/ Approach	A Beka—Scope and Sequence
Text/ Materials	*Biology: God's Living Creation Student Text* (A Beka), *Biology: God's Living Creation Field and Laboratory Manual* (A Beka), *Biology: God's Living Creation Test Booklet* (A Beka)
Course Description	This course allows the student to learn about biology through the completion of reading assignments, in-text questions, and quizzes/tests, as well as through laboratory work. The student will also be able to engage in an in-depth study of three major biology topics by completing projects focusing on any aspect of each topic that appeals to him.
Length/ Credits	Two semesters/one and a half credits
Major Topics	Flowering seed plants, structure and function of leaves, flowers, fruits, and seeds, stems and roots, variety in plant world, bones and muscles, nervous system, nutrition and digestion, circulation and respiration, excretory and endocrine systems, disease and the body's immune system, natural history and scientific investigation, evolution, mammals, birds, reptiles and amphibians, fish, arthropods, variety in the world of invertebrates, cytology, heredity, DNA, laboratory work: dissections, microscopy, field studies, nutrition, cellular biology, genetics.
Assignment/ Projects	Complete text reading assignments, textbook questions, unit tests, fourteen lab assignments, and three major projects related to botany, human physiology, and zoology.

Course Title	French I and Lab
Curriculum/ Approach	A Beka—Scope and Sequence
Text/ Materials	*Nouveaux Chemins A and B Student Texts* (A Beka), *Nouveaux Chemins Vocabulary Workbook* (A Beka), *Nouveaux Chemins Test Book* (A Beka), *French Computer CD—Learn French Now!* (Transparent Language), *Multilingual Talking Picture Dictionary by Princeton Review*, A Beka French Vocabulary Cassettes
Course Description	This is an introductory course to the French language with an emphasis on building vocabulary, introducing and reinforcing grammar, building writing, and conversational skills.
Length/ Credits	Two semesters/one credit
Major Topics	Grammar, vocabulary, writing, conversation skills
Assignment/ Projects	Complete textbook reading and writing assignments and unit tests. Complete lab time consisting of speaking and listening with computer CD.

Key Points

- ☐ Prepare course descriptions so colleges will know what each course covered.
- ☐ Keep a record of your child's extracurricular activities.
- ☐ Print copies of course descriptions and important schoolwork and store in a safe place.
- ☐ Make electronic backup of computer files.

CHAPTER 26

Preparing Portfolios

The definition of the word "portfolio" varies. For our purpose, a portfolio means a packet of information a child will use as part of the college admission process. The contents of this packet will depend primarily on the criteria of the college or university to which your child is applying. Some schools have specific requirements for a portfolio, others require a portfolio but leave the format up to the student—which is a "test" in itself—and some schools don't want anything to do with portfolios. Some schools may require an electronic portfolio while others want a paper version. Transcripts are generally more important to a school than a portfolio.

Portfolio Guidelines

There are some general guidelines applicable to every kind of portfolio:

- Neatness, correct spelling, and grammar
- Accuracy of information (names, dates, and addresses)
- Ensuring that the format and content of the portfolio meets the school's guidelines

■ The student being knowledgeable about the contents of the portfolio and being able to speak intelligently about it

Some of the requirements for the contents of a portfolio may include the following:

1. Application form
2. Application fee
3. Copy of high school transcripts (and possibly course descriptions as "proof")
4. Copy of transcripts from other high schools or colleges
5. Admission test scores
6. Letters of recommendation
7. Essay
8. Statement of philosophy
9. Résumé
10. Academic work samples

Items 1–5 on the list above are fairly self-explanatory or we've already reviewed them elsewhere in this book. Here are some recommendations for items 6–10:

6. Letters of recommendation: Letters of recommendation from credible and important sources, such as teachers, coaches, and employers, are essential. Letters from relatives, family friends, or peers are not a good idea. Make sure to provide the clean original letter of recommendation in the portfolio. It might be a good idea to keep extra copies to provide to an admission counselor. The letter writer may have to send the original, signed letter directly to the school to make it "official." Some schools have specific forms for letters of recommendation that must be used.

7. Essay: The essay is an important part of the application. Schools will judge the student's academic abilities by her writing skills. Not only do spelling and grammar count, but so do organization, structure, style, and content. Sometimes a school will provide the essay topic and other times the student is required to choose the topic. Often a topic offered by the school is designed to gain more information about the student—keep this in mind if the student is allowed to pick the topic. In either case, what the student writes should reflect well on her.

Although it may be tempting to help a child write the essay, it is usually better to restrict coaching to grammar and spelling and provide minimal guidance about the content and style. Essays should reflect the student's best abilities and her personality. Remember, your child may have to "live up to" the essay during a personal interview. Practicing interviews is a great school project.

8. Statement of Philosophy: Some schools may want to know the student's philosophy on life, education, or other topics. Often these statements are the hardest to write for students because they may never have tried to put their philosophies into words. Writing and explaining personal philosophical statements is a great academic exercise to include in your curriculum.

> For extra college prep and good academic exercise, consider preparing your child for the admission process. Practice interview skills through mock interviews with your child. Provide opportunities for your child to write a statement of personal philosophy.

9. Résumé: For extra college prep and good academic exercise, consider preparing your child for the admission process. Practice interview skills through mock interviews with your child. Provide opportunities for your child to write a statement of personal philosophy.

It may seem funny to think of a résumé in conjunction with a college portfolio. We usually think of résumés in relation to employment. Yet, college is, in many ways, a student's *employment* for a period of time, so developing a detailed résumé can be appropriate when applying for admission to school.

There are too many possibilities for résumé layout and format to cover in this book. Quite often, the format is a matter of personal preference. However, the basics of an effective résumé remain constant:

1. Personal information—name, address, phone number, and e-mail address
2. Statement of objective(s)—related to education and admission
3. Work history in chronological order indicating the name of the employer, city and state, dates of employment, positions held, and primary duties for each position
4. Educational history with the names of the schools and their locations, courses or programs in which the individual was enrolled, dates attended, and if appropriate the completion status (diploma, certificate, and so forth)
5. Extracurricular activities, club or organizational memberships, locations, community involvement with dates, positions held, and duties performed
6. Specific skills, certifications, or related accomplishments
7. List of references (three to five preferably professional references with the individual's full name, job title, home address, home phone, and home e-mail—use the individual's work phone and e-mail only with permission)
8. The résumé should be neatly typed, organized effectively, reflect proper spelling and grammar, and be printed on heavy-bond, white paper with black ink. It isn't appropriate to use colored paper or ink on a résumé— even though it may reflect the student's personality.

9. A cover letter may also be in order. As with a job, the cover letter should (in about three to four paragraphs) be addressed to a specific person or the specific institution to which the child is *applying* and indicate the purpose of the letter, the student's interest in the school, her intentions and skills, and contact information. The letter should be dated with the current date and should be signed in black ink. Again, the letter should be printed on white, heavy-bond paper with black ink.

10. In some ways, the most challenging item on the list of potential portfolio contents is the last one: academic work samples. If the school doesn't provide any guidance about this area, you and your child will have to exercise a good deal of common sense to impress the school's official rather than bore or overwhelm her. It's also important to reflect the student's best work in a professional manner, rather than having it look like a hodge-podge of samples in a scrapbook.

10. Academic work samples: What you included as academic work samples is really up to you and your child. Here are our suggestions about what you might want to include:

- A paper or essay written for a school assignment—no more than three to five typed pages (single side and double-spaced)
- Articles written for a newspaper, yearbook, or another type of publication (preferably clean copies of the entire page or pages from the original source, but tastefully highlighted to direct the reader to the student's article)
- Samples (portions) of poems, stories, or songs written by the student
- Photographs of academic projects completed (such as for a science fair), models built, sew-

ing or needlecraft work, or culinary creations. Photographs should be in color and clearly show what the project was in as much detail as possible. The student should also be in the photo. If needed, include a brief, typed explanation of what the photo shows.

■ Copies of certificates, awards, or letters of commendation from academically related competitions or events

■ Photographs taken by the child (if photography is a hobby)

■ Copies of art work (if art is a hobby)

■ Other items that help build a positive image of the child's personality, academic ability, and overall potential to succeed in higher education

Format of the Portfolio

The format of the portfolio depends on your preferences and the school to which your child is applying. We usually prefer neatly laid out sheets of paper put into top-loading sheet protectors and then organized in a thin binder, but you may have another method that works best for you. However, some items, such as the application, essay, and resume, may need to be kept separate from the rest of the information to aid the school in filing their paperwork.

Key Points

❑ Ensure the accuracy of information (names, dates, and addresses).

❑ Check portfolio items for neatness, correct spelling, and proper grammar.

❑ Make sure the format and content of the portfolio meets the school's guidelines.

❑ Make sure your child is knowledgeable about the contents of the portfolio and is able to speak intelligently about it.

CHAPTER 27

The End of High School: A New Beginning

IT TAKES A LOT OF TIME AND ENERGY to homeschool your child. At times you may get bogged down in the planning, preparation, and daily routine. As you plan and move through your program, it helps to remember why you chose homeschooling and what you and your child want to achieve—the "end" of your homeschooling program.

Our oldest son recently asked us about an old song he wanted to learn to play on his guitar. The song, "Turn, Turn, Turn" by Pete Seeger, is based on the Book of Ecclesiastes, which speaks of a time for everything—to everything there is a season. His interest in the song and its message came at a time when we were working on this final chapter, and it encouraged us to reflect on all of our experiences and efforts as a homeschooling family and on the purpose of this book.

For us, homeschooling was the right choice. We learned about homeschooling at a time when our oldest daughter, Holly, was transitioning from preschool—a time for drawing, reading, and playing—to a time for starting the formal process of education. At that time we weren't sure how to best meet her learning needs given her hearing impairment and our concerns about her education and safety in the public school environment.

We've learned much since then. Chandra and I work well together as a couple, discussing what is going well in our program and what isn't, and considering the children's needs and what we can do for them. As a result, we've developed and modified our teaching approaches to find a system that works well for them and us.

When Holly and Cameron reached the end of elementary school, we knew our earlier teaching approaches weren't going to be as effective during the high school years. Our elementary program was too pedagogical—too focused on us being subject-matter experts and having the children answer textbook questions with little or no real understanding of the material. We saw warning signs when we would ask the children about their work or what they had read in their books recently only to receive blank stares and long periods of silence in return. We knew that although they were scoring well on their textbook assignments and tests, they weren't really getting anything out of their education. With the time approaching for the children to go off to college, we knew we had to do something different.

We first looked at our materials. We then looked at the children's ability to learn. We also took a look at our teaching approach. We made changes in all three. My formal education and experience teaching college greatly influenced the changes we made to our program. We evaluated the problems with our program from the viewpoint of not only what would help the children get into college, but what would help them to succeed once they got there.

Using some of the weaknesses I saw in my college students over the years, we identified some key skills and behaviors we wanted the children to develop during high school. We then examined a variety of teaching approaches and theories that are used in homeschools and higher education to identify the best approaches to help us prepare the children for college. Lastly, we looked for ways to make our program fun and manageable for all of us. What we came up with became the basis of this book.

Were we successful? Well, Holly has graduated from homeschool high school and has been accepted to the university of her choice. She plans to major in English and creative writing and then go on for a master's degree in library science. That's impressive for a girl who was never supposed to learn to read, write, or speak! We have no doubt that she will achieve any goals she sets her mind to accomplishing.

Cameron is now only a year away from finishing high school and is being actively recruited by a couple of schools. He has been taking a variety of upper-level mathematics courses at the local community college to prepare him for admission into a university where he plans to major in meteorology. While he may change his mind a dozen times before he graduates from college, we know he has the skills he needs to achieve his goals.

Both of the children are happy, well-adjusted individuals with tremendous confidence. They both love to learn and they both have a desire to succeed in college and life. Yes, we'd say that we have been successful with teaching our children at home.

At the time this book is being published, we have children going into third grade, second grade, pre-kindergarten, and preschool. So, even as one chapter in our lives is closing with Holly going off to college and Cameron following right behind, we are starting all over again. To everything there is a season.

We hope this is just the beginning of new adventures for you whether you are already teaching your high school student at home or are just considering doing so. Either way, our desire is that you now have a new perspective and appreciation for homeschooling through high school in order to determine if it is the right thing for you. We also hope we have provided you with expert information about the high school and college levels of education and how homeschooling fits into it all.

We wanted to provide you with the perspective of colleges, universities, and professors with regard to children being prepared for higher education so you can effectively plan your homeschool high school program accordingly. It was our goal to give you practical academic knowledge with directions and advice based on real-life experience upon which you could base your program to help prepare your child for college. Even if you decide not to homeschool through high school, we hope you feel like you now are able to make an informed decision to that end.

Finally, we hope that if you do decide to teach your children at home through high school, you will do so with confidence. We want you to be able to enjoy this time with your children, as they can be among the best years you'll ever spend with them.

REFERENCES

Adelman, C. (2006). *The Toolbox Revisited: Paths to Degree Completion From High School Through College.* Washington, DC: US Department of Education.

Aiex, N. (1994). *Home schooling and socialization of children* [Electronic Version]. *Bloomington, IN:* ERIC Clearinghouse on Reading English and Communication, 1–4, (ED372460).

Alfassi, M. (2003). Promoting the will and skill of students at academic risk: An evaluation of an instructional design geared to foster achievement, self-efficacy, and motivation [Electronic Version]. *Journal of Instructional Psychology, March 2003, 30*(1).

Anderson, A. and Krathwohl, D. (Eds). (2001). A taxonomy for learning, teaching, and assessing. Addison-Wesley Longman, Inc.

Apple, M. (2000). The cultural politics of home schooling [Electronic Version]. *Journal of Education, 2000, 75*(1/2).

Arai, A. (1999). Homeschooling and the Redefinition of Citizenship [Electronic Version]. *Education Policy Analysis Archives, 7*(27), 1–18.

Armstrong, T. (1994). *Multiple intelligences in the class-room.* Alexandria, VA: Association of Supervision and Curriculum Development.

Ascough, R. (2002). Designing for online distance education: Putting pedagogy before technology [Electronic Version]. *Teaching Theology and Religion,* 5(1).

Balla, J. and Boyle, P. (1994). Assessment of student performance: A framework for improving practice [Electronic Version]. *Assessment and Evaluation in Higher Education, 1994, 19*(1).

Battistini, J. (1995). From theory to practice: Classroom application of outcome-based education [Electronic Version]. Eric Digest Clearinghouse, ED3777512.

Bers, T. (2001). Measuring and reporting competencies [Electronic Version]. *New Directions for Institutional Research, 110, Summer 2001.*

Biggs, J. (1996). Assessing learning quality: Reconciling institutional, staff, and educational demands [Electronic Version]. *Assessment and Evaluation in Higher Education, March 1996, 21*(1).

Bishop, C. (1991). *Home schooling parent support groups in groups in Kansas: A naturalistic inquiry into their concerns and functions.* Unpublished doctoral dissertation, Kansas State University.

Bluedorn, H. and Bluedorn, L. (1994). *A comparison of different methods and approach to homeschooling.* Trivium Pursuit Online. Retrieved February 19, 2003, from http://www.triviumpursuit.com/articles/comparison_approaches.htm

Bluedorn, H. and Bluedorn, L. (2002). *The trivium in a capsule.* Trivium Pursuit Online. Retrieved April 30, 2004, from http://www.triviumpursuit.com

Borja, R. (2003). Oregon mulls relaxing test mandate for home schoolers [Electronic Version]. *Education Week, 4/30/2003, 22*(33).

Brookfield, S. (1987). *Developing Critical Thinkers.* San Francisco: Jossey-Bass. ISBN 1-55542-055-9.

Brookfield, S. (1994). Interview with Stephen Brookfield [Electronic Version]. *A* Review of General Semantics, Spring 1994, 51(1).

Brookfield, S. (1995). *Becoming a critically reflective teacher.* San Francisco: Jossey-Bass. ISBN 0-7879-0131-8.

Brookfield, S. (1998). Understanding and facilitating moral learning in adults. [Electronic Version]. Journal of Moral Education, September 1998, 27(3).

Brookfield, S. (1999). *Discussion as a way of teaching.* San Francisco: Jossey-Bass. ISBN 0-7879-4458-0

Brougher, J. (1997). Creating a nourishing learning environment for adults using multiple intelligence theory [Electronic Version]. *Adult Learning, March/April 1997, 8*(4).

Brualdi, A. (1998). Gardner's theory [Electronic Version]. *Teacher Librarian, November/December 1998, 26*(2).

Buchanan, S. (1987). Evolution of parental rights in education [Electronic Version]. *Journal of Law and Education, 16*(3), 339–349.

*Bullen, M. (n.d.). Andragogy and university distance education. Retrieved October 16, 2003, from http:itesm.cstudies.ubc.ca/561g/Canada/resources/bullen1.html

Bunday, K. (1999). *Socialization: A great reason not to go to school.* Retrieved February 20, 2003, from http://www.learninfreedom.org/socialization.html

Campbell, B.J. (1991). Planning for a student learning style [Electronic Version]. *Journal of Education for Business, July/August 1991, 66*(6).

Cardiff, C. (1998). *The seduction of homeschooling families* [Electronic version]. The Freeman, Ideas on Liberty.

Chambers, E. (1992). Work-load and the quality of student learning [Electronic Version]. *Studies in Higher Education, 1992, 1*(2).

Checkley, K. (1997). The first seven ... and the eighth [Electronic Version]. *Educational Leadership, September 1997, 55*(1).

Chemers, M., Hu, Li-tze, and Garcia, B. (2001). Academic self-efficacy and first-year college student performance and adjustment [Electronic Version]. *Journal of Educational Psychology, March 2001, 93*(1).

Christa McAullife Academy. (2004). *FAQ.* Retrieved April 21, 2004, from http://www.cmacademy.org/db/about/FAQ

Chyung, S. and Stepich, D. (2003). Applying the "congruence" principle of—_Bloom's taxonomy to designing online instruction [Electronic Version].

The Quarterly Review of Distance Education, 4(3), 317–330.

*CNN.com. (1999, August 17). *School violence helps spur rise in home schooling.* Retrieved December 10, 2002, from http://www.cnn.com/US/9903/17/home.schooling/

*CNN Student News. (2003). *How did poor study habits net stellar grades?* Retrieved January 27, 2003, from http://www.cnn.com /2003/ EDUCATION /01/27/ college.freshmen.ap /index.html

Cohen, C. (2000). *And What About College?* Cambridge, MA: Holt Associates, Inc.

Collins, J. (1998). Seven kinds of smart [Electronic Version]. *Time, 10/19/98, 152*(16).

Cornford, I. (1999). Imperatives in teaching for life-long learning: Moving beyond rhetoric to effective educational practice [Electronic Version]. *Asia-Pacific Journal of Teacher Education, 27*(2).

Dugdale, S. (1982). What's the student doing? A crucial aspect of instructional design [Electronic Version]. *Educational Leadership, February 1982.*

Duvall, S., Delquardi, J., and Greenwood. 1997. *An exploratory study of home school instructional* environments and their effects on the basic skills of students with learning disabilities [Electronic Version]. Education and Treatment of Children (20).

Duvall, S., Delquardi, J., and Ward, L. 2004. A preliminary investigation of the effectiveness of homeschool instructional environment for students with attention-deficit/hyperactivity *disor-*

der [Electronic Version]. School Psychology Review, 2004, 33(1).

Eisner, E. (1994). Commentary: Putting multiple intelligences in context: Some questions and observations [Electronic Version]. *Teachers College Record, Summer94, 95*(4).

Eisner, E. (2000). Benjamin Bloom [Electronic Version]. *Prospects: The Quarterly Review of Comparative Education, September 2000, XXX*(3).

Ewell, P. (2003). Assessment (Again) [Electronic Version]. *Change, January/February 2003, 35*(1).

Fasko, D. (2001). An analysis of multiple intelligences theory and its use with the gifted and talented [Electronic Version]. *Roeper Review, April 2001, 23*(3).

Flottemesch, K. (2000). *Building effective interaction in distance education: A review of the literature. The 2001/2002 ASTD Distance Learning Yearbook.* McGraw-Hill, May 2001.

*Fortnet.org (2004). *Waldorf FAQ: Frequently asked questions about Waldorf education.* Retrieved April 28, 2004, from http://www.fortnet.org/rsws/wadorf/faq.html

*Fox News (2003). Homeschooling on the rise in Black communities. Fox News Channel. (2003, May 19). Retrieved May 19, 2003, from http://www.foxnews.com/printer_friendly_story0,3566,8728600.html

Frame, R. (2002). A strengths-based approach and student retention rates [Electronic Version]. *Christianity Today, 11/18/02, 46*(12), 100–101.

Francis, B. (1990). Many lives to lead: The adult professional's quest. *New Direction for Adult and Continuing Education; 45, Spring 1990*, San Francisco: Jossey-Bass Inc.

Frost, E. A. and Morris, R. C. (1988). Does home schooling work? Some insights for academic success [Electronic Version]. *Contemporary Education, 59*(4), 223–227.

*Gaddis, B. (1999). Application of adult learning theories to constructivist learning environments. Retrieved January 28, 2003, from http://web.uccs.edu/bgaddis/leadership/topicfocus2D1.htm

Gall, M., Gall, J., and Borg, W. (2003). *Educational Research, an introduction.* Boston: Allyn & Bacon.

Gardner, H. (1994). Intelligences in theory and practice: A response to Elliot W. Eisner, Robert J. Sternberg, and Henry M. Levin [Electronic Version]. *Teachers College Record, Summer 1994, 95*(4).

Gardner, H. (1995). Reflections on multiple intelligences [Electronic Version]. *Phi Delta Kappan, November 1995, 77*(3).

Gardner, H. (1999). *Intelligence reframed: Multiple intelligences for the 21st century.* New York: Basic Books.

Gibbons, H. and Wentworth, G. (2001). Andrological and pedagogical training differences for online instructors. Retrieved October 16, 2003, from http://www.westga.edu/~distance/ojdla/fall43/gibbons_wentworth43.html

Gibson, B. and Govendo, B. (1999). Encouraging constructive behavior in middle school classrooms:

A multiple-intelligences approach [Electronic Version]. *Intervention in School and Clinic, September 1999, 35*(1).

Gordon, W. M., Miles, A., and Russo, C. J. (1991). *Home Schooling.* (EDRS Document Reproduction Service No. ED 332 291).

Greany, T. (2003). What makes an effective lifelong learner? [Electronic Version]. *Adults Learning, March 2003, 14*(7).

Greenhawk, J. (1997). Multiple intelligences meet standards [Electronic Version]. *Educational Leadership, September 1997, 55*(1), 62–65.

Guskey, T. (2003). Assessment learning [Electronic Version]. *Educational Leadership, February 2003,* 7–11.

Hearne, D. and Stone, S. (1995). Multiple intelligences and underachievement: Lessons from individuals with learning disabilities. *Journal of Learning Disabilities, August/September 1995, 28*(7).

Hiemstra, R. and Sisco, B. (1990). Moving from pedagogy to andragogy [Electronic Version].Retrieved January 28, 2003, from http://www-distance.syr.edu/andraggy.html

Hill, P. (2000). Home schooling and the future of public education [Electronic Version]. *Peabody Journal of Education, 2000, 75*(1/2).

Homeschool.com (n.d.). Homeschooling approaches: Multiple intelligences. Homeschool.com. Retrieved April 22, 2004, from http:www.homeschool.com/approaches/MultipleIntelligences.asp

Hopper, B. and Hurry, P. (2000). Learning the MI way: The effect on students' learning of using the theory of multiple intelligences [Electronic Version]. *Pastoral Care in Education, December 2000, 18*(4), 26–32.s

HSLDA. (2004). Homeschooling grows up [Electronic Version]. Retrieved from April 21, 2004, from http://nche.hslda.org/research/ray2003/default.asp

Illinois H.O.U.S.E. (n.d.). *We've grown up and we're okay: Studying home-educated adults.* Retrieved February 20, 2003, from http://www.illinoishouse.org/a05.htm

Imel, S. (1989). Teaching adults: Is it different? [Electronic Version]. Eric Clearinghouse on Adult Career and Vocational Education, Columbus, OH, ERIC Digest No. 82.

Ishizuka, K. (2000). *The unofficial guide to homeschooling.* Foster City, CA: IDG Books Worldwide, Inc.

James, W. and Gardner, D. (1995). *New Directions for Adult and Continuing Education, 67, Fall 1995.* San Francisco: Jossey-Bass Inc.

*King, J. and Doerfert, D. (n.d.). Interaction in the distance education setting. Retrieved January 28, 2003, from http://www.ssu.missouri.edu/ssu/AGEd/NAERM/s-e-4.htm

Knowles, J. G. (1988). Introduction: The context of home schooling in the United States [Electronic Version]. *Education and Urban Society, 21*(1), 5–15.

Knowles, J. G. (1988). Parents' rationales and teaching methods for home schooling [Electronic Version]. *Education and Urban Society, 21*(1), 69–84.

Knowles, J. G., Marlow, S. E., and Muchmore, J. A. (1992). From pedagogy to ideology: Origins and phases of home education in the United States, 1970–1990. *American Journal of Education, 100*(2), 195–235.

Krathwohl, D. (2002). A revision of Bloom's taxonomy: An overview [Electronic Version]. *Theory into Practice, Autumn 2002, 41*(4).

LaRue, J. and LaRue, S. (1991). Is anybody home? Home schooling and the library. *Wilson Library Bulletin, 66*(1), 32–37.

Leamnson, R. (2002). It's never too late: Developing cognitive skills for lifelong learning [Electronic Version]. *Interactive Learning Environments, 2002, 10*(2), 93–103.

Limbaugh, D. (2002). California takes on homeschoolers [Electronic Version]. *Human Events, 9/9/2002, 58*(33).

Lines, P. (2000). Homeschooling comes of age [Electronic Version]. *The Public Interest, No. 140, (Summer 2000),* 74–85.

Lubienski, C. (2000). Whither the common good? A critique of home schooling [Electronic Version]. *Peabody Journal of Education, 75*(1 and 2), 207–232.

Lyman, I. (1998). Homeschooling: Back to the future? [Electronic Version]. *Cato Policy Analysis, 294,* 1–17.

*Lyman, I. (1998). "What's behind the growth in homeschooling (public school problems prompt parents into homeschooling)" *USA Today Magazine.* September 1998, Society for the Advancement of Education. Retrieved January 2003 from http://www.findarticles.com /cf_0/m1272/n2640 _v127/21114547/print.jhtml

MacDonald, S. (1997). Giving first-year students what they deserve [Electronic Version]. *College Teaching, Spring 1997,45*(2), 42–45.

Mahan, B. M. and Ware, B. J. (1987, July). *Home schooling: Reasons some parents choose this alternative form of education and a study of the attitudes of home schooling parents and public school superin tendents toward the benefits of home schooling.* Paper submitted to the School of Education, University of Dayton, Ohio.

Marshak, R. (1983). What's between pedagogy and andragogy? [Electronic Version]. *Training and Development Journal, October 1983,* 80–81.

Martin, R. (2004). Philosophically based alternatives in education [Electronic Version]. *Encounter: Education for Meaning and Social Justice, Spring 2004, 17*(1), 17–27.

*Masland, M. and Ross, M. (2003). Teach your children well—at home. *MSNBC News, (2003, August 29).* Retrieved August 29, 2003, from http://www.msnbc.com/news/93723.asp?0cl-cR

*Mattox, W. (1999). "Homeschooling benefits children less preoccupied with peer acceptance." *San Francisco Chronicle,* Chronicle Sections. Retrieved February 20, 2003, from http://www.sfgate.com/

cgiin/article.cgi?file=/chronicle/archive/1999/
03/19/ED71809. DTL

Mayberry, M. and Knowles, J. G. (1989). Family unity
objectives of parents who teach their children:
Idcological and pcdagogical oricntation to homc
schooling. *The Urban Review*, *21*(4), 209–225.

McCusker, C. (2002). Homeschoolers arrive on cam-
pus [Electronic Versio—-n]. *Insight on the News*,
(2002, September 9). 47.

McLean, C. (1998). Virtual school, real benefits [Elec-
tronic Version]. *Alberta Report Newsmagazine, 12/
28/98, 26*(2), 36.

McNeir, G. (1993). Outcome-based education [Elec-
tronic Version]. *Eric Digest Clearinghouse 85*.

Medline, R. (2000). Home schooling and the question
of socialization [Electronic Version]. *Peabody Journal of Education, 2000, 75*(1/2).

Merriam, S. and Caffarella, R. (1991). Learning in
adulthood. San Francisco: Jossey-Bass. ISBN 1-
55542-312-4.

Mettetal, G., Jordan, C., and Harper, S. (1997). Attitudes toward a multiple intelligences curriculum [Electronic Version]. *The Journal of Educational
Research, November/December 1997, 91*(2), 115–
122.

Mezirow, J. (1997). Transformative learning: Theory
to practice [Electronic Version]. *New Directions
for Adult and Continuing Education, Summer 1997,
74*, 5–12.

Mezirow, J. (1997). Transformation theory out of context [Electronic Version]. *Adult Education Quarterly, Fall 1997, 48*(1).

Miller, K. (1993). Assisting our communities: Critical Awareness and self-direction [Electronic Version]. *The Community Services Catalyst, Winter 1993, XXIII*(1).

Myers, M. (1996). Liberal arts colleges prepare students for life [Electronic Version]. *Christian Science Monitor 6/17/96, 88*(141), 18.

National Education Association. (2004). *Guide to online high school courses.* Retrieved April 21, 2004, from http://www.nea.org/technology/onlinecourseguide.html

*National Teaching and Learning Forum. (2004). Benjamin Bloom's taxonomy on cognitive behaviors. *The National Teaching and Learning Forum Newsletter, 8*(4). Retrieved April 15, 2004, from http://www.ntlf.com/html/lib/faq/bl_ntlf.htm

Nebraska Department of Education. (2003). *A report on participants in Nebraska exempt schools, 2002/03 school year.* Nebraska Department of Education, Educational Support Services, March 2003.

Nebraska Department of Education. (2004). *A report on participants in Nebraska exempt schools, 2003/04 school year.* Nebraska Department of Education, Educational Support Services, March 2004.

Notar, C., Wilson, J, and Ross, K. (2002). Distant learning for the development of higher-level cognitive skills [Electronic Version]. *Education, Summer 2002, 122*(4).

Oliver, A. (1997). Plugging into multiple intelligences [Electronic Version]. *Education Digest, February 1997, 62*(6).

Omaha World Herald (2003). Increasingly home is where the school is (2003, November 12.), 12A.

Osguthorpe, R. and Graham, C. (2003). Blended learning environments definitions and directions [Electronic Version]. *The Quarterly Review of Distance Education, 4*(3), 2003, 227–233.

Palloff, R. and Pratt, K. (1999). *Building learning communities in cyberspace.* Jossey-Bass: San Francisco.

*Park Point University. (2004). Syllabus construction: Educational objectives. Retrieved April 15, 2004, from http://www.ppc.edu/academics/syllabus construction.shtml

Rachal, J. (2002). Andragogy's detectives: A critique of the present and a proposal for the future [Electronic Version]. *Adult Education Quarterly, May 2002, 52*(3), 210–227.

Rakestraw, J. F., and Rakestraw, D.A. (1990). Home schooling: A question of quality, an issue of rights. *The Education Forum, 55*(1), 66–77.

*Rauchut, E. and Patton, J. (2002). *Home schooling: An American tradition.* Retrieved December 13, 2002, from Bellevue University, Web site: http://academic.bellevue.edu/-jpatton/homeschool.html

Ray, B. (2002). Customization through homeschooling [Electronic Version]. E*ducational Leadership, April 2002,* 50–53.

Ray, B. (2004). Home educated and now adults. Salem, Oregon: NHERI Publications.

Reich, R. (2002). The civic perils of homeschooling [Electronic Version]. *Educational Leadership, April 2002, 59*(7), 56–60.

Revenaugh, M. (2000). A classroom that never dismisses [Electronic Version]. *Curriculum Administrator, May 2000, 36*(5), 22.

Revised Statutes of Nebraska, Section 79-318 R.R.S., Nebraska Department of Education. (2002).

Romanowski, M. (2001). Common arguments about the strengths and limitations of homeschooling [Electronic Version]. *The Clearing House, November 1, 2001, 75*(2), 79.

Rossman M. and Rossman, M. (1995). Facilitating distance education. *New Directions for Adult and Continuing Education 67, Fall 1995,* San Francisco: Jossey Bass, Inc.

Shavelson, R. and Huang, L. (2003). Responding responsibly to the frenzy to assess learning in higher education [Electronic Version]. *Change, January/February 2003, 35*(1).

*Shaw, I. (n.d.). How can I teach you? Let me count the ways [Electronic Version]. Family Education.com. Retrieved April 22, 2003, from http://newsletters.fen.com/article/print/0,1303,58-19342,00.html?obj_gra

Silver, H., Strong, R., and Perini, M. (1997). Integrating learning styles and multiple intelligences [Electronic Version]. *Educational Leadership,* September 1997.

Small, R. (2000). Motivation in instructional design [Electronic Version]. *Teacher Librarian, June 2000, 27*(5).

Smith, M. and Razzouk, N. (1993). Improving classroom communication: The case of the course syllabus [Electronic Version]. *Journal of Education for Business, March/April 1993, 68*(4).

Spector, J. Michael (2001). A philosophy of instructional design for the 21st century [Electronic Version]. *J. Struct. Learn. and Intel. Sys., 14: 307-318, 2001.*

Sweet, S. (1998). A lesson learned about multiple intelligences [Electronic Version]. *219*(17).

Thompson, B. and Thornton, H. (2002). The transition from extrinsic to intrinsic motivation in the college classroom: A first-year experience [Electronic Version]. *Education, Summer 2002, 122*(4).

Thoms, K. (n.d.). They're not just big kids: Motivating adult learners [Electronic Version]. Retrieved January 28, 2003, from http://www.mtsu.edu/~itconf/proceed01/22.pdf

Traub, J. (1998). Multiple intelligence disorder [Electronic Version]. *New Republic, 10/26/98.*

US Department of Education. (2001). *Homeschooling in the United States: 1999* [Electronic Version]. National Center for Education Statistics, Statistical Analysis Report, July 2001, National Household Education Survey Program. Retrieved April 20, 2004, from http://nces.ed.gov/pubsearch/pubsinfo.asp?pubid=2001033

Vandenberg, D. (2002). The transcendental phases of learning [Electronic Version]. *Educational Philosophy and Theory, 34*(3).

Vos, H. (2000). How to assess for improvement of learning [Electronic Version]. *European Journal of Engineering Education, September 2000, 25*(3). *Educational leadership, November 1998, 56*(3).

*Wahl, M. (n.d.). Multiple intelligences power up math teaching [Electronic Version]. Retrieved April 22, 2004, from http://www.resourcefulhomeschool. com/files/MarkWahlMathArticle.html

Weiss, R. (2000). Howard Gardner talks about technology [Electronic Version]. *Training and Development, September 2000, 54*(9), 52–56.

Weston, M. (1996). Reformers should take a look at home schools [Electronic Version]. Education Week, April 3, 1996.

Wichers, M. (2001). Homeschooling: Adventitious or detrimental for proficiency in higher education [Electronic Version]. *Education, Fall 2001, 122*(1), 145–150.

Winters, R. (2000). Education/school testing/home schoolers: From home to Harvard homeschooled kids have earned a college of their own—and admission to elite, traditional campuses. *Time, September 11, 2000,* 55.

WorldNet Daily. (2003). CBS Warns of homeschooling's 'dark side' (2003, October 15). Retrieved October 15, 2003, from http://www.worldnetdaily.com/ news/printer-friendly.asp?ARTICLE_ID=35082

Yarbrough, D. (2002). The engagement model for effective academic advising with undergraduate college students and student organizations [Electronic Version]. *Journal of Humanistic Counseling, Education and Development, Spring 2002, 41*(1), 61–67.

Zehr, M. (2003). More home schoolers registering in Indiana [Electronic Version]. *Education Week, 6/11/2003, 22*(40).

Zheng, L. and Smaldino, S. (2003). Key instructional design elements for distance education [Electronic Version]. *The Quarterly Review of Distance Education, 2003, 4*(2).

*   Although the reference was valid at the time the research was conducted, due to the ever-changing nature of the World Wide Web, these particular URLs are no longer active. However, armed with the names of the authors, the documents, and the dates, other options for finding this information may exist, such as contacting the original source (like CNN.com) and getting access to their archives, looking for other instances of the document on other sites, utilizing a research library to find the articles, and so on.

Appendix A

An Historical Overview of Homeschooling in the United States

By David Byers, Ph.D.

DURING THE EARLY HISTORY of the United States, educating children at home was more of a necessity than a choice. Due to the lack of schools or the general inaccessibility of schools, children learned practical-life skills and academics at the hands of their parents by working on their parents' ranches and farms or in their parents' trade shops. Academics, when taught, came from stories told by their parents, excerpts read from the Bible, and occasionally, structured lessons in arithmetic, reading, and writing (Bishop, 1991).

The Tenth Amendment to the Bill of Rights in 1791 gave the power of providing education to the states. However, since attendance was still not compulsory and public schools were not tax-supported, state schools were not generally available (Rakestraw and Rakestraw, 1990). Therefore, parents remained in control of their children's education, a duty that was viewed to be more the parents' responsibility than a right (Buchanan, 1987).

As formal schools were developed, some parents took advantage of the opportunity to have their children enjoy the privilege of a free public school education. Yet many chose not to, and some children were unable to consistently attend school due to conflicts with chores, work schedules, or family beliefs.

Even in the early 1900s, when every state had established public schools, parents retained some control by refusing to send their children to school if the subjects being taught were considered objectionable. Parents wanted schools to adhere to community values and treated education as a service provided for their benefit—if they desired it. They also wanted schools to recognize that parents alone had full authority over their children (Rakestraw and Rakestraw, 1990).

The advent of child labor laws occurred at about the same time that compulsory education laws went into effect. In the early twentieth century, the balance of power shifted—the government began to gain control of childhood education. Although parents still had the option of private or religious schools, teaching children at home was considered an idea of the past (Bishop, 1991).

When compulsory attendance took effect, a public school education soon became a status symbol by which many measured themselves and others to determine just how "American" they were. Public school education was the means to an end. The goal was two-fold: the welfare of children in general and the benefit of society as a whole.

By providing all children with adequate education, federal and state governments hoped to ensure that American ideals would flourish and children would be taken care of in lieu of neglectful parenting. The government also sought to create an American culture through the public schools by helping eliminate some of the ethnic differences of the numerous immigrant families who were flocking to the United States (Knowles, Marlow, and Muchmore, 1992).

In this light, public education flourished until the mid-twentieth century when, in the midst of the Cold War, the Soviet Union launched Sputnik. As a result of the Russians beating the Americans into space, many Americans began not only to fear for their national security, but also to question American educational systems (Rakestraw and Rakestraw, 1990). For some, public schools became a scapegoat for many societal problems.

It is to this point in time that the origins of many educational reform movements can be traced. Since the American public became not only fearful of losing its superior place in global affairs, but fearful of Communist aggression as well, educators and parents began to look for alternatives to the "failing" public education systems. Since all aspects of the public school system were under close scrutiny, faults—which may or may not have existed prior to Sputnik—became the target of criticism and were brought to the attention of the public via the media (Knowles, 1988). The media helped open the door for the acceptance of homeschooling.

Social Change Agents

Parents who teach their children at home are, often unwittingly, social change agents or leaders of a social movement. Although few homeschooling parents identify themselves as social activists just because they made the decision to educate their children themselves, they have indirectly made a social statement and have become part of the larger social movement—often without knowing much about its origins.

Although homeschooling has been part of the United States since the beginning of the country's history, the *current* movement can be traced at least in part back to two individuals: Raymond Moore and John Holt. These two led the grass-roots homeschooling movement of the 1960s and 1970s (Lyman, 1998).

John Holt, an alternative-school teacher in the 1960s, became a principal force in the homeschooling movement. Holt's concern was that a typical day in a traditional school was akin to the types of bleak daily jobs most of the children would have as adults. Eventually, Holt founded a method of homeschooling now popularly referred to as unschooling (Lyman, 1998).

Raymond Moore and his wife, Dorothy, studied research that had been conducted about developmental problems in children, such as hyperactivity, nearsightedness, and dyslexia. They later concluded that the majority of these problems were the result of children's nervous systems being overwhelmed by formal education at too early an age. As a result of their research, the Moores supported delaying formal education until children were at least eight years old and even supported delays up to the age of twelve. Eventually, the Moores became interested in homeschooling and advocated an approach that balanced study with work in and out of the home—both of which should be adjusted to the child's developmental abilities (Lyman, 1998).

As the homeschooling movement began to take shape in the 1960s, the general reaction of the public was one of confusion and concern—some considered those who homeschooled as extremists. Families who chose to homeschool for religious reasons were sometimes viewed as extremists on the right side of the political spectrum, while those who chose to homeschool as a rebellion against government-run public schools were viewed as extremists on the *left* side (Lyman, 1998).

However, the extremist view of homeschoolers has changed in the last several years. As the number of homeschoolers has grown, homeschooling families have become even more diverse. As a result, homeschooling has become accepted by some as being mainstream.

General Acceptance Despite Continued Resistance

The increased popularity of homeschooling raised general public awareness of the movement. Ultimately, public support and acceptance of homeschooling came from the same forces that belittled the public schools: the media (Knowles, 1988).

Growth in the number of children being educated at home was also partially due to the growing tolerance, if not acceptance, by public school educators, superintendents, and legislators following court rulings favoring homeschool parents. By 1986 homeschooling was allowed in every state, though some states reserved varying degrees of educational control (Gordon, 1991). Some states regulate homeschooling severely, while others don't regulate it at all (Lyman, 1998).

Some states that initially regulated homeschooling heavily have begun to at least consider loosening some of their requirements. In 2003 the Oregon Senate passed a bill removing the requirement that homeschoolers take standardized tests and that they notify their school districts of their intent to homeschool. Arkansas loosened its homeschool requirements in 1997. Arizona and New Mexico repealed their testing requirements in the mid-1990s and in 2001, respectively. Maine and New York have similar bills pending (Borja, 2003). Although the state-level legislative trend toward homeschooling seems to indicate a growing tolerance and acceptance of the movement, some states are still maintaining or increasing levels of regulation (Borja, 2003).

One reason homeschooling has not been completely deregulated is because opponents express concern about limiting the state's control and influence over homeschooled children. In a 1981 court case in West Virginia, a judge ruled against a homeschool family attempting to change compulsory attendance laws. The judgment indicated that doing so could possibly allow homeschooling parents to keep their children ignorant in an environment akin to something from a Charles Dickens novel—an environment away from the helpful influences of the state's social services and welfare agencies (Frost and Morris, 1988).

Concerns espoused by homeschooling opponents come to the forefront when homeschooling receives any negative publicity, such as the case of a fourteen-year-old homeschooler in North Carolina who killed himself and two of his siblings. News anchorman Dan Rather reported about the North Carolina incident in a manner that was seen by homeschool advocates as being biased even in its title: "A Dark Side to Homeschooling." The news special hinted heavily at the need for regulation to protect homeschooling children from their parents (WorldNetDaily, 2003).

Through organizations such as the Home School Legal Defense Association (HSLDA) and through grass-root politics, homeschoolers have become more politically aware. Homeschoolers as an organized, collective entity have increased their abilities to combat negative publicity, as well as to oppose regulation. As a result of the political resistance of homeschoolers, attempts to increase regulation failed in the early 1990s in states such as Maine, South Dakota, North Dakota, Kansas, and Michigan (Weston, 1996).

Success in preventing new regulation and reviewing or overturning existing regulation may be in part because the battle is contained at the state level. Neither the US Constitution nor the Bill of Rights established public education, therefore the public education of children remains a state-level issue (Lyman, 1998).

Homeschooling opponents have tried to take their concerns to the federal level. In 1996 homeschoolers successfully lobbied against a bill in Congress that would have required homeschooling parents to have teaching certificates. After politicians were swarmed with phone calls from homeschooling parents, the vote in the House was 424 to 1 in favor of homeschoolers (Lyman, 1998). This decision seemed to indicate that while the federal government may address concerns about quality of teaching or socialization within homeschools, it is not prepared to oppose homeschooling outright. The government has refrained from interfering partly due to even larger issues surrounding homeschooling, such as family unity and religious freedom.

The Homeschool Debate

Since the time of the modern homeschool movement, religious grounds have been the main socially acceptable reason for homeschooling. Religious education in the home reflects parents' right to choose how best to raise their children. In the area of religious education, laws concerning separation of church and state and banning prayer in the public schools worked in favor of homeschooling parents because it was one area with which public school officials concurred (Mahan and Ware, 1987). To keep religion out of schools, parents who chose religious education were allowed to provide it—at home.

Although not all families who homeschool do so for religious reasons, some states, like Virginia and Pennsylvania, offer parents the option to use religion as their official justification for not sending their children to public school. In Michigan parents are not required to have teacher certification if they declare religious exemption. In Nebraska homeschooling parents were required annually to submit a notarized form indicating that sending their children to public schools violated their religious principles. Since 2005, Nebraska homeschoolers have an option to declare that public schooling interferes with their ability to direct their children's education (Revised Statutes of Nebraska, n.d.).

Research indicates that religion is increasingly becoming a minor factor in parental decisions to homeschool their children (Lyman, 1998). Many parents are concerned about public-school quality and safety, socialization and family unity, and academics. As a result of the different types of motivations homeschooling parents have, researchers now break homeschoolers into two primary groups: pedagogues and ideologues. Pedagogues are primarily concerned about practical aspects of educating their children, and ideologues are primarily concerned about their children's spiritual development (Romanowski, 2001). However, individuals in one group may share the concerns of the opposite group.

The current debate over homeschooling generally centers on pedagogical grounds. Practical issues such as safety, quality of education, and socialization are becoming bigger factors in many parents' decisions to homeschool. Opponents often point to socialization and educational quality as weaknesses of homeschooling.

Academic Considerations

In the face of adverse publicity, public schools continue trying to meet the needs of the students and parents they serve. The increasingly complex and diverse needs of children and their families, combined with ever-rapidly growing numbers of students, are key to one of the primary concerns homeschool parents have about public schools: children receive very little individual attention, and their individual needs are not being met effectively. Some research indicates that public school students often receive less than ten minutes of individual instruction per day (LaRue and LaRue, 1991).

Children who are taught at home benefit from smaller class sizes, more individualized attention, and the flexibility to work on academic activities as their abilities and interests dictate. In addition, experts believe homeschooled children are able to spend more time working on their studies—not only quantity time, but also quality time. Some homeschooling advocates indicate that parents understand the needs of their children and therefore are able to establish a curriculum and learning pace that best meets those needs (Romanowski, 2001).

Opponents of homeschooling also express concern regarding academics—specifically about the quality of academic instruction students receive at home. One expert cited his belief that homeschooling parents lack the ability to teach complex subjects and that they are incapable of providing their children with the type of peer interactions that take place in the public school in order to learn effectively (Romanowski, 2001).

Despite such concerns, homeschoolers as a group have demonstrated greater academic aptitude than students of public schools. In 1994 average test scores of a group of 16,311 homeschooled students from fifty states were in the 77th percentile compared to the standard 50th percentile benchmark among public school children (Weston, 1998).

Several studies have been conducted comparing the academic performance of homeschool students to that of public-school students, including the Hewitt Research Foundation Study, the Christian Liberty

Academy Study, the Alaska Department of Education Study, and the Illinois Study. In each case, homeschool students consistently outscored public school counterparts by a significant margin.

In the Hewitt Research Study, homeschoolers scored in the 80th percentile on standardized tests compared to the national norm of 50 percent. In the Christian Liberty Academy Study, homeschool children were an average of two to three grade levels ahead of public school children of the same age and grade (Frost and Morris, 1988).

These test results were impressive, but their validity was questioned because homeschool parents themselves administered the tests. The Illinois Study was considered particularly important, as it used an independent researcher to examine homeschool academics. The researcher tested seventy-four homeschool students in a five-county area in Illinois. Using the same Iowa Tests of Basic Skills, homeschooled children outperformed Illinois public-school students in almost every area (Frost and Morris, 1988).

Similar results were presented in a 1995 study conducted by the Ohio Department of Education (Wichers, 2001). Experts attribute the academic performance of homeschoolers in such studies to the individualized attention they receive and to the practical application of the information they acquire through their studies (LaRue and LaRue, 1991).

Concerns About Public Schools

Even though the quality and quantity of time spent on learning in public schools is a major concern for homeschooling parents, an even greater concern for some is the safety of their children. Both teachers and children have increasingly become victims of violence in or near their public schools (Lyman, 1998).

Public-school violence can range from common bullying to multiple killings. The most notorious and brutal events make the local, national, and even international news. The more significant the reports of violence, the more convinced some homeschooling parents are that they made the right decision to keep their children at home. Similarly, shocking stories of violence in the public schools motivate additional parents to consider the homeschooling option. After the 1999 mass shooting in Columbine, Colorado, parents there showed increased interest in homeschooling (CNN, 1999).

As the media continues to disclose disturbing research about the lack of effectiveness of public schools, some parents and educators continue to blame much of the perceived social, moral, and academic decline in the United States upon the public educational system. Some of these parents and professionals have worked to gather data about public school students, such as poor scores on standardized tests, high drop-out rates, use of drugs and alcohol, increased numbers of teen pregnancies, and an escalation of violence/gang activity within the schools. Reports, books, and articles based on this information have acted as a catalyst to entice many families away from public schools. This decision is often made based on concern for the physical, moral, and intellectual well-being of the students.

In the early and mid-twentieth century, the main discipline problems facing public school teachers included students chewing gum, talking in class, getting out of line, and running in the halls. In recent years, public school teachers have had to deal with rape, arson, robbery, bombings, murder, gang warfare, and student suicides, as well as numerous other issues not associated with teaching and learning (Bishop, 1991). Inspired or frightened into action by such facts, some parents believe they can certainly do no worse than the public schools when educating their children at home. Many are convinced they can do much better.

Socialization Issues

For many opponents to homeschooling, socialization is a main concern because of the perception that homeschooled children lack daily exposure to other children. Homeschooling advocates are quick to point out the various activities in which their children are involved and how their socialization is much more positive than their interactions with public school children would be. However, some public school advocates are not convinced. Opponents maintain that homeschoolers do not get a diverse enough exposure to people and cultures (Romanowski, 2001).

The issue of socialization for homeschooled children has been the topic of many studies. Many, if not all, of the studies seem to conclude that homeschoolers not only have the academic abilities necessary to be successful, but that they are socially adept as well. Some studies indicate that homeschoolers have greater amounts of self-confidence and a better concept of self than public school children do (Aixe, 1994).

Some parents, keenly aware of the criticism about socialization, spend a great deal of time making sure their homeschooled children get numerous opportunities for social interaction in a variety of settings. Common activities include organized sports, church events, dance classes, scouting, volunteer work, apprenticeships, field trips, and simply playing with friends and neighbors (Mattox, 1999, and Ray, n.d.).

The question of where children best learn social skills comes down to where and with whom they spend the majority of their time. Homeschooled children typically learn social norms at the hands of their parents or guardians and other family members. Children attending public schools, due to the amount of time they spend away from their families each day, learn more about social norms from their teachers and peers (Mattox, 1999).

In addition to these indirect influences, there is often a radical difference between how public schools and homeschools overtly teach concepts of socialization and self-esteem. As public schools have struggled to meet the needs of a wide variety of students and to combat numerous social ills, classes have been required to address topics such as drug/alcohol abuse, sexual safety, tolerance, handling violence, stranger safety, and reporting potential threats to the school. To help children cope with the world around them, some public schools have also incorporated a variety of approaches teaching the secular concept of self-esteem.

Homeschoolers, particularly those with strong religious motivation, also teach their children to have positive self-esteem. However, the focus is often on an intrinsic concept of self that stems from their relationships with others through God, rather than an extrinsic notion of worth that stems from relationships with peers and their opinions (Bunday, 1999). Some research tends to support homeschooling advocates' claim that proper exposure to other children, away from the problematic influences of group norms, positively affects children's social development.

Many children in public, private, and even parochial schools are subject to dealing with conformity to group norms at one time or another. Sometimes a group norm involves a behavioral issue such as drug or alcohol use. Sometimes a group norm is simply related to the type of clothes children are wearing. Occasionally, the pressure to conform to the group leads children to engage in violence, join gangs, and commit crimes. Some children resort to suicide as a means to avoid or deal with this sort of peer pressure (LaRue and LaRue, 1991).

Yet, despite what would seem like well-documented social problems in public schools and the factual concerns of parents for the safety and well-being of their children, homeschool parents are criticized by some for protecting their children too much. Homeschool advocates do cite concerns about public school violence as one of their reasons for keeping their children at home. In addition, homeschoolers often see the issue of protecting their children as part their parental responsibility to prepare children for their roles in society, rather than as a complete removal from it (Mayberry and Knowles, 1989).

The concern that some individuals and groups have about the social skills of homeschooled children may result from different interpretations of socialization. Some consider socialization to be interacting with individuals or groups with whom one has a common frame of reference. To others, socialization is an exposure to individuals or groups who are culturally and even behaviorally different (Medline, 2000). Public-school advocates argue that homeschooled children do not engage in activities with a diverse array of individuals or groups. As a result, some imply that homeschooling is undermining the very nature of a public school education, causing the decline of public schools in general and having the potential to negatively impact democracy in the United States (Lubienski, 2001, and Reich, 2002).

Homeschool advocates counter these arguments with research indicating that homeschoolers are heavily involved in the democratic process and civic duties. Researchers have found that homeschooling families are more active in civic affairs than public school families (Lines, 2000, and Ray, 2004).

For fundamentalist Christians, many of whom homeschool, the notions of civic duty and religion go hand-in-hand. For example, history textbooks created by A Beka and Bob Jones University Press heavily emphasize the symbiotic roles of religion and democracy in the development of the United States. In this way, some homeschoolers learn a sense of civic responsibility through programs that combine religious beliefs with academic instruction (Arai, 1999, and Ray, n.d.).

In 2003 HSLDA hired Dr. Brian Ray of the National Home Education Research Institute (NHERI) to conduct a survey of 7,300 adults who had been homeschooled; over 5,000 of these adults had been taught at home for at least seven years. Ray's research evaluated socialization by asking questions relating to community and civic involvement (HSLDA, 2003).

Ray compared his findings to data from other researchers about the civic involvement of adults in the United States. Compared to the general adult population, the percentage for homeschool respondents who were involved in community service, who were members of community organizations, and who attended religious services at least once a month was twice as much or more than the general adult population. Similarly, only 4.2% of homeschool graduates found politics and government too complicated to understand compared to 35% of other US citizens. In the age bracket of 18–24 years old, 76% of homeschool graduates have voted within the last five years compared to 29% of the general population (HSLDA, 2003).

Socialization used to be a primary concern for both sides of the homeschooling issue. However, valid research has helped many to see that ample socialization is possible for children taught at home at any level of their education. While there will always remain a likelihood of cases of homeschooled children who have less-developed socialization skills than their public school counterparts, they are generally in the minority compared to the number of children whose parents work hard to provide numerous and varied opportunities and social activities.

The Politics of Homeschooling

Despite evidence that seems to refute opponents' concerns about the academic performance and socialization of homeschool students, other concerns remain. The crux of these concerns may be more political in nature, particularly in relation to control of state education funds.

Annual increases in the number of homeschoolers present a financial concern for some educators and legislators. Although homeschooling families continue to pay federal and state taxes supporting the public school system, the absence of their children in the system reduces the amount of funding available to individual schools.

Some homeschooling families spend less money annually per student than the public schools do and yet seem to produce better results, which may represent a threat to some who favor the public education system. Some research indicates that an average homeschooling family spends just one tenth of what public schools spend to educate one child. When a homeschooling child doesn't attend a public school, the average amount the public school loses in per pupil funding is about $6,000 per year—a national average of several billion dollars a year (Cardiff, 1998).

In addition to the loss of funding, some opponents express concern that homeschoolers seem to have a consumerist mentality with regard to their children's education. The ability of homeschoolers to customize their children's education is something that some public schools may not be able to do (Reich, 2002).

Although homeschooling represents a loss of income for public schools, it also represents a reduction in costs for them as well. In areas where the population of students is growing rapidly, more homeschoolers means less of a burden for public schools regarding facilities and staff—both of which can be costly.

Although independently operated homeschools don't directly take money away from public schools like vouchers or charter schools do (Hill, 2000), some charter schools do receive public funds and in turn offer educational programs to homeschoolers. In some instances, charter schools buy educational materials produced by conservative religious groups; therefore, these public-school funds may be seen as being used to provide homeschoolers with religious education (Apple, 2000).

For public-school advocates, funding is a serious political consideration in the argument against homeschooling, and it may be the primary issue for some administrators and government officials. The debate also raises practical issues for public school teachers, since a lack of funds makes it difficult, if not impossible, to buy adequate supplies and provide services for students.

For teachers, administrators, and government officials who have the educational interests of children in mind, the philosophical issues of academics and socialization may represent the central issue of the homeschool debate. However, for both opponents and advocates of homeschooling, what binds all three aspects together is control over the education of children (Limbaugh, 2002).

Since the responsibility for educating children falls on individual states, there are valid reasons why state governments are involved in making sure each child receives an appropriate level of education and is adequately prepared socially for a role in the world. These goals are difficult for many states to accomplish within their own public school systems, and restrictive budgets make the task even more difficult.

Some states' attempts to regulate homeschools more heavily may be motivated in part by a need to acquire the funding lost when homeschooled students don't attend public schools. Regulations also attempt to ensure that homeschooled students receive adequate education and a chance to develop necessary social skills to prepare them for life—a goal shared by homeschooling parents.

Homeschooling Resources

Throughout the book, especially in the sections about the history of homeschooling, we reference many authors whose books and articles David studied to prepare his dissertation. As we've prepared this book, we have found the work of certain individuals to be extremely noteworthy, and some have influenced our approach to teaching our own children. We share their names and some of their books with you below:

1. Terrie Bittner—Terrie is a homeschooling parent and freelance writer with numerous credits to her name.

- *Homeschooling: Take a Deep Breath, You Can Do This!* Mapletree Publishing Company. Denver. *(2004).*
- Web site: www.terriebittner.com

2. Dr. Stephen Brookfield—Dr. Brookfield has done extensive research and written prolifically about critical thinking. We recommend at least the follow-

ing of his books:

- Brookfield, S. (1987). *Developing Critical Thinkers*. San Francisco: Jossey-Bass. ISBN 1-55542-055-9.
- Brookfield, S. (1995). *Becoming a critically reflective teacher*. San Francisco: Jossey-Bass. ISBN 0-7879-0131-8.
- Brookfield, S. (1999). *Discussion as a way of teaching*. San Francisco: Jossey-Bass. ISBN 0-7879-4458-0.

3. Terri Camp—Terri is a homeschool mother of eight whose book *Ignite the Fire!* provides tremendous insight into the joy homeschooling can be for parents and children when the focus is on learning and having fun. Terri has written other books and has her own Web site.

- *Ignite the Fire!* Self-published. Palmer, IA. (2000)
- http://www.terricamp.com/ignitethefire.htm

4. Cafi Cohen—Cafi has written a variety of books and in many ways really broke the ground for discussing the subject of teaching children through high school.

- Cohen, C. (2000). *And What About College?* Cambridge, MA: Holt Associates, Inc.
- Cohen, C. (2000). *Homeschooling the Teen Years: Your Complete Guide to Successfully Homeschooling the 13- to 18-Year-Old*. Roseville, CA. Prima Publishing.

5. Dr. Howard Gardner—Dr. Gardner, a psychologist and university professor, has written some groundbreaking material about the concepts of intelligence. His work has greatly impacted the field of education, and there is tremendous opportunity for homeschooling parents to review and incorporate his thoughts in their programs.

■ Gardner, H. (1999). *Intelligence reframed: Multiple intelligences for the 21ˢᵗ century*. New York: Basic Books.

6. Kathy Ishizuka—Kathy authored a book with input from several homeschooling experts. The book provides a tremendous overview of how to homeschool and even touches on the subjects of teaching children at home during high school. She also provides a variety of useful resources in the appendices of her book.

■ Ishizuka, K. (2000). *The unofficial guide to homeschooling*. Foster City, CA: IDG Books Worldwide, Inc.

7. Dr. Brian Ray—Dr. Ray is a noted authority on the subject of homeschooling and has conducted research into the validity of homeschool education from a variety of viewpoints, such as evaluating the adult lives of individuals who were taught at home.

■ Ray, B. (2004). Home Educated and Now Adults. Salem, Oregon: NHERI Publications.

■ Web site: http://www.nheri.org/

Organizations

We have found certain organizations that help parents educate and raise their children at home.

1. Focus on the Family—This organization founded by Dr. James Dobson has been instrumental for many years in helping parents effectively raise their children in a loving, Christian environment. The works they have either developed themselves or that they promote on their site about homeschooling are useful and inspirational.

■ http://www.family.org/resources/search.cfm?tflag=1&qry=homeschool&pg=3

2. Home School Legal Defense Association—
HSLDA provides a variety of services directly and indirectly to homeschool parents. For those who join
the association, legal services are available to protect their homeschooling rights. For all homeschooling
families, HSLDA is active in lobbying the government,
affecting legislations, and generally seeking to right
any wrongs against homeschooling through timely
action that helps promote the acceptance and understanding of the value of homeschools throughout the
country.

■   http://www.hslda.org/

Appendix C

Course-Specific Resources

WE OFTEN GET QUESTIONS ABOUT which resources we like to use in our program—especially since we don't use standardized texts exclusively. This section contains a list of resources we've found useful.

We've grouped the classes from our program into major subject areas. The list includes course descriptions, teaching methods, and assignment types, as well as the resources we used for each class. We've also indicated the grade levels in which we taught each subject, but this is not critical. The format we've used is an example of detailed course descriptions that can be given to a college or university to accompany formal high school transcripts.

For simplicity, we have listed all of the courses that both our son and daughter completed, which were for the most part identical. However, our son chose to study French while our daughter studied Spanish. Other differences occurred in the physical education courses, their choices of electives, and certain social studies courses. It's not necessary for one student to complete all of the classes we've included.

English

We took a comprehensive approach to teaching English in our high school program. As a result, our children ended up with multiple credits in English for their transcripts and a broad understanding of reading and writing.

We incorporated spelling and grammar into our high school program during the first two years, using standard textbooks from A Beka publishers. While we only required these subjects for grades nine and ten, there are materials all the way through grade twelve. However, since our children were doing well in spelling and grammar at the end of the tenth grade, we chose to focus on writing skills during their last two years to help them develop their vocabulary.

Two courses focused on writing thesis papers in APA format, a formal writing format used by many colleges and universities. APA stands for American Psychological Association. Other styles are also available, such as Modern Language Association (MLA) format. MLA and APA are similar, but not exactly the same. In addition to the books we reference here, many resources are available online for both formats.

We developed creative writing courses with several types of writing assignments, including short stories, poetry, and newsletters. The children also took two journalism classes. The first class focused on formal journalistic writing exercises. In the second they published their own newsletters using some of the skills they had developed.

Part of what makes children good writers is the ability to read well, a skill that requires practice. We first used A Beka materials to introduce World Literature in a formal way so we could easily assess reading comprehension of formal literature. An American Literature course is also available, though we chose not to use it.

We then moved on to the use of actual novels

and other materials. We chose to have the children read a variety of books—some of which they had read in elementary school but understood differently in high school. We also added books to their reading lists that were new to them—often these were books that are common for college reading and writing courses.

No education would be complete without a study of Shakespeare. Shakespeare is often difficult for children to understand and his works are often referenced, if not studied, in college. The texts we chose presented the original version of each play along with a modern translation on the facing page, which helped with comprehension.

Course Title	English Grammar and Composition 9
Grade	Ninth
Curriculum/ Approach	A Beka Homeschool Publishing—Scope and Sequence
Text/ Materials	*Grammar and Composition III Work Text for Grade* (A Beka)
Course Description	This course is a traditional approach to grammar and composition via workbook explanations and exercises. It is a continuation of a series from the seventh and eighth grades, as well as a continuation into the tenth grade.
Length/ Credits	Two semesters/one credit
Major Topics	Capitalization rules, punctuation rules, kinds of sentences and diagramming, eight parts of speech and their uses, diagramming eight parts of speech, sentence structure, manuscript form, writing process, the library, outlining, book reports, paragraphs, exposition, writing letters, character sketch and type sketch, the research paper, improving writing style
Assignment/ Projects	Complete workbook assignments and exercises.

Course Title	College Thesis Paper/APA Style I
Grade	Eleventh
Curriculum/ Approach	This course is designed to teach students how to write a college-level thesis paper in APA style.
Text/ Materials	*Publication Manual of the American Psychological Association, Fifth Edition* (American Psychological Association (APA); Fifth edition (July 2001) Washington, DC, United States), *Mastering APA Style—Student's Workbook and Training Guide* (Harold Gelfand, Charles J. Walker, and The American Psychological Association, 2002, Washington, DC), *Mastering APA Style—Instructor's Resource Guide* (Harold Gelfand, Charles J. Walker, and The American Psychological Association, 2002, Washington, DC), *Concise Rules of APA Style* (American Psychological Association, 2005, Washington, DC)
Course Description	This course is designed to provide the student with the opportunity to write a college-level thesis paper in APA style.
Length/ Credits	One semester/1/2 credit
Major Topics	Thesis paper writing, APA style
Assignment/ Projects	Research and complete a three-to-five-page thesis paper using APA format

Course Title	College Thesis Paper/APA Style II
Grade	Twelfth
Curriculum/ Approach	This course is designed to reinforce the skills required to write a college-level thesis paper in APA style
Text/ Materials	*Publication Manual of the American Psychological Association, Fifth Edition* (American Psychological Association (APA); Fifth edition (July 2001) Washington, DC, United States), *Mastering APA Style—Student's Workbook and Training Guide* (Harold Gelfand, Charles J. Walker, and The American Psychological Association, 2002, Washington, DC), *Mastering APA Style—Instructor's Resource Guide* (Harold Gelfand, Charles J. Walker, and The American Psychological Association, 2002, Washington, DC), *Concise Rules of APA Style* (American Psychological Association, 2005, Washington, DC)
Course Description	This course is designed to provide the student with the opportunity to write a college-level thesis paper in APA style.
Length/ Credits	Two semesters/one credit
Major Topics	Thesis paper writing, APA style
Assignment/ Projects	Research and complete two, fifteen-to-twenty-page thesis papers using APA format

Course Title	Creative Writing I
Grade	Tenth
Curriculum/ Approach	Independent study and completion of multiple writing projects
Text/ Materials	While there are many texts designed to help students write creatively, we chose not to use any specifically. However, essential help with this subject is provided by the use of a dictionary and thesaurus-two resources students should be able to use. Other resources that may be useful include the following: *Pocket Book of Quotations* (Davidoff, Pocket; Reissue edition, April 1, 1990), *Scholastic Dictionary of Spelling* (Marvin Terban, 1998, Scholastic, NY), *Scholastic Dictionary of Synonyms, Antonyms, Homonyms* (Scholastic, 1965, NY), *Scholastic Rhyming Dictionary* (Sue Young, 1998, Scholastic)
Course Description	This is an independent study class in which the student can choose to complete any combination of writing assignments to meet the requirement of twelve complete projects. Students may write short stories, plays, poems, songs, interviews, biographies, autobiographies, news stories, or advertisements.
Length/ Credits	One semester/1/2 credit
Major Topics	Writing, editing, revising, composition, spelling, grammar, design, organization
Assignment/ Projects	Complete twelve writing projects and "package" them in an attractive fashion

Course Title	Creative Writing II
Grade	Eleventh
Curriculum/ Approach	Independent study
Text/ Materials	N/A
Course Description	This is an independent study class in which the student can explore writing in greater depth by focusing on one or more writing projects, such as writing chapters of a book, short stories, poetry, and so on.
Length/ Credits	Two semesters/one credit
Major Topics	Writing, editing, and revising stories. Exploring character and plot development and the use of literary skills.
Assignment/ Projects	Create a contract at the beginning of the school year defining the work to be accomplished broken down into two semesters. Turn in one major project each semester as described in the contract.

Course Title	Poetry Studies
Grade	Eleventh
Curriculum/ Approach	Course designed by Dr. David Byers using independent reading assignments, student-written journals, and hands-on projects.
Text/ Materials	*A Child's Anthology of Poetry*-Edited by Elizabeth Hauge Sword (Edited by Elizabeth Hauge Sword, 1995, Scholastic, NY), *A Poetry Handbook by Mary Olive*r (Mary Oliver, 1994, Harcourt Brace & Co., Orlando, FL, USA), *Scholastic Dictionary of Synonyms, Antonyms, Homonyms* (Scholastic, 1965, NY), *How to Write Poetry* (Paul B. Janeczko, 1999, Scholastic, NY), *Poetry Patterns* (Eleanor Orndoff, 1990, Evan-Moor), *Scholastic Rhyming Dictionary* (Sue Young, 1998, Scholastic), *The Best Loved Poems of the American People* (Doubleday, 1936, NY, USA)
Course Description	This is a two-part course that focuses on exposing the student to the beauty of poetry. The student will participate in a poetry class to learn how to read, write, and analyze poetry.
Length/ Credits	One semester/1/2 credit
Major Topics	Read poems, analyze elements of poetry, practice poetry writing skills
Assignment/ Projects	Identify and define key terms associated with reading, writing, and analyzing poetry; identify and define various types of poetry; create a rough draft of at least six types of poems; engage in critical thinking to analyze and understand the meaning of selected poems; discuss and debate the differences between poetry and prose for effectively conveying a message; identify and discuss the benefits of analyzing poetry; discuss the expectations of college professors related to analyzing and discussing poetry and other subjects

Course Title	Journalism I
Grade	Tenth
Curriculum/ Approach	Independent study—completion of text assignments
Text/ Materials	*Writing for Publication* (Sheryl Lee Hinman, Thomas E. Winski, The Center for Learning, 2000, USA)
Course Description	This course introduces the student to the terminology and basic components of journalism by having them write news stories, sports articles, editorials, and features in the style required for newspaper publication.
Length/ Credits	One semester/1/2 credit
Major Topics	Journalism terminology, newspaper writing styles
Assignment/ Projects	Completion of weekly writing assignments focusing on major sections of a newspaper.

Course Title	Journalism I
Grade	Eleventh
Curriculum/ Approach	Independent reading assignments, student-written journals, and hands-on projects utilizing publishing software.
Text/ Materials	*Microsoft Home Publisher*
Course Description	This course allows the student to practice both creative writing and journalism skills by producing her own newsletter, as well as to write for the homeschool newspaper.
Length/ Credits	One semester/1/2 credit
Major Topics	Writing and publication of a newsletter
Assignment/ Projects	Use creative writing and journalism skills to produce three "newsletters" during the year by the dates assigned.

Course Title	World Literature
Grade	Ninth
Curriculum/ Approach	A Beka Homeschool Publishing—Scope and Sequence
Text/ Materials	*Themes in Literature Student Text* (A Beka), *World Literature Student Text* (A Beka), *Themes in Literature Student Test and Quiz Book* (A Beka), *World Literature Student Test and Quiz Book* (A Beka)
Course Description	This course introduces students to the beauty of literature through short stories, poems, and excerpts of classical prose works of writers from the United States and throughout the world.
Length/ Credits	Two semesters/one credit
Major Topics	Literature appreciation, character development, plot, theme, setting, and imagery
Assignment/ Projects	Complete reading assignments, answer textbook discussion questions, complete review tests, write theme papers

Course Title	Great Books I
Grade	Ninth
Curriculum/ Approach	Course focusing on reading, thinking, and writing skills
Text/ Materials	*Treasure Island* (Robert Louis Stevenson), *The Incredible Journey* (Sheila Burnford), *Around the World in 80 Days* (Jules Verne), *The Time Machine* (Jules Verne), *The Red-Headed League* (Sir Arthur Conan Doyle), *Tom Sawyer* (Mark Twain), *The Magician's Nephew* (C.S. Lewis), *The Lion, the Witch, and the Wardrobe* (C.S. Lewis)
Course Description	This course introduces students to the beauty of literature through classical prose.
Length/ Credits	Two semesters/one credit
Major Topics	Literature appreciation, character development, plot, theme, setting, and imagery
Assignment/ Projects	Read each book, write a book report for each

Course Title	Great Books II
Grade	Eleventh
Curriculum/ Approach	Course focusing on reading, thinking, and writing skills
Text/ Materials	*Great Expectations* (Charles Dickens), *Oliver Twist* (Charles Dickens), *Tale of Two Cities* (Charles Dickens), *The Iliad* (Homer), *The Odyssey* (Homer), *The Grapes of Wrath* (John Steinbeck), *All Quiet on the Western Front* (Erich Maria Remarque)
Course Description	This course focuses on exposing the student to the beauty of classical literature. The student will independently read several classic novels and discuss them with the instructor.
Length/ Credits	Two semesters/one credit
Major Topics	Character development, plot, imagery, metaphors, similes, symbolism, foreshadowing, theme, setting, and literature appreciation
Assignment/ Projects	Read classical novels, discuss with professor, and write book reports

Course Title	Shakespeare Studies
Grade	Eleventh
Curriculum/ Approach	Course designed by Dr. David Byers using independent reading assignments, student-written journals, and hands-on projects
Text/ Materials	*The Essential Shakespeare Handbook* (Leslie Denton-Downer and Alan Riding, DK, 2004), *Shakespeare Made Easy* (Alan Durband, 1994, Barron's Educational Services, Inc.), *Romeo and Juliet, Hamlet, Macbeth, The Tempest, A Midsummer Night's Dream, Julius Caesar, King Lear*
Course Description	This course provides the student with an introduction to some of Shakespeare's plays with materials designed to help the student understand the written words of the plays, as well as to understand some of the context of the plays and the time period in which they were written.
Length/ Credits	One semester/1/2 credit
Major Topics	Shakespeare, plays, characters, iambic pentameter, stage productions, Globe theater
Assignment/ Projects	Read the Essential Shakespeare handbook. Read select plays of Shakespeare and answer questions using critical thinking skills. Use artistic skills to draw one scene and create a detailed color drawing of what you think the set, props, and costumes would look like for a stage production of the plays.

Mathematics

We used a variety of approaches to teach mathematics during high school, including traditional texts and community college courses. Teaching advanced mathematics was beyond either of our abilities. We taught what we could at home and then had the children take courses at a community college to complete their credits and reinforce their knowledge prior to taking the ACT.

While our daughter completed only the basic mathematic requirements to complete high school and to get into college, our son went on to take other courses at the community college, including college geometry, algebra II, statistics, trigonometry, and physics.

Course Title	Algebra I
Grade	Ninth
Curriculum/ Approach	A Beka Homeschool Publishing—Scope and Sequence
Text/ Materials	*Algebra 1 Student Text* (A Beka), *Algebra 1 Student Test Book* (A Beka)
Course Description	This course focuses on developing the student's mathematical skills through an understanding of algebra.
Length/ Credits	Two semesters/one credit
Major Topics	Linear equations in one variable, algebraic numbers, graphs, formulas, positive and negativenumbers, fundamental operations, special products and factoring, fractions, ratio, proportion and variation, linear systems of equations, powers and roots, exponents and radicals, quadratic equations, numerical trigonometry
Assignment/ Projects	Complete text exercises and unit tests

Course Title	Beginning College Algebra
Grade	Eleventh
Curriculum/ Approach	Community college course—Scope and Sequence
Text/ Materials	*Elementary Algebra for College Students,* (2004) Sixth Edition by Allen R. Angel, Published by Pearson Education, Inc.
Course Description	This course is designed for the student who needs to learn basic algebra skills.
Length/ Credits	Three quarter hours = two semesters or one high school credit
Major Topics	Positive and negative real numbers, solving linear equations, and applications of linear equations
Assignment/ Projects	Completion of problems in the text and attendance

Course Title	Beginning College Algebra, Part 2
Grade	Eleventh
Curriculum/ Approach	Community college course—Scope and Sequence
Text/ Materials	*Elementary Algebra for College Students,* (2004) Sixth Edition by Allen R. Angel, Published by Pearson Education, Inc.
Course Description	This course begins with a review of solving linear equations and their applications.
Length/ Credits	Five quarter hours = 3.33 semesters or 1.5 high school credits
Major Topics	Integer exponents, operations with polynomials, factoring, rational expressions, equations of lines, and graphing of equations and inequalities
Assignment/ Projects	Completion of problems in the text and attendance to class

Course Title	Consumer Mathematics
Grade	Eleventh
Curriculum/ Approach	A Beka—Scope and Sequence
Text/ Materials	*Consumer Mathematics* (A Beka)
Course Description	This course focuses on teaching teens the basics about personal finances.
Length/ Credits	One semester/1/2 credit
Major Topics	Personal finances, bookkeeping and accounting, business formulas, Metric-English conversions, investments, taxes, banking, the small business
Assignment/ Projects	Completion of text exercises
Course Title	Plane Geometry
Grade	Tenth
Curriculum/ Approach	A Beka Homeschool Publishing—Scope and Sequence
Text/ Materials	*Plane Geometry Student Text* (A Beka)
Course Description	This course focuses on developing the student's mathematical skills through an understanding of algebra.
Length/ Credits	Two semesters/one credit
Major Topics	Rectilinear figures, circles, proportions, similar polygons, surface polygons, regular polygons and circles, solutions of right triangles by means of ratios
Assignment/ Projects	Complete in-text exercises and unit tests.

Course Title	Intermediate Algebra
Grade	Twelfth
Curriculum/ Approach	Community college
Text/ Materials	*Intermediate Algebra (2004)*. Ninth Edition by Margaret L. Lial, John Hornsby, and Terry McGinnis. Published by Pearson Education, Inc.
Course Description	Basic algebra skills are extended in this course to provide the background necessary for further mathematics courses.
Length/ Credits	4.5 quarter hours = 3 semesters or 1.5 high school credits
Major Topics	Linear, quadratic, polynomial, radical, and rational equations; systems of linear equations; rational exponents and polynomial factoring; rational and radical expressions; complex numbers; and graphs of linear and quadratic functions
Assignment/ Projects	Weekly assignment of problems, quizzes, and tests

Social Sciences

We felt it was important for the children to study our country's government. Yet, social science isn't simply a study of governments or countries. Therefore, we included several other courses in our social science curriculum.

We also required them to get involved in the community through various community service projects. By the twelfth grade, we didn't require community service hours each year because the children were regularly involved in such activities anyway. In addition, both were holding down part-time jobs, and that involvement in the world provided valuable learning opportunities as well.

Course Title	American Government I
Grade	Tenth
Curriculum/ Approach	Course designed by Dr. David Byers using independent study approach and non-textbook materials for research and review
Text/ Materials	Required readings: *A Brilliant Solution: Inventing the American Constitution*—Carol Berkin (Harcourt, 2002), *All the People 1945–1999*—Joy Hakim (Oxford Univer-sity Press, 1999), *Everything American History* (Loriann Hoff-Oberlin, Adams Media Corp. 2001), *Kids at Work*—Russell Freedman (Clarion Books, 1998), *The Bill of Rights: A User's Guide*—Linda R. Monk (Close-up Foundation, 1991), *To the Best of My Ability: The Am-erican Presidents*—James M. McPherson (DK, 2001), *We Were There Too*—Phillip Hoose (DK, 2001), *Why Am-erican is Free*—Kenneth E. Hamburger, Ph.D (Society of the Cincinnati, 1998), *Words that Built a Nation*—Marilyn Miller (Scholastic, 1999)
Course Description	This course allows the student to read a variety of non-textbook materials to obtain a broader understanding of American history. The student will read and review multiple materials of primary source collections, as well as secondary source materials in order to learn more about the people and events that shaped US history. The student will then complete one major paper about a related subject of her own choosing.
Length/ Credits	One semester/1/2 credit
Major Topics	Events and people in American history
Assignment/ Projects	Complete multiple reading assignments of primary source collections and secondary materials. Write one major paper about a topic of student's choice relating to the subject matter studied.

Course Title	American Government II
Grade	Eleventh
Curriculum/ Approach	Course designed as an independent study with reading assignments, hands-on activities, and workbooks
Text/ Materials	*Weekly Reader—The Road to the White House 2004, Electing a President: The Process* (Weekly Reader, 2004), *A Brilliant Solution: Inventing the American Constitution*—Carol Berkin (Harcourt, 2002), *To the Best of My Ability: The American Presidents*—James M. McPherson (DK, 2001), *Words that Built a Nation*—Marilyn Miller (Scholastic, 1999), *Presidential Election, Second Edition*—Syl Sobel (Barrons Educational Series, 2001)
Course Description	This course is designed to give the student an opportunity to learn more about the presidential election process and the workings of the federal government.
Length/ Credits	Two semesters/one credit
Major Topics	Presidential election process, branches and functions of the federal government
Assignment/ Projects	Read various books and materials, as well as view videos about the US government and the election process to identify and define key terms, utilize the US Constitution to identify the process and laws associated with electing the president of the United States and with the order of succession, complete projects to build an understanding of the functions and duties of the three branches of the federal government.

Course Title	American History
Grade	Ninth
Curriculum/ Approach	Course designed to help the student focus on reading, thinking, and writing skills in relation to American History by focusing on people, places, and events from a variety of perspectives using literature, as well as primary and secondary sources
Text/ Materials	*To the Best of My Ability: The American Presidents*—James M. McPherson (DK, 2001), *We Were There Too*—Phillip Hoose (DK, 2001), *Why America is Free*—Kenneth E. Hamburger, Ph.D (Society of the Cincinnati, 1998), *Words that Built a Nation*—Marilyn Miller (Scholastic, 1999), *Huckleberry Finn* (Mark Twain), *When the Legends Die* (Hal Borland), *A Separate Peace* (John Knowles), *To Kill a Mockingbird* (Harper Lee), *Diary of Anne Frank* (Anne Frank, and others)
Course Description	This is an introductory course to US history and the events that shaped our country. Students are also able to read classical literature relating to events or time periods from US history. Finally, students are able to complete multiple projects of their own design through which they are able to study events, persons, or time periods from US history.
Length/ Credits	Two semesters/one credit
Major Topics	People, events, and time periods of US history
Assignment/ Projects	Complete reading assignments, write book reports, and complete four history projects relating to people, events, or time periods of US history

Community Service Ninth Grade	One hundred hours of community service: No credit Assist librarians at public library one time per week for two hours on miscellaneous projects including checking in books, organizing shelves, preparation of art materials for classes Work as needed at church functions including craft fairs, Christmas giving program, and church picnic booths
Community Service Tenth Grade	One hundred hours of community service: No credit Assist librarians at public library one time per week for two hours on miscellaneous projects including checking in books, organizing shelves, preparation of art materials for classes Work as needed at church functions including craft fairs, Christmas giving program, and church picnic booths
Community Service Eleventh Grade	Two hundred hours of community service: No credit Assist librarians at public library one time per week for two hours on miscellaneous projects including checking in books, organizing shelves, preparation of art materials for classes Work as needed at church functions including craft fairs, Christmas giving program, and church picnic booths

Course Title	Economics
Grade	Tenth
Curriculum/ Approach	Course designed as an independent study approach with non-textbook materials for research and review
Text/ Materials	*Young Investor*—Katherine R. Bateman (Chicago Review Press, 2001), *Marketing Simulations*—(Teacher Created Materials, 2002), *Math at Work*—Nancy Brown (T.S. Denison, 2001)
Course Description	This course introduces the student to basic information about US economics by focusing on a variety of approaches, including advertising, how the stock market works, and how basic mathematical principles are applied in the workplace.
Length/ Credits	One semester/1/2 credit
Major Topics	Stock market, marketing, mathematics, investing, economics
Assignment/ Projects	Complete the in-text exercises from the three books for the course

Course Title	Ethics
Grade	Tenth
Curriculum/ Approach	Course designed as an independent study approach with non-textbook materials for research and review
Text/ Materials	*All the People 1945–1999*—Joy Hakim (Oxford University Press, 1999), *The Bill of Rights: A User's Guide*—Linda R. Monk (Close-up Foundation, 1991), *We Were There Too*—Phillip Hoose (DK, 2001), *Words that Built a Nation*—Marilyn Miller (Scholastic, 1999)
Course Description	In this course students are able to explore any aspect of US history that they desire from the aspect of ethical behavior.
Length/ Credits	One semester/1/2 credit
Major Topics	Ethics, American history
Assignment/ Projects	Write one major paper about a subject relating to the topic and give an oral report on the same

Course Title	World Geography
Grade	Tenth
Curriculum/ Approach	Course designed as an independent study approach with non-textbook materials for research and review
Text/ Materials	Internet and library materials
Course Description	This course allows the student to explore an aspect of world geography that is of interest to him. Students may focus on climatology, topography, meteorology as it affects geography or any of the natural wonders of the world.
Length/ Credits	One semester/1/2 credit
Major Topics	The world in which we live
Assignment/ Projects	Complete one major project including a written paper related to the subject

Course Title	World History
Grade	Tenth
Curriculum/ Approach	A Beka—Scope and Sequence
Text/ Materials	*World History and Cultures 10*—Student Text (A Beka), *World History and Cultures 10*—Test and Map Book (A Beka)
Course Description	This is an introductory course to world history and the events that shaped our world from ancient history to modern times.
Length/ Credits	Two semesters/one credit
Major Topics	Ancient history, Asian and African cultures in a unique ancient-to-modern style, in-depth study of the Greco-Roman culture, Middle Ages, Dark Ages, medieval history and culture, current history, France, England, America, Industrial Revolution, Victorian Era, nineteenth century Europe, twentieth century, WWI, Communism, WWII, Cold War era, world events, history of ideas, types of government, political events, and economic conditions
Assignment/ Projects	Complete text reading assignments, textbook questions, unit tests, map work

Course Title	World History—Advanced Studies
Grade	Eleventh
Curriculum/ Approach	Course designed to focus on war and how it shaped history
Text/ Materials	*The Battles that Changed History* (Fletcher Pratt, Dover Publications, 2000), *Battle 100: The Stories Behind History's Most Influential Battles* (Michael Lee Lanning, Sourcebooks, May 2003), *50 Battles That Changed the World: The Conflicts That Most Influenced the Course of History* (William Weir, Career Services, 2001)
Course Description	The purpose of this class is to study how wars/battles have shaped world history. Utilize a variety of resources to research information about wars or battles from at least three different time periods in history.
Length/ Credits	Two semesters/one credit
Major Topics	Famous battles and wars and their impact on world history
Assignment/ Projects	Write three, five-to-ten-page term papers in APA format about the battles or wars during each time period selected and address each of the questions below: 1. Describe the time period and the major persons and events in world history during that period beyond the battle/war to be discussed. 2. For the battle or war during the time period, explain what was the original cause or purpose. Explain who fought and why. 3. Explain whether or not the battle/war was necessary and if it could have been avoided. If so, how? 4. Explain what were the short-term and long-term outcomes and impacts of the battle/war on the people, governments, and lands of the time period, as well as on world history. Consider things like improvements in science/technology, knowledge, art, as well as changes in governments/countries. 5. Explain what might have been the impact on world history if the battle/war had not been fought or if the outcome had been different. 6. What lessons can be learned from the battle/war? Have we (humans) learned these lessons? If so, how? If not, why not?

Natural Science

Natural science subjects, like mathematics, can be done well at home if parents have the expertise and materials available to them. We felt comfortable teaching science at home using a variety of resources. Another option we could have chosen was to enroll our children in courses at the community college, as we did for math.

Course Title	Physical Science and Lab
Grade	Ninth
Curriculum/ Approach	A Beka—Scope and Sequence
Text/ Materials	*Physical Creation Student Text* (A Beka), *Physical Creation Test Book* (A Beka), *Janice Van Cleve's Earth Science Experiments* (Janice Van Cleve, 1991, John Wiley and Sons), *Janice Van Cleve's Chemistry Experiments* (Janice Van Cleve, 1991, John Wiley and Sons), *Janice Van Cleve's Physics Experiments* (Janice Van Cleve, 1991, John Wiley and Sons)
Course Description	This course introduces the student to the components of physical (earth) science through reading assignments, lab experiments, and project work.
Length/ Credits	Two semesters/one and a half credits
Major Topics	The atmosphere, Earth's weather, a survey of the seas, foundations of chemistry, molecules and chemistry, chemistry in action, foundations of geology, rocks and minerals, weathering and erosion, interpreting the fossil record, physics of motion, waves and sound, light and color, electrostatics and magnetism, and electricity
Assignment/ Projects	Complete text reading assignments, textbook questions, unit tests, and thirty experiments in chemistry, earth science, and physics from the Van Cleve text. Complete four projects of own choosing-one each for topics of chemistry, earth science, geology, and one other physical science topic.

Course Title	Biology and Lab
Grade	Tenth
Curriculum/ Approach	A Beka—Scope and Sequence
Text/ Materials	*Biology: God's Living Creation Student Text* (A Beka), *Biology: God's Living Creation Field and Laboratory Manual* (A Beka), *Biology: God's Living Creation Test Booklet* (A Beka)
Course Description	This course allows the student to learn about biology through the completion of reading assignments, in-text questions, and quizzes/tests, as well as through laboratory work. The student will also be able to engage in an in-depth study of three major biology topics by completing projects focusing on any aspect of each topic that appeals to him.
Length/ Credits	Two semesters/one and a half credits
Major Topics	Flowering seed plants; structure and function of leaves, flowers, fruits, and seeds; stems and roots; variety in plant world; bones and muscles; nervous system; nutrition and digestion; circulation and respiration; excretory and endocrine systems; disease and the body's immune system; natural history and scientific investigation; evolution; mammals; birds; reptiles and amphibians; fish; arthropods; variety in the world of invertebrates; cytology; heredity; DNA; laboratory work: dissections, microscopy, field studies, nutrition, cellular biology, genetics
Assignment/ Projects	Complete text reading assignments, textbook questions, unit tests, fourteen lab assignments, and three major projects related to botany, human physiology, and zoology

Course Title	Chemistry and Lab
Grade	Eleventh
Curriculum/ Approach	A Beka—Scope and Sequence
Text/ Materials	*Chemistry: Precision and Design Student Text* (A Beka), *Chemistry: Precision and Design Field and Laboratory Manual* (A Beka), *Chemistry: Precision and Design Test Booklet* (A Beka), *Smithsonian Institute Chemistry Lab*
Course Description	This is an introductory chemistry course that reviews basic principles in chemistry while giving the students hands-on experience with chemistry experiments.
Length/ Credits	Two semesters/one and a half credits
Major Topics	Matter: The substance of chemistry, elements and compounds, chemical reactions, gases, chemical thermodynamics, light, electrons, atomic structure, Periodic Table, chemical bond and intermolecular forces, selected nonmetals and their compounds, selected metals and semimetals, solutions and colloids, chemical kinetics, chemical equilibrium, acids, bases, salts, oxidation-reduction reactions and electrochemistry, nuclear chemistry, organic chemistry, weekly laboratory studies
Assignment/ Projects	Text reading assignments, textbook questions, unit tests, lab work, and complete seventeen experiments. Maintain experiment record/journal, text reading journal, and complete one project of own design relating to chemistry.

Foreign Languages

Foreign languages can be studied independently, but typically students learn best when they are able to immerse themselves into practice of the spoken language—both hearing and speaking it. While our son studied French at home, we also chose to have him study Spanish through the community college. Our hearing-impaired daughter was able to grasp only some of the verbal portions of Spanish, but she did very well with grammar and writing in that language. She plans to study sign language in college.

Course Title	Spanish I and Lab
Grade	Ninth
Curriculum/ Approach	A Beka—Scope and Sequence
Text/ Materials	*Por todo el mundo A and B Student Texts* (A Beka), *Por todo el mundo Vocabulary Workbook* (A Beka), *Por todo el mundo Test Book* (A Beka), *Learn Spanish Now!* (CD-ROM, Transparent Language), *Spanish—Multilingual Talking Picture Dictionary* (CD-ROM, Princeton Review), *501 Spanish Verbs* (Christopher Kendris, Barron's Educational Services, Inc. 1996), *Webster's New Explorer Spanish-English Dictionary* (1999, Merriam-Webster, USA)
Course Description	This is an introductory course to the Spanish language with an emphasis on building vocabulary, introducing and reinforcing grammar, and building writing and conversational skills.
Length/ Credits	Two semesters/one credit
Major Topics	Grammar, vocabulary, writing, conversation skills
Assignment/ Projects	Complete textbook reading and writing assignments and unit tests. Complete lab time consisting of speaking and listening with computer CD.

Course Title	Spanish II and Lab
Grade	Tenth
Curriculum/ Approach	A Beka—Scope and Sequence
Text/ Materials	*Más que vencedores A and B Student Texts* (A Beka), *Más que vencedores Vocabulary Workbook* (A Beka), *Más que vencedores Test Book* (A Beka), *Learn Spanish Now!* (CD-ROM, Transparent Language), *Spanish-Multilingual Talking Picture Dictionary* (CD-ROM, Princeton Review), *501 Spanish Verbs* (Christopher Kendris, Barron's Educational Services, Inc. 1996), *Webster's New Explorer Spanish-English Dictionary* (1999, Merriam-Webster, USA)
Course Description	This is a continuation course of the Spanish language with an emphasis on building vocabulary, introducing and reinforcing grammar, and building writing and conversational skills.
Length/ Credits	Two semesters/one credit
Major Topics	Grammar, vocabulary, writing, conversation skills
Assignment/ Projects	Complete textbook reading and writing assignments and unit tests. Engage in lab time of speaking and listening practice using computer CDs.

Course Title	French I and Lab
Grade	Ninth
Curriculum/ Approach	A Beka—Scope and Sequence
Text/ Materials	*Nouveaux Chemins A and B Student Texts* (A Beka), *Nouveaux Chemins Vocabulary Workbook* (A Beka), *Nouveaux Chemins Test Book* (A Beka), *Learn French Now!* (CD-ROM, Transparent Language), *Multilingual Talking Picture Dictionary* (CD-ROM, Princeton Review), *French Vocabulary Cassettes* (A Beka), *Big Blue Book of French Verbs* (David M. Stillman and Ronni L. Gordon, 2003, McGraw-Hill), Oxford French Dictionary (Berkley; Bilingual edition, July 1, 2003)
Course Description	This is an introductory course to the French language with an emphasis on building vocabulary, introducing and reinforcing grammar, and building writing and conversational skills.
Length/ Credits	Two semesters/one credit
Major Topics	Grammar, vocabulary, writing, conversation skills
Assignment/ Projects	Complete textbook reading and writing assignments and unit tests. Complete lab time consisting of speaking and listening with computer CD.

Course Title	French II and Lab
Grade	Tenth
Curriculum/ Approach	A Beka—Scope and Sequence
Text/ Materials	*Langue et louange A and B Student Texts* (A Beka), *Langue et louange Vocabulary Workbook* (A Beka), *Langue et louange Test Book* (A Beka), *Learn French Now!* (CD-ROM, Transparent Language), *Multilingual Talking Picture Dictionary* (CD-ROM, Princeton Review), *Big Blue Book of French Verbs* (David M. Stillman and Ronni L. Gordon, 2003, McGraw-Hill), *Oxford French Dictionary* (Berkley; Bilingual edition, July 1, 2003)
Course Description	This is a continuation course of the French language with an emphasis on building vocabulary, introducing and reinforcing grammar, and building writing and conversational skills.
Length/ Credits	Two semesters/one credit
Major Topics	Grammar, vocabulary, writing, conversation skills
Assignment/ Projects	Complete textbook reading and writing assignments and unit tests. Engage in lab time of speaking and listening practice using computer CDs.

Electives

Electives are an important part of our high school program. There were some courses we required both the children to take while we allowed them to explore their own personal interests with other courses of their choice. Often, we either designed the course for them or we worked together on designing it. Some courses were offered outside the home using community resources.

Course Title	ACT Prep/College Skills
Grade	Tenth
Curriculum/ Approach	ACT Practice Computer CD/Practice and Review College Level Skills course designed and facilitated by Dr. David Byers using independent reading assignments, hands-on activities, and workbooks
Text/ Materials	*ACT Practice* CD-ROM (Princeton Review), *A Guide to College Survival* (William F. Brown, American College Testing Program; Revised edition, January 1987), *The College Admission Mystique* (Bill Mayher, 1998, Farrar, Straus and Giroux), *College Level Skills* (Course by Dr. David Byers)
Course Description	In this course students review the lessons on the ACT/SAT CD to prepare for the ACT test. The students also investigate colleges they may want to attend by using the Internet and attending a college fair. The students also attend an instructor-facilitated course to explore the skills students need to succeed in college.
Length/ Credits	Two semesters/1/2 credit
Major Topics	ACT testing and skills needed to succeed in college
Assignment/ Projects	Complete ACT practice tests, register for ACT test, attend college fair, research potential colleges, practice for ACT test, review and evaluate colleges that student may want to attend, attend an instructor-facilitated course to learn about the skills required to succeed in higher education

Course Title	Aerobics
Grade	Tenth
Curriculum/ Approach	YMCA—hands-on practice
Text/ Materials	N/A
Course Description	This course is led by a certified aerobics instructor in a group setting at the YMCA.
Length/ Credits	One semester/1/2 credit
Major Topics	Body conditioning, muscle toning
Assignment/ Projects	Attend aerobics class one hour per week for the semester

Course Title	Art
Grade	Ninth
Curriculum/ Approach	Locally-owned art studio run by two art majors graduates—direct instruction and hands-on practice
Text/ Materials	Painting materials
Course Description	This course focuses on drawing and painting objects with an emphasis on improving technique.
Length/ Credits	One semester/1/2 credit
Major Topics	Drawing and painting focusing on perspective, composition, technique, coloring, shading, lighting
Assignment/ Projects	Complete two eight-week courses with weekly instruction of 1.5 hours followed by hands-on practice in the studio and at home-completion of four paintings.

Course Title	Art 104 Drawing and 2-D Design
Grade	Tenth
Curriculum/ Approach	Community college course. Scope and Sequence
Text/ Materials	Drawing from Observation—*Brian Curtis (McGraw-Hill, 2002)*
Course Description	Community college course. Visual problem solving. These include the creation of independent visual images as well as the preparatory process leading to finished work. Traditional media is used.
Length/ Credits	4.5 quarter hours = 3 semesters or 1.5 high school credits
Major Topics	Two-dimensional design principles and elements are integrated into the process of acquiring drawing skills. Drawing is addressed as an activity that includes observation, imagination, aesthetic inquiry, and critical thinking.
Assignment/ Projects	Reading assignments, in-class and homework art assignments, tests

Course Title	Driver's Education
Grade	Tenth
Curriculum/ Approach	Hands-on practice
Text/ Materials	*Nebraska Driver's Manual* (Nebraska Motor Vehicle Division)
Course Description	This course lets the student learn how to safely operate a motor vehicle.
Length/ Credits	One semester/1/2 credit
Major Topics	Driving basics, defensive driving, safety on the road
Assignment/ Projects	Study the driver's manual and take the test to obtain a driver's permit. Practice driving each week with an adult.

Course Title	Home Economics I
Grade	Ninth
Curriculum/ Approach	Course designed as hands-on practice with parent/instructor guidance
Text/ Materials	No text except for use of cookbooks as needed
Course Description	This is a hands-on course teaching the student some of the basic skills related to crafts, cleaning, meal preparation, baking, and household budgeting.
Length/ Credits	Two semesters/1/2 credit
Major Topics	Meal preparation, baking, grocery shopping/budgeting, pet care, care of home environment, completion of sewing projects
Assignment/ Projects	Plan, shop for, and prepare weekly dinner meal and monthly dessert/baking item for family-figure cost of meal and keep recipe for dessert. Take care of pets, daily/weekly chores in and around the home. Complete one or more craft projects each semester.

Course Title	Home Economics II
Grade	Tenth
Curriculum/ Approach	Course designed as hands-on practice with parent/instructor guidance
Text/ Materials	No text except for use of cookbooks as needed
Course Description	This is a hands-on course teaching the student some of the basic skills related to sewing, cleaning, cooking, and budgeting.
Length/ Credits	Two semesters/1/2 credit
Major Topics	Meal preparation, baking, grocery shopping/budgeting, pet care, care of home environment, completion of sewing projects
Assignment/ Projects	Plan, shop for, and prepare weekly dinner meal and monthly dessert/baking item for family-figure cost of meal and keep recipe for dessert. Take care of pets, daily/weekly chores in and around the home. Complete four sewing or craft projects each semester.

Course Title	Home Economics III
Grade	Eleventh
Curriculum/ Approach	Course designed as hands-on practice with parent/instructor guidance
Text/ Materials	No text except for use of cookbooks as needed
Course Description	This is a hands-on course teaching the student some of the basic skills related to sewing, cleaning, cooking, and budgeting.
Length/ Credits	Two semesters/1/2 credit
Major Topics	Meal preparation, baking, grocery shopping/budgeting, pet care, care of home environment, completion of sewing projects
Assignment/ Projects	Plan, shop for, and prepare weekly dinner meal and monthly dessert/baking item for family-figure cost of meal and keep recipe for dessert. Take care of pets, daily/weekly chores in and around the home. Complete four sewing or craft projects for the year.

Course Title	Photography
Grade	Tenth
Curriculum/ Approach	Course designed as an independent study approach and non-textbook materials for research and review
Text/ Materials	*Absolute Beginner's Guide to Taking Great Photos*—Jim Mistke (Prima Publishing, 2002), *101 Essential Photography Tips*—DK Publishing, 1995
Course Description	This course allows the student to explore the joys of photography by learning the basics and then trying out different techniques.
Length/ Credits	One semester/1/2 credit
Major Topics	Photography basics
Assignment/ Projects	Use color and black/white film to take a variety of photos. Compile and neatly present your photos into a memory book.

Course Title	Religion
Grade	Tenth
Curriculum/ Approach	Course designed as an independent study with reading assignments, hands-on activities, and workbooks
Text/ Materials	Bible
Course Description	This is an independent study course that allows the student the opportunity to reflect on readings from the scriptures in conjunction with her own life. The student will read the scriptures each week, reflect on them, and write a journal with regard to her thoughts and reflections.
Length/ Credits	Two semesters/1/2 credit
Major Topics	Scripture readings, religion, personal values
Assignment/ Projects	Reading the scriptures, maintaining a weekly journal

Course Title	Swimming
Grade	Ninth
Curriculum/ Approach	YMCA—hands-on practice
Text/ Materials	N/A
Course Description	This is an advanced swimming course offered through the YMCA that focuses on refining various swimming strokes.
Length/ Credits	One semester/1/2 credit
Major Topics	Swimming strokes
Assignment/ Projects	Complete lessons and free swim practice two hours per week for sixteen weeks

Course Title	Typing I
Grade	Ninth
Curriculum/ Approach	Mavis Beacon—hands-on drill and rote practice
Text/ Materials	*Mavis Beacon Typing* (CD-ROM)
Course Description	This is an introductory course focusing on the development of typing skills through drill and practice.
Length/ Credits	One semester/1/2 credit
Major Topics	Home row keys, finger placement, special characters, drill, and practice
Assignment/ Projects	Complete a series of lessons for practice followed by speed drills using video game approach

Course Title	Sports Studies
Grade	Tenth
Curriculum/ Approach	Independent study
Text/ Materials	*Sports: The Complete Visual Reference* (Editor, Francois Fortin, Firefly Books, Ltd., 2000)
Course Description	This course allows the student to learn about a wide variety of sports and then focus on learning about certain sports to a greater depth through completion of a project.
Length/ Credits	One semester/1/2 credit
Major Topics	Sports-rules, equipment, history
Assignment/ Projects	Read the book. Write three reports about sports of your own choosing that demonstrate your knowledge of the history of each sport, how it is played, and the rules.

Course Title	Physical Education I
Grade	Ninth
Curriculum/ Approach	Hands-on participation in team activities facilitated by coach
Text/ Materials	N/A
Course Description	This is a course in which the student can participate in an organized flag football league for three months, as well as in an organized physical education class that meets twice per month for two semesters.
Length/ Credits	One semester/1/2 credit
Major Topics	Sports, physical education, conditioning, team work
Assignment/ Projects	Participate in flag football for three months, participate in physical education class twice a month for both semesters
Course Title	Physical Education I
Grade	Tenth
Curriculum/ Approach	Hands-on participation in team activities facilitated by coach
Text/ Materials	N/A
Course Description	This is a course in which the student can participate in an organized flag football league for three months, an organized physical education class that meets twice per month for two semesters, and a bowling league that meets once per month for two semesters.
Length/ Credits	One semester/1/2 credit
Major Topics	Sports, physical education, conditioning, team work
Assignment/ Projects	Participate in flag football for three months, participate in physical education class twice a month for both semesters, participate in bowling league once per month for both semesters

BIBLIOGRAPHY

O<small>THER</small> <small>REFERENCE</small> <small>MATERIALS</small> we owned that the children used in conjunction with their courses and the research they conducted (not necessarily direct course texts), are listed below:

Advertising: Information or Manipulation?
Nancy Day, 1999, Enslow Publishers, Inc.

Algebra Survival Guide
Josh Rappaport, Singing Turtle Press, 2000

Algebra Survival Guide Workbook
Josh Rappaport, Singing Turtle Press, 2000

Algebra Word Problems
Anita Harnadek, 2001, Critical Thinking Books and Software

All the People 1945–1999
Joy Hakim, Oxford University Press, 1999

American Heritage New History of the Civil War
Bruce Catton, Edited by James M. McPherson, 1996, American Heritage Publishing Co., Inc.

American History Volume 1
Michael S. Mayer, 2003, Greenhaven Press

American History Volume 2
Michael S. Mayer, 2003, Greenhaven Press

American Tall Tales
Mary Pope Osborne, 1991, Scholastic, NY

Art of Construction
Mario Salvadori, Chicago Review Press, 1990

Baseball Math
Christopher Jennison, Good Year Books, 2001

A Brilliant Solution: Inventing the American Constitution
Carol Berkin, Harcourt, 2002, Orlando, FL)

CIA World Factbook
Central Intelligence Agency, Potomac Books, 2004

Constitution of the United States
Consumer Reports 2004 Buying Guide

Data Analysis
McGraw-Hill, Margaret Thomas, 2002

Declaration of Independence

Don't Know Much About American History
Kenneth C. Davis, Scholastic, 2003

Economics in Action
National Council on Economic Education, 2003, Jane
S. Lopus and Amy M. Willis, Editors

Everything American History Book
Loriann Hoff-Oberlin, Adams Media Corp. 2001, Avon,
MA

Eyewitness Books American Revolution
DK, 2002, USA

Financial Times: World Desk Reference
DK, 1994, NY

Get the Picture?
Jim Piper, Allworth Press, 2001

Algebra Word Problems
Anita Harnadek, 2001, Critical Thinking Books and Software

In the Line of Fire: Presidents' Lives at Stake
Judith St. George, Scholastic, 1999, NY

In Their Own Words: Abraham Lincoln
George Sullivan, 2000, Scholastic, NY

It Happened In America
Lila Perl, 1992, Henry Holt and Company, NY

Kids at Work
Russell Freedman, Clarion Books, Scholastic, 1998, NY

LIFE: Man in Space
2003, Time, Inc., USA

LIFE: ONE NATION America Remembers September 11, 2001
Little, Brown and Company, 2001, Time, Inc., USA

LIFE: Our Century in Pictures
Edited by Richard B. Stolley, Little, Brown, and Company, 1999

Marketing Simulations
Teacher Created Materials, Inc., 2002

Math in the Real World of Architecture
Shirley Cook, Incentive Publications, 1996

Math of Sports
2000, J. Weston Walch, Publisher, USA

Poetry for Young People: Carl Sandburg
Scholastic, 1995, Edited by Frances Schoonmaker Bolin

Poetry for Young People: Edgar Allen Poe
Scholastic, 1995, Edited by Brod Bagert

Poetry for Young People: Emily Dickinson
Scholastic, 1994, Edited by Frances Schoonmaker Bolin

Poetry for Young People: Robert Browning
Scholastic, 2001, Edited By Eileen Gillooly

Poetry for Young People: Robert Frost
Scholastic, 1994, Edited by Gary D. Schmidt

Poetry for Young People: Rudyard Kipling
Scholastic, 2000, Edited by Eileen Gillooly

Poetry for Young People:William Shakespeare
Scholastic, 2000, Edited by David Scott Kastan and Marina Kastan

Probability and Statistics
Margaret Thomas, McGraw-Hill, 2001

Scholastic Encyclopedia of the Civil War
Catherine Clinton, 1999, Scholastic, NY

Scholastic Encyclopedia of the Presidents and Their Times
David Rubel, Scholastic, 1994, NY

Scholastic Encyclopedia of the United States at War
June A. English, Thomas D. Jones, 1998, Scholastic, NY

Stock Market Simulations
Teacher Created Materials, Inc., USA, Editor Gisela Lee, 2000

Teach Yourself Film Studies
Warren Buckland, McGraw-Hill, 2003

The Bill of Rights: A User's Guide
Linda R. Monk, Close-up Foundation, 1991, US

Timelines of World History
DK, 2002, NY

Timetables of American History
Laurence Urdang, Editor, 1984, Touchstone, NY

To the Best of My Ability: The American Presidents
James M. McPherson, DK, 2001

We Shall Not Be Moved—The Women's Factory Strike of 1909
Joan Dash, 1996, Scholastic, NY

We Were There Too!
Phillip Hoose, DK, 2001, US

What Are My Chances?
Linda Griffin and Glenda DeMoss, McGraw-Hill, 1998

Why America is Free
Kenneth E. Hamburger, Ph.D., Society of the Cincinnati, 1998, Washington, DC

Words that Built a Nation
Marilyn Miller, Scholastic, 1999, NY

World War II Encyclopedia
General Editor: John Keegan, 1999, PRC Publishing, Inc.

About the Authors

About David

I always wanted to be a teacher. When I went to college, I let myself be talked out of pursuing a degree in education because those who were older and wiser than I said there were no jobs (and no money) to be had in that career field. So I steadily pursued a variety of college courses until I had enough credits for a bachelor's degree in speech communication with an emphasis in theater. While I never actively pursued a career in speech or theater, my education and experience with both have helped me throughout my career.

Although I didn't end up with an undergraduate degree in education, the desire to be an educator never left me. As a result, my career path has consistently involved teaching in one capacity or another.

I was born and raised in Denver, Colorado. After earning a bachelor's degree in speech communication with an emphasis in theater and then a master's degree in adult and continuing education, Chandra and I moved to Omaha in 1996 to work as Family Teachers at the famous Boys Town facility. After leaving Boys Town, I took a position as a trainer for a corporation in the Omaha area and worked there for eight years during which time I also started teaching management courses part-time for Bellevue University.

Near the end of my corporate trainer career, I went back to school to earn my Ph.D. in education with a specialization in teaching and learning. I work full-time as an assistant professor and program director for the master of arts in leadership at Bellevue University.

I have been married to my beautiful wife for over twenty years. We have six children, three girls and three boys, ranging in ages from two to eighteen. We have been teaching them at home for over twelve years.

About Chandra

I've always wanted to be a stay-at-home-mom. I joke with people that the only reason I went to college was to get my M.R.S. degree—otherwise known as finding a husband. However, that's not entirely true. I went to college thinking that was what I was supposed to do, but I never had any great interest in a particular career field other than being a full-time mother and wife. Although that particular vocation is often frowned upon by our society, David has always supported me in my chosen career.

While I never thought I'd be a homeschool teacher, I can now look back and see what a positive impact homeschooling has had on our children. I wouldn't trade the experiences we've had over the last several years for anything in the world. Even though we've been homeschooling for quite a few years and our oldest two are almost ready for college, I still can't say that I'm 100% comfortable with being a teacher. However, I am convinced that I want to be able to teach the rest of our children at home all the way through high school.

In addition to mothering and teaching, I've worked part-time over the years in a variety of fields from secretarial work to data entry. I even worked in the childcare field with David for a period of time as a teacher's aide. At one time I ran my own business as a seamstress, which was interesting and stressful. I much prefer to sew, quilt, and crochet for my own family—as time allows, of course.

Index